A
DICTIONARY
OF
COMMON
FALLACIES

BOOKS BY PHILIP WARD

Poetry

Collected Poems, 1960
Seldom Rains, 1967
At the Best of Times, 1968
The Poet and the Microscope, 1969
Maps on the Ceiling, 1970
A House on Fire, 1973
Impostors and their Imitators, 1977
The Keymakers, 1977

Drama

A Musical Breakfast, 1968
Garrity and other Plays, 1970
Pincers, 1973
Television Plays, 1976

Travel

Touring Libya, 3 vols., 1967-9
Tripoli, 1969
Touring Iran, 1970
Sabratha, 1970
Motoring to Nalut, 1970
Touring Cyprus, 1971
The Way to Wadi al-Khail, 1971
Touring Lebanon, 1971
Come with me to Ireland, 1972
The Aeolian Islands, 1973
Bangkok, 1974
Indonesia: a Traveler's Guide
(as 'Darby Greenfield'), 2 vols., 1975–6

Fiction and Essays

The Okefani 'Song of Nij Zitru', 1966
Ambigamus, or The Logic Box, 1967
Apuleius on Trial at Sabratha, 1968
The Quell-Finger Dialogues, 1969
A Lizard and other Distractions, 1969
A Maltese Boyhood, 1976

Librarianship

Simplified Cataloguing Rules (with R. Cave), 1959
A Survey of Libyan Bibliographical Resources, 1964
The Libyan Research Library Catalog, 1970
Planning a National Library Service, 1973
Indonesia: the Development of a National Library
Service, 3 vols., 1976

Literature

Spanish Literary Appreciation, 1969
Indonesian Traditional Poetry, 1975
The Oxford Companion to Spanish Literature, 1978

A
DICTIONARY
OF
COMMON
FALLACIES

PHILIP WARD

Second Edition
Volume One

THE OLEANDER PRESS

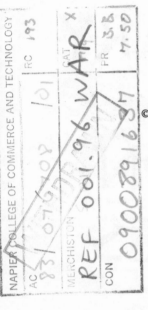

The Oleander Press
17 Stansgate Avenue
Cambridge CB2 2QZ

The Oleander Press
210 Fifth Avenue
New York, N.Y. 10010, U.S.A.

1st edition in 1 volume
ISBN 0 900891 14 9

1st impression 1978
2nd impression 1978
3rd impression 1978
© 1980 2nd edition in 2 volumes

British Library Cataloguing in Publication Data

Ward, Philip
  A dictionary of common fallacies.—2nd ed.
  Vol. 1.—(Oleander reference books series; 3).
  1. Errors, Popular
  I. Title
  001.9'6'03   AZ999

  ISBN 0-900891-63-7
  ISBN 0-900891-65-3   Set of 2 vols.

Printed and bound at
The Burlington Press (Cambridge) Ltd.,
Foxton, Royston, Herts., England

PREFACE

A Dictionary of Common Fallacies deals not only with the narrow field of purely logical fallacies, but also with a number of important ideas or theories common either now or in the past which have been proved wrong by scientific experiment or observation, or are so intrinsically improbable that their widespread acceptance should be questioned.

The Latin word 'fallere' (to escape from, deceive) gave the Vulgar Latin 'fallire' (to commit a fault, deceive, fail), and the adjective 'fallax' (deceptive), which provided the English adjective fallacious through 'fallaciosus'. In classical logic, a fallacy is understood to denote an argument violating the laws of correct demonstration; more generally, it refers to any mistaken statement used in argument, while in common parlance is understood in the even wider sense of a mistaken view which is held by a relatively large number of people in spite of its having been disproved by some form of scientific or logical test.

"For a mind, let us not say exactly ignorant, but shall we say superficial, a work on popular errors might appear quite useless. Why, indeed, he might complain, give the slightest attention, the least emphasis to those daydreams which occupy the brain of the common people, old wives, nurses, and children?" asked Louis Pierre François Adolphe, Marquis de Chesnel de la Charbouclais, in mock despair, before contributing 1360 closely-printed columns of popular fallacies to Migne's *Troisième et dernière encyclopédie théologique* . . . (Paris, 1856, vol. 20).

Why indeed! As if it were not provocation enough to read newspapers and magazines still containing horoscopes in the 1970s, to see shelf upon shelf of fashionable occult 'literature' in otherwise reputable bookshops, fanatic religious sects springing up to make claims of miracle-working and Messianity, extremist political groups seeking converts among the badly-educated and the confused, and pseudo-sciences making untestable and incredible claims. However, a dictionary which exhaustively attempted to examine all the various fallacies which have bewitched, beguiled, and bemused the minds of men (and women) would fill an anti-encyclopedia more voluminous than that of the Marquis de Chesnel de la Charbouclais. The intention of the present work is not so ambitious: it merely offers to anatomize some of the popular beliefs which have been shown to be false by those without a vested interest in deceiving the multitude for power, wealth or prestige.

The compiler has taken to heart the three mildly sceptical attitudes proposed by Bertrand Russell in *Let the people think* (London, 1941, p. 2):

(1) That when the experts are agreed, the opposite opinion cannot be held to be certain;
(2) That when they are not agreed, no opinion can be regarded as certain by a non-expert;
(3) That when they all hold that no sufficient grounds for a positive opinion exist, the ordinary man would do well to suspend his judgment.

"These opinions may seem mild", wrote Russell, "yet, if accepted, they would absolutely revolutionize human life. The opinions for which people are willing to fight and persecute all belong to one of the three classes which this scepticism condemns. When there are rational grounds for an opinion, people are content to set them forth and wait for them to operate. In such cases, people do not hold their opinions with passion; they hold them calmly, and set forth their reasons quietly. The opinions that are held with passion are always those for which no good ground exists; indeed the passion is the measure of the holder's lack of rational conviction."

There is no sign that impostors, charlatans, and the plain misguided have diminished in numbers since the Middle Ages. The steep rise in population since the Crusades has been accompanied by the fragmentation of a greatly increased quantity of scientific knowledge, so that fewer and fewer possess a clear understanding of a smaller segment of knowledge and their scepticism about their own 'truths', healthy as it is, leaves ample scope for the less scrupulous to protest the truth of new 'religions', occultist movements varying in integrity and intelligence, pseudo-sciences, and obsessions touted as facts.

Excluded from this catalogue of common fallacies are a majority of the phenomena generally classified as *hallucinations and delusions* of an individual or of a closely-knit group which are evidently not shared by the generality of mankind; *hoaxes* except insofar as they have led to fallacious conclusions; mere *ignorance* before major discoveries, inventions, or new patterns of awareness pervade the times; *miracles* of the various churches which have a vested interest in advertising the power of their magic or the ease with which they can obtain favours from a deity; simple *mistakes* which are subsequently recognized and rectified; *occult* beliefs which appeal, however irrationally, to a sector of the consciousness allegedly different from that to which known scientific principles can be seen to apply; *religious systems* which, through their dogma of faith, claim to be immune from the process of verification which is logically applicable to them as to everything else; *superstitions*, which are by their nature irrational and, as their name suggests, constitute survivals of religious systems now abandoned; and *unsolved mysteries*, which are stated with data that are normally either incomplete or prejudiced.

The compiler has not fallen into the predictable trap of believing that his is the whole truth, or even most of it (whatever 'truth' is). He would be very grateful for suggestions as to ways in which the *Dictionary* might be improved by omission, correction, or addition. Describing an idea as a 'common fallacy' does not of course thereby automatically make it so; the intention is merely to reflect the best scholarly opinion currently available and the reader's indulgence is craved for mistakes and distortions which, regrettably, as the book demonstrates, are all too obviously part of the human condition.

ACKNOWLEDGEMENTS

As the frequent citation of sources in the text and notes proves, the compiler has relied on hundreds of authorities more dependable than himself in the fields of art and archaeology, anthropology and biology, cosmology, geology, religion, philosophy, medicine, mathematics, engineering, literature and philology. Most of the authorities are cited at the appropriate point to assist further exploration, but the general bibliography should also be consulted by those more deeply fascinated by the human propensity to get things wrong.

An especial debt is that to the staff of the Cambridge University Library, and to their open-shelf policy, envied by scholars of many other nations, which makes browsing a never-ending delight.

HOW TO USE THE BOOK

A. Readers not looking for any subject in particular may start anywhere and find cause for amusement or concern, depending on their temperament.
B. Readers interested in one particular subject should:
1. Look up that name or subject in the INDEX. If no reference seems to be present, seek synonyms or heteronyms.
2. Should there be no reference at all, check the PREFACE for the categories deliberately omitted from the book.
3. Should there be a reference, consult the TEXT of the dictionary and, if desired, note the source (where given) for verification.
4. Refer to the BIBLIOGRAPHY for general or specialized studies on fallacies in your field of interest.

"Are you clear in your mind in regard to the following (some people would call them platitudes)?

That an idea or belief is not necessarily true or false because your parents, your friends, or you or your children have believed it.

That an idea is not necessarily false because you would hate to believe it, or true because you would like to believe it.

That an idea is not necessarily true or false because it is new, or because it is old.

That asserting a statement an infinity of times does not in itself make that statement true.

That the repeated denial of the existence of a thing does not dispose of its existence."

—ABEL J. JONES, *In search of truth* (London, 1945)

ABIOGENESIS

The production of living by not-living matter, or 'spontaneous generation'. The term was introduced by Prof. T. H. Huxley in *Brit. Assoc. Rep.* LXXVI, but it is a fallacy repeated many times in the history of pseudo-science. Aristotle taught as a fact that animals spring from putrid matter, and it was not until 1668 that the Italian Redi conclusively proved that no maggots were 'bred' in meat on which flies were prevented by wire screens from laying their eggs.

Pasteur refuted abiogenesis in the microscopic world, and it is now generally agreed (except by theosophists and some other sectarians) that all known living organisms rise only from pre-existing living organisms. However, Huxley refuted only contemporary abiogenesis, noting that there was probably once a primordial archebiosis which remains unknown; in other words, in the remote past protoplasm may have developed from non-living matter by a series of steps which are not yet understood, and may possibly never be understood.

Among the well-known abiogenetic fallacies are those of

1

Andrew Crosse, an Englishman who claimed in 1836 to have produced living creatures by passing an electrical current through certain chemical mixtures; of John Butler Burke, whose book *The origin of life* (1906) created wild interest because of its claim that the author had produced primitive artificial forms half living and and half crystalline; and of a third Englishman, Morley Martin, who died in 1937 after claiming to produce from the fossil-free Azoic rock what he described as 'primordial protoplasm'.

Sources include: Mrs C. H. A. Crosse, *Memorials of Andrew Crosse* (1857), and Borderland Science Research Associates of San Diego, *The Morley Martin experiments* (1948).

LEGALIZING ABORTION ONLY OCCURRED AFTER WORLD WAR II

No: the U.S.S.R. legalized abortion in 1920, and though the practice was later discontinued for a time, it is once again national policy there.

THE EFFICACY OF 'ABRACADABRA'

The Kabbala, or esoteric 'science' of the Jewish rabbis which appeared in the form we know it today in thirteenth-century Europe, is responsible for many worthless charms, amulets, and talismans, none more widespread or useless than the charm ABRACADABRA. It was worn on parchment or metal round the neck like a scapular, and was reputed to cure fever and intestinal diseases.

```
A B R A C A D A B R A
A B R A C A D A B R
A B R A C A D A B
A B R A C A D A
A B R A C A D
A B R A C A
A B R A C
A B R A
A B R
A B
A
```

Source: Maurice Bessy, *A pictorial history of magic and the supernatural* (London, 1963, p. 92).

THE 'CHICKEN BEFORE THE EGG' FALLACY, OR THE ERROR OF ABSOLUTE PRIORITY

It is not true that there must be an absolute first term in any causal series, and that if event A_1 can be said to cause event B_1, the same cannot be said of B_1 and A_2.

American historians, for instance, have traditionally over-simplified the problem of causality between the observable cultural (not *racial*) inferiority of American negroes and prejudice against negroes.

Gunnar Myrdal has persuasively argued that there was a vicious circle, in which intense anti-negro cultural prejudice from the very beginning of modern American history was a contributing factor in the situation, but others no less potent included the nature of an African negro's cultural heritage, the nature of Anglo-American culture, and the nature of the acculturative process. These factors placed the negro in a position of cultural inferiority from the very start.

THE ADVERTISING EXECUTIVE IS IN AN UNSTABLE JOB

Many sensational novels and films have portrayed account executives in peril of putting a foot wrong with the avenging client, and thus losing both the account and his job. In reality only a very small proportion of all advertising employees are account executives, and this category of personnel is one of the most stably employed groups in agencies. Another advertising fallacy is that intellectuals are snatched from more worthwhile occupations: in fact the intellectual calibre of most advertising people is below that in academic life or the professions, and the salaries are proportionately low.

Source: Jeremy Tunstall, *The advertising man in London advertising agencies* (London, 1964, p. 13).

AETHERIUS SOCIETY

The best-organized minor religious group which relates itself to superior beings from outer space, with several thousand supporters. Its beliefs include divine healing, arduous pilgrimages, chanting, and the leadership of its founder and leader, Mr George King of Maida Vale. It dates from March 1954, when Mr King heard a voice saying, "Prepare yourself. You are to become the voice of Interplanetary Parliament".

King was subsequently taken under the control of 'Master Aetherius' who comes from a highly-civilized Venus (he may have moved following recent space probes indicating a total absence of highly-civilized life on Venus) and brought the news that King was to be the 'primary terrestrial channel' for the Interplanetary Parliament, which meets on Saturn.

Jesus Christ is alive and well, and living on Venus or Mars. *Aetherius Speaks on Earth* magazine, started in 1955 to spread the word, later became *The Cosmic Voice*, issued from the society's headquarters at No. 757 in London's Fulham Road. A completely new text of the Lord's Prayer was delivered to a Los Angeles audience in 1961. Contrary to the findings of theoretical astronomy and actual space probes, the solar system is stated to be fully inhabited (except for Mercury).

As if all this were not sufficient evidence to damn the pretensions of the Aetherius Society, a number of clever, though not particularly sophisticated, hoaxes were perpetrated on the Society in the 1950s by such eminent scientists as Dr Walter Wümpe (who reported radio signals coming from a planetary system 43 light-years distant), Dr Egon Spünraas, Dr Dominic Fidler (who wrote on 'Mescaline and Flying Saucers'), Professor Huttle-Glank, Dr N. Ormuss, Drs Houla and Huizenass, and even a Dr L. Pullar. The Society even then sensed nothing wrong until *Psychic News* exposed the genial hoaxes.

The Aetherius Society is still in existence as we go to press, and the self-styled Rev Dr King has left for Hollywood. See also **FLYING SAUCERS EXIST!**

Sources: *Cosmic Voice*, no. 5 (1956), and Chris Evans, *Jesus is alive and well and living on Venus* in *New Humanist*, October 1973, pp. 191-3.

HUMAN BEINGS CAN LIVE TO A GREAT AGE

Every two or three years there is an excited press comment somewhere in the world, usually from Georgia or Azerbaijan in the Soviet Union, or from a South American 'lost valley' in Ecuador, Colombia, or Bolivia, that a race of men has lived to fantastic ages: anywhere from 130 to 180 in some cases. Solemn interviews are reported, during which the recipe for long life is variously stated: 'an outdoor existence', 'a wholly milk-related diet', 'pure air and vigorous daily exercise', and 'abstinence from smoking' are some of the most common.

The curious common factor in these reports is the absence of a proportionate number of elders between 70 and 90 years of age. The facts are that no birth records are maintained for those individuals; great age is venerated so it is in one's interest to exaggerate it; they are illiterate or semi-literate with no accurate idea of time; and (in the case of Soviet citizens) many males added years to their age to avoid military service under the Tsar and induced their wives to do likewise.

No genuine case is recorded so far of a person older than 114 years. The highest recorded expectation of life at birth for males is 71.4 years, in the Netherlands (1956-60) and for females 74.92 years, in Sweden (1960).

BRAIN ACTIVITIES AND OTHER ABILITIES ARE IMPAIRED WITH INCREASING AGE

Though ageing is of course a process which often involves deterioration of certain abilities, there are brilliant exceptions which make this observation no reason for complacency among the elderly.

Mrs Winifred A. Mould took the B.A. at London University at the age of 70 and was reported in *The Times* of London (6 July 1976) to be continuing her studies, while Havergal Brian wrote his Symphony no. 30 in 1967 at the age of 91 (one of three written that year).

Some of Robert Graves' most passionate and sensitive love poems were written in his 60s and 70s.

These examples could be multiplied a hundredfold.

BRIDES WALK UP THE AISLE

Not unless they lose their way they don't. 'Aisle' (from the French *aile*, wing) is one of the lateral passages of a church. The bride walks along the central passage.

ALECTRYOMANCY

Divination by means of a cockerel. Jean-Baptiste Belot described this popular error as follows: "He then who desires to know concerning some matter, whether it be a robbery, a larceny, or the name of a successor, must make upon a very smooth spot a circle which he shall divide into as many parts as there are letters in the alphabet [which alphabet? Ph.W.]. This done, he shall take grains of wheat and shall place them on each letter, beginning with A and so continuing, while he says this verse, *Ecce enim veritatem*, etc. [Latin: 'Behold then the truth'.]. The wheat being thus placed, let him take a young cock or cockerel, perfectly white, and cut its claws; then, having set down this cock, he must take care to watch upon which letters he eats the grain of corn, and, having noted or written these letters upon paper, he must gather them together and then will find the name that he desires to know".

Unless of course the cockerel is so hungry that he eats all the grain, in which case presumably the alectryomancer will accuse ABCDEFGHIJLMNOPQRSTUVX of the robbery or larceny. A fallacy for the anagrammatist.

Source: É. Grillot de Givry, *Picture museum of sorcery, magic and alchemy* (New York, 1963, p. 302).

KING **ALFRED** BURNT THE CAKES, DISGUISED HIMSELF AS A MINSTREL AND FOUNDED THE UNIVERSITY OF OXFORD

Alfred (849-901) was too practical to allow his supper to be burnt on the hearth, too wary to go masquerading as a minstrel in the Danish camp, and the first note of students at Oxford occurs in the 12th century. Three fallacies out of three. The legends which gathered around the names of Theseus, Alexander the Great, Roland, and King Arthur, have suffered similar nationalistic and mystic accretions which obscure serious archaeology and historical explanation.

About 1600 a forger interpolated into Asser's *Life of King Alfred* a statement dating to 877 the destruction of a large Danish fleet off Swanage. It was only in Stevenson's edition of Asser (1912) that the forged paragraphs were clearly shown to be interpolated.

Source: Frederic Harrison, *The life of Alfred the Great* (1899).

THAT BY **ALGEBRA** ONE CAN MAKE 2=1

The notion has been current since George Bernard Shaw first admitted to being hoodwinked by a schoolboy friend.

"Mr Shaw's youthful experience about *x* and *a* are so highly instructive that I cannot refrain from dwelling upon them for a moment. His friend induced him to "let $x=a$" and Mr Shaw—not expecting that x would take any mean advantage of the permission —granted the request. But he did not understand that in letting $x=a$ he was also letting $xt-a=0$, and the proof (of the proposition, $2=1$) that "followed with rigorous exactness," assumed that $x-a$ did *not* equal 0.

Source: Philip H. Wicksteed, *The common sense of political economy* (Rev. ed., 2 vols., London, 1948, vol. II, p. 726).

ALMANACS

The U.S. Weather Bureau, attacked for its inability to provide weather forecasts for more than a day or two in advance by irate individuals who use popular, fallacious almanacs such as Hicks' (U.S.) or Old Moore's (U.K.), replied in E. B. Garriott's *Long range weather forecasts* (Bulletin 35 of the U.S. Weather Bureau), brought up to date since. As Hering observes, "the futility of protesting in that way against the almanac forecasts is plain, since the latter keep on appearing at short and regular intervals, with constant reiteration, while the reports of scientific tests or investigations are published but once, and then meet the eyes of few readers—perhaps of none who especially ought to see them".

Source: Daniel Webster Hering, *Foibles and fallacies of science* (New York, 1924, pp. 38-57).

ALTARS ARE OF CHRISTIAN ORIGIN

Quite the reverse. The earliest Christians had no altars, and were taunted for this by the pagans, who used them for offerings to pre-Christian deities. Celsus charged the Christians with being a secret society for their refusal to build temples or raise altars, to which Origen replied that the altars were the heart of every Christian.

Altars have been found from the earliest remains of Babylonian cities, from Egypt and from Palestine.

Source: *Encyclopaedia Britannica*, 11th ed. (1910-11), art. *Altar*.

AMULETS

An amulet is a charm (see **CHARMS**) worn on some part of the body, usually around the neck or wrist. Most of the ancient amulets are of ancient Eastern provenance, but E. A. W. Budge showed (*Amulets and Talismans*, New York, 1961) that all cultures have suffered the delusions of the amulet's power. "The truth seems to be", wrote Budge, "that primitive man believed that every object which he used as an amulet possessed, either as a result of its natural formation or through the operation of some supernatural spirit which had incorporated itself in it, a power which to him was invisible. It was this power which, existing in everything, animate and inanimate, turned every object into an amulet, and as such it became a prized possession".

The amulet is merely a superstitious object, but the real belief in its efficacy, which seems widespread not only in the miscalled 'primitive' cultures but also in the literacy-based cultures, is a fallacy.

WE SHOULD RESPECT THE OPINIONS OF OUR ANCESTORS

The fallacy of authority is committed whenever one states something like "As old age is wiser than youth, we should respect the opinions of our ancestors". This error is neatly refuted by W. P. Montague in *The ways of knowing* (London, 1925, p. 44): "If our ancestors were now alive they would be very old, and their opinions, as the outcome of generations of experience, would indeed be worthy of reverence. But when our ancestors uttered the opinions which are now hoary with age and which we are asked to revere, they were as young in years as ourselves, and the world in which they lived was much younger in the matter of racial experience. Their opinions, however old they may be, express the childhood of the race, not its maturity. And the age of an opinion or dogma actually affords a presumption against its truth rather than in favour of it. The conservative tends to accord to old ideas and opinions, and especially to old customs and institutions, the same tenderness and respect which he pays to old persons. This is psychologically natural, for old persons and old institutions are associated ideas; but it is logically absurd, inasmuch as the age of an opinion is only an indication of the immaturity of the generation which expressed it. In all that makes for wisdom we are not younger but older than our ancestors."

THERE WERE ANGELS AT MONS

On 29 September 1914, *The Evening News* published a story they had commissioned from Arthur Machen (1863-1947) to favour the patriotic mood of the day. This story, 'The Bowmen', is a fantasy in which Machen imagined St George in shining armour at the Battle of Mons at the head of angels in the guise of English archers at the Battle of Agincourt.

Alas for human credulity! Despite persistent and wearied disavowals from the author throughout the rest of his life, his fantasy was received as truth not only by the readers of *The Evening News* in England, but also by those who had participated 'under the guidance of St George' in the retreat at Mons. Credence was given to a statement that 'dead Russians had been found on the battlefield with arrow wounds in their bodies' but regrettably no arrows were brought back as mementoes.

Many letters were published from scores of soldiers who wrote to the newspapers that they had actually seen St George and the angels at Mons. Edward Clodd quotes Machen in *The question* (1917, p. 177): "It is all somewhat wonderful: one can say that the whole affair is a psychological phenomenon of considerable interest".

THE ANT AND THE GRASSHOPPER

An inconvenience of animal fables is that they are often based on a fallacy: none more so than this. The ant is supposed to labour all summer to provide for the winter. But the harvester ants which do in fact lay up stocks are uncommon. Most ants live on food that could not be stored anyway, but they wouldn't need it even if it could, for they are usually torpid in winter.

The grasshopper, alleged to beg from the ant, does no such thing: the ant steals from the grasshopper.

Source: Jean Henri Fabre, *Social life in the insect world* (London, 1923, pp. 6-8).

THE APATHETIC FALLACY

An error of "treating living creatures as though they were inanimate", according to Toynbee (in *A study of history*, London, 1935, vol. I, p. 18). Two outstanding examples current at the present day, and throughout the last half-century and more, are classical Freudian theory and the doctrine of historical materialism.

As W. H. Walsh wrote in *Philosophy of history* (New York, 1962, pp. 102-3), "Marxists and Freudians, in their different ways, have taught us all to look for non-rational causes for ideas and

9

beliefs which on the surface look perfectly rational, and have convinced some that rational thinking as such is an impossibility. But though we cannot (and should not) return to the naive confidence of our grandfathers in these matters, it must none the less be pointed out that the anti-rationalist case here cannot be stated without contradiction. It undermines not only the theories of which its proponents disapprove, but itself as well. For it asks us to believe, as a matter of rational conviction, that rational conviction is impossible. And this we cannot do".

Norman's Brown's once fashionable *Life against death* (Middletown, Conn., 1959) combines the apathetic fallacy with the fallacies of metahistory, as explained by Arthur C. Danto in *Analytical philosophy of history* (Cambridge, 1965).

WATER IS AN APHRODISIAC

Not many substances *are* aphrodisiac (sex appeal is after all rather a subjective matter, not easily induced unless there is a marked propensity for it) but Nicolas Venette, in *La génération de l'homme* (Paris, 1690) went altogether too far: "After all", he wrote, "the celebrated Tiraqueau could not have engendered thirty-nine legitimate children, if he had not been a drinker of water: and the Turks would not have had several wives today, if wine had not been prohibited to them".

Alcohol is often thought to have aphrodisiac qualities, but alcohol does not so much increase the appetite for love as decrease the fear of its consequences. Modern aphrodisiac lore places the mistaken faith in raw eggs that Casanova placed in oysters, the Elizabethans in prunes, potatoes and tobacco, and classical antiquity in onions. All the remedies are thought to be inefficacious of themselves.

THE APOSTLES WROTE THE 'APOSTLES' CREED'

False. Nobody knows who wrote the Creed, but it was written within the Western Church during the fourth century A.D. or perhaps a little earlier. It is based structurally on Matthew 28. 19.

According to *The Oxford dictionary of the Christian Church* (Oxford, 1966) though the Creed's "affirmations can be supported by New Testament evidence, the formula itself is not of apostolic origin".

EVE GAVE ADAM AN **APPLE** IN THE GARDEN OF EDEN

St Jerome, translating *Genesis*, possibly influenced by the Greek myth of Aphrodite according to some authorities, turned the Hebrew 'the *fruit* of the tree which is in the midst of the Garden' into 'the *apple*'. Since Adam and Eve dressed themselves in fig-leaves after eating of the fruit, it must have been a fig-tree.

However, as most Biblical commentators now realize, the Garden of Eden is a universal myth and as myths fall outside the scope of this work, the reader is directed to a work such as Peake's *Commentary on the Bible* (1928). Among other theories is that put forward by Sir J. G. Frazer that *Genesis* combines a Hebrew myth of a tree of knowledge with a much earlier myth of the tree of life. The Creator left man free to choose between the tree of life and the tree of death, hoping he would choose the former; but the serpent learnt the secret and persuaded the woman to eat of the tree of death, thus leaving the tree of life to it.

Frazer's point is made not in his classic *Golden bough* but in a contribution to *Essays and studies presented to William Ridgeway* . . . (Cambridge, 1913).

THE **ARCTIC** IS AN AREA OF ETERNAL SNOW AND UNENDURABLE COLD

These popular errors stem from an ignorant assumption that cold increases in close proportion to distance north (or south) of the Equator. But more snow falls in Virginia, U.S.A., than in the Arctic lowlands. Reykjavik, Iceland's capital, is only just below the Arctic Circle, but its mean annual temperature is actually higher than that of New York City. Montana has recorded a temperature 10 degrees Fahrenheit colder than the North Pole's record.

Source: Merle Colby, *A guide to Alaska* (New York, 1939, p. xliv).

ARGENTAURUM

A fallacy which falls into the category of the failure to transmute metals into gold. Many thousands invested in the alleged production of 'Argentaurum' (Lat. compound: 'silver-gold') by Dr Stephen H. Emmens from 1896.

Emmens, a New York chemist, professed to obtain from silver a substance which he regarded as the "raw material out of which both gold and silver were constructed by the hand of nature".

And this substance he called 'Argentaurum'. He insisted that his work was not alchemical, but in strict conformity to the existing state of chemical science; that the periodic law of the elements plainly indicated an allotropic form of silver or gold, or of a substance intermediate between them.

In the *Engineering and Mining Journal* of 5 September 1896, Dr Emmens stated that "the metal which we have made from silver answers every test to which the U.S. Government Assay Office subjects the gold offered to them for sale. It is, therefore, gold to all intents and purposes. This metal made from pure silver by the process discovered by us could be proved to be gold in a court of law. It not only answers every test of the Government mints, but it also has every quality required by the gold of commerce, having the same color, weight and strength".

As Hering writes, "Extraordinary as were the statements about argentaurum, it neither excited the interest of the public nor enlisted the support of capitalists, and the whole matter simply dropped out of sight. Its quiet disappearance was as remarkable as its appearance".

Source: D. W. Hering, *Foibles and fallacies of science* (New York, 1924, pp. 66-69).

NOAH'S ARK

The first edition of the *Encyclopaedia Britannica* (1768-1771) had no doubt of the factual existence of the Biblical ark, and only wondered about the location of Noah's cabin and disposition of the numerous animals! By the 11th ed. (1911) the story had come to be described as a 'myth', which makes it even more amusing that *The Pathfinder*, 3 July 1944 (p. 26), announced the finding of 'the Ark' by a Russian pilot while flying over Mount Ararat, the traditional site of the lodging of the Ark on land. A Turkish expedition declared that it had found the Ark in 1875, but was unable to collect any scientific data because it was 'haunted'.

Source: Bergen Evans, *The natural history of nonsense* (London, 1947, p. 17).

FALLACIES IN ART

The best general work on such topics as false perspective and optical illusions in art is E. H. Gombrich's *Art and illusion: a study in the psychology of pictorial representation* (London, 1960; 2nd ed., 1962).

Gombrich illustrates (p. 184) the 'Fraser spiral' which is a fallacy, since it only appears to be a spiral: closer examination reveals a series of concentric circles. This illusion operates through the spectator's tendency to take on trust the continuation of a series which turns out to be less simple than one had thought. Leonardo da Vinci's *sfumato*, the deliberately blurred image, works on the same principle of reducing the amount of information on a canvas to stimulate the spectator's powers of projection. Titian's contemporary, Daniele Barbaro, writes of the technique of *sfumato* which leads us to 'understand what one does not see'. The fallacy is that one could often be persuaded to swear that what one imagines is actually 'there', a technique used by certain film directors too.

Trompe l'oeil (deception of the eye) relies on the spectator's reinforcement of expectation over the artist's illusion. Dutch art is full of such effects, in still life and in architectural compositions, the most interesting perhaps being the peepshow box painted by Samuel van Hoogstraten (1627-1678) in the National Gallery, London. One can see, through two peepholes at opposite ends of the box, typical tiled floors and various 'rooms' with a range of illusionistic effects including coats and hats 'hung up' and a 'dog' awaiting the visitor who is presumably oneself.

The most ingenious *trompe l'oeil* demonstrations yet devised are probably those by Adelbert Ames, Jr. In one peepshow he allows us three peepholes, through each of which we apparently see a chair: we recognize the apparent shape of a chair, and because we recognize it we wish it to be a chair. However, only the first is a chair-object; the right-hand object is a distorted object which assumes the appearance of a chair *only* from the one angle at which we viewed it through the peephole; the middle object is merely a variety of wires extended in front of a backdrop on which is painted what we took to be the seat of a chair.

William Hogarth's engraving *False perspective* (1754), said to be a satire on a dilettante nobleman whom he wished to ridicule, indicated a number of visual fallacies against the laws of perspective. Maurits Cornelis Escher, a Dutch artist born in 1898, has devoted much of his life to creating impossible (and hence fallacious) waterfalls, buildings, staircases, and spiral forms which can exist in the two dimensions of the print but are incapable of reproduction in three dimensions (see his *Graphic work*, 2nd ed., London, 1967 for reproductions and the artist's commentary). A cube-shaped building, for instance, has openings in five visible walls on to three different landscapes. "Through the topmost pair one looks down, almost vertically, on to the ground; the middle two are at eye-level and show the horizon, while through the bottom pair one looks straight up to the stars. Each plane of the building, which unites nadir, horizon and zenith, has a threefold function. For instance, the rear plane in the centre serves as a *wall* in relation to the horizon, a *floor* in connection with the view through the top opening, and a *ceiling* so far as the view up towards the starry sky is concerned."

Fakes and forgeries in art, such as the 'Vermeers' passed off by van Meegeren to Hermann Goering as original during World War II, show the fallacy that it is possible for an expert to detect the difference between an original and a fake. Alceo Dossena (1878-1937) had forged a vast number of sculptures from Greek to Gothic and Renaissance styles before the characteristics of his style were detected, and even now it is almost certain that much of his work is still at large, credited to the period which he was copying. Jean-Baptiste-Camille Corot's landscapes were and are among the easiest masterpieces to copy. The Jousseaume collection of 2,414 spurious Corots was acquired over many years, mainly from obscure dealers and at very low prices: none appeared in Robaut's catalogue of Corot's works published in 1905 and so a mysterious rumour about Corot's 'secret' output was invented and the worthless legacy of Jousseaume was turned into a goldmine.

ASTROLOGY

A former Astronomer Royal, Sir William Christie, sent the following duplicated reply to those who plagued him with questions on astrology:

Sir or Madam,

I am directed by the Astronomer Royal to inform you that he is unable to rule your planets. Persons professing to do so are rogues and vagabonds.

I am, yours faithfully,

.... (*Secretary*).

If you or anyone in your household is ever tempted to 'read the stars' or 'have your fortune told, dearie', please recall the stern legal warning from 5 Geo. IV c. 83 which is still in force:

"And be it further enacted that . . . every Person pretending or professing to tell Fortunes, or using any subtle Craft, Means, or Device, by Palmistry or otherwise, to deceive and impose on any

14

of His Majesty's Subjects . . . shall be deemed a Rogue and Vaga-
bond, within the true Intent and Meaning of this Act; and it shall
be lawful for any Justice of the Peace to commit such Offender . . .
to the House of Correction, there to be kept to hard Labour for
any Time not exceeding Three Calendar Months . . .".

Those who smile at astrologists and excuse them on the grounds
that we should not have had astronomy without an interest in
superstitious astrology are forgetting that ignorance is excusable
only before the state of knowledge has so advanced that further
preying on ignorance can be construed only as fraud.

There is of course no possible correlation between the stars or
the planets in their movements and the fate of human beings on
earth, their character, or their luck. The ignorance characteristic
of all earnest astrologers can be illustrated from the modern prediction that a man will catch cold with unusual frequency if he
was born when Saturn is opposite the sun in the sky *because*
Saturn is the coldest planet! Even if there were any connection
between a man's health and the planets (which there is not), it
must now be told that Saturn was only the coldest planet known
until the discovery of Uranus, Neptune and Pluto . . . .

The fallacy in the study of cosmic objects and events is their
'interpretation' as portents and heralds of human fate. The study
of the heavens with this intent developed astrology. It required the
study of the celestial positions and movements for interest in their
laws alone to establish astronomy. Not only *motive* but the *level
of logical method* shapes inquiry; the beliefs of astrology proceed
on the folklore level, elaborated by learned doctrines; the conclusions of astronomy are framed—with whatever measure of error
and imperfection—on the scientific level of investigation.

Patrick Moore wrote a simple, careful explanation of the fallacy
of astrology in *Can you speak Venusian?* (London, 1976, pp.
121-8).

"The horoscope remains as the blue ribbon exhibit of the misuse
of intelligence", concluded Joseph Jastrow in his *The story of
human error* (New York, 1936).

One frightening feature of superstitious astrology (which is the
only kind of astrology there is) is the unknown degree of its power
over *every* human mind—not only mine but his, hers, and yours.
Even the most intelligent sceptic glances cynically yet compul-
sively over any horoscope he is shown. In *The dawn of magic* (London, 1963), Louis Pauwels and Jacques Bergier offer unsubstantiated figures which, if correct, constitute a terrible indictment of

15

human credulity. In the early 1960s there were "in the United States more than 30,000 astrologers, and 20 magazines exclusively devoted to astrology, one of which [had] a circulation of 500,000". More than 2,000 newspapers had an astrological column, and it is reasonable to suppose that if that number has been reduced, it is because of the mortality among newspapers rather than among astrological columns. Pauwels and Bergier claimed that in 1943 five million Americans followed the advice of these 'prophets' and spent U.S. $200 million on buying prophecies and advice based on these prophecies.

François Le Lionnais has studied this problem in *Une maladie des civilisations: Les fausses sciences* in *La Nef* (no. 6, June 1954), finding that in France during the mid-50s there were 40,000 'healers' and 50,000 practising occultists of all types. Le Lionnais estimated that fees paid to 'prophets', radiesthetists, clairvoyants and such amounted to Frs. 50,000 million a year *in Paris alone* and probably Frs. 300,000 million a year throughout the nation, which was far more than the total budget for scientific research.

Pauwels and Bergier are "sure that the fact that occultism and the pseudo-sciences are at present in such high favour with an enormous public is an unhealthy symptom. It is not cracked mirrors that bring bad luck, but cracked brains".

Sources include: Rupert T. Gould, *Oddities*, 2nd ed. (London, 1944) and *The Humanist* (Buffalo, N.Y.), September-October 1975 (studies by Bart J. Bok and Lawrence E. Jerome), with signatures against astrology by 186 leading scientists, including eighteen Nobel Prizewinners.

ATLANTIS

The myth that an 'Atlantis' once existed occurs first in Plato, where the imaginary island, full of pomp and luxury, is sited near the Straits of Gibraltar, 'beyond the Pillars of Hercules'. Plato says he heard of Atlantis from Solon, who had heard it from Egyptian priests, who dated the flooding of Atlantis to 9,000 years before Solon's birth. Regrettably for this theory, the present level of the Atlantic Ocean has remained constant for several million years, according to geologists and oceanographers. The civilization described by Plato is not altogether dissimilar to the Minoan culture centred on Crete, which disappeared abruptly late in the 15th century B.C. But recent archaeological findings suggest that the Minoan Empire was destroyed by a single volcanic explosion.

Thera (the largest of three islands in the small archipelago now called Santorini) is a volcanic island in the *Eastern* Mediterranean which suffered an eruption in 1470 B.C., its mountain about 4,900 feet high exploding so violently that the centre of the island dropped into a hole about 1,200 feet below sea level. The island was covered in a hundred feet of volcanic ash, but this was *900* not 9,000 years before Solon's birth, so that both time and place are radically different from Plato's story in the *Critias* and the *Timaeus*.

The most remarkable fantasies concerning the fallacious belief in an actual Atlantis were perpetrated by the Minnesota Irishman Ignatius Donnelly, known as the U.S. Prince of Cranks, in *Atlantis, or the Antediluvian World* (New York, 1882), a work of immense popularity not only in Victorian times (when it was absorbed by Madame Blavatsky into her *Secret doctrine* of 1888) but right up to the present day, when successive editions are appearing with the enthusiastic revisions of Egerton Sykes (the latest in 1970).

Briefly, Donnelly asserted that Atlantis was the Biblical Paradise which existed on a huge continent in the Atlantic Ocean. Mankind there arose from barbarism after a glacial epoch and developed the world's first civilization which worshipped the sun. Colonizers from Atlantis spread their advanced technological knowledge all over the world, and were the first to inhabit Asia, Europe, and the Americas. Atlantean kings and queens became the gods and goddesses of the ancient religions. Atlantis was entirely submerged about 13,000 years ago by floods which followed a volcanic cataclysm.

William Ewart Gladstone, whose logical abilities may be assessed from his argument that the ancient Greeks were colour-blind because few colour-words occur in Homer, asked the British Cabinet for funds to send a ship into the Atlantic to trace the outline of the sunken continent. The otherwise eminent folklorist Lewis Spence, a Scottish Presbyterian, thought that the Atlanteans were a composite race with large brains, and that their first colonists of Europe were of the Cro-Magnon type. "If a patriotic Scotsman may be pardoned the boast", he wrote in *The problem of Atlantis* (London, 1924), "I may say that I devoutly believe that Scotland's admitted superiority in the mental and spiritual spheres springs almost entirely from the preponderant degree of Cro-Magnon blood which certainly runs in the veins of her people . . ." (See ONE NATION'S **BLOOD** IS SUPERIOR TO ANOTHER NATION'S). Of the thousands of books and pamphlets on Atlantis which have gushed from the presses of the world since the Middle Ages, Spence's *Atlantis in America* (London, 1925) and *The history of Atlantis* (London, 1926) are among the *least* peculiar.

The connections between the occultists and Atlantis, fostered by Blavatsky and the Theosophists, were strengthened by the clairvoyant methods of Rudolf Steiner and the Anthroposophists, whose theories of Atlantis were based on W. Scott-Elliot's *The story of Atlantis and the lost Lemuria* (1914), a theosophical work speculating on the seven sub-races whom Scott-Elliot believed to have inhabited Atlantis in succession.

Steiner's own *Atlantis and Lemuria* (1923) claimed occult knowledge from the Akashic record (a hypothetical bank of all events, ideas and emotions that have ever occurred said by some occultists to be preserved in the 'astral plane') to describe Atlantean history. According to Steiner, the Atlanteans used the energy latent in plants to drive airships.

The occultist Edgar Cayce predicted that Atlantis would rise again in 1968 or 1969, a fallacy of the type AT THE MILLENNIUM THE MESSIAH WILL RETURN (q.v.).

The British witch Alex Sanders, in reviewing Francis King's *Ritual magic in England* (London, 1970), claimed that the book's appendices had been 'brought through by the Hidden Masters from Atlantis'.

The search for Atlantis is never-ending because there is nothing to find. If the continent was totally destroyed, how is it possible for enthusiasts to demonstrate that artefacts claimed to be Atlantean do in fact survive? Exactly how is their knowledge obtained if all Atlanteans perished with Atlantis? If it is all a parable or metaphor, why does not somebody, somewhere, say so? Jürgen Spannuth's quest for Atlantis, published in 1956, ended 'off Heligoland'.

Karl Georg Zschaetzsch believed the Atlanteans to have been the original Aryans, and the only survivors of the destruction of Atlàntis to have been Wotan, his daughter, and his pregnant sister, who sought refuge in a cave among the roots of a giant tree beside a cold geyser. Wotan's sister died in childbirth and a she-wolf suckled her infant. The pure, noble 'blood' of these Wagnerian characters was inevitably mingled with that of non-Aryans on the European continent: Zschaetzsch's pernicious nonsense was merely one of the strands in Hitler's occultist mania to purify the world.

Another hypothesis identifying Atlantis with Corsica was answered at the Congress of the Society for Atlantis Studies held in Paris in 1929 by the hurling of tear-gas bombs.

Thus is the irrational answered by the irrational. See also **LEMURIA.**

Sources include: Martin Gardner, *Fads and fallacies in the name of science* (New York, 1957) and A. G. Galanopoulos and Edward Bacon, *Atlantis: the truth behind the legend* (London, 1965).

AN **AURA** OF COLOURED LIGHT AROUND SOME HUMAN BEINGS OR OBJECTS CONSISTS OF A SUPERNATURAL LIFE FORCE

This long-standing idea appears finally to have been repudiated by Rudolph P. Guzik, contributing 'Is the Kirlian aura a life force or a fact of life?' to the Unesco magazine *Impact*, vol. 24, no. 4 (1975).

The Kirlian effect is found in photographs showing human beings or objects (such as leaves) surrounded by an 'aura' of coloured light. Parapsychologists have seized on this aura as a manifestation of a supernatural life force, but Guzik shows that the objects thus photographed are connected to a high voltage source, and considers the aura to be due to corona discharge through the ionized air surrounding the object. Guzik described the underlying physical conditions responsible for the Kirlian effect.

"During the early transatlantic voyages", writes Guzik, "sailors were comforted by what they believed to be the presence of St Elmo, the patron saint of seamen: on a dark night, at the tip of the mast, they could see a blue-violet glow against the sky. These were probably the first recorded observations of a corona discharge, and the phenomenon was attributed to supernatural forces as the Kirlian 'aura' is today by some people.

Guzik concludes that "it would be arrogant for physicists to presume that their model of nature is complete or irrefutable, but the model can explain a phenomenon such as the Kirlian aura if sufficient care is taken with experimental constraints . . . Physicists rely on the laws of cause and effect because they believe that Mother Nature is not a mystic. Were a physicist of today called upon, however, to explain the glow at the tip of a mast to sailors of five or six centuries ago, the scientist would undoubtedly be thrown overboard or burnt at the stake. Not because he could not make himself understood but because St Elmo's fire implied the presence of the sailor's patron and that presence was a comfort. It is possible that life force and 'psionic aura' are a similar comfort to today's parapsychologists".

AUTOBIOGRAPHICAL FALLACIES

"It is doubtful whether it is humanly possible to write entirely true autobiography. If a man deals frankly with his weaknesses he may be merely an exhibitionist. Dr Johnson once said that all condemnation of self was oblique praise: it was to show how much a man can spare. On the other hand most men are too modest to speak openly of their achievements.

Volumes of reminiscences are often full of inaccuracies, due to their being written, for the most part, many years after the events. E. F. Benson, in his last work, *Final edition* (published posthumously), gives several examples from published reminiscences of reported incidents that could never have occurred. On one of these writers he commented: "It is not his memory that had failed, but his imagination that had flowered".

I am fond of reading autobiographies, but I read them for their anecdotes and the glimpses they afford into the character of the writer; I realise that they are among the least reliable of historical literature so far as truth is concerned". See also **HISTORICAL FALLACIES.**

Source: Abel J. Jones, *In search of truth* (London, 1945, pp. 110-1).

AUTOMATIC WRITING

Nobody denies the human ability to write connected and intelligible prose without full attention: the practised writer can even be thinking of another book while writing a first, especially if the subject-matter is not particularly taxing.

The fallacy is that the credulous believe that in all or some cases the subconscious writing is 'dictated' by an allegedly 'spiritual' source such as angels or demons. Such motor automatisms are, however, both familiar and understood by psychologists. Limited consciousness can occur not only in so-called 'automatic' writing, but also in other activities such as painting (as in the cases of Madge Gill or Frederic Thompson) and music (as in the case of Mrs Rosemary Brown). These automatists are simply compelled to create by subconscious urges, and nothing unnatural or supernatural occurs. See also **OUIJA BOARD** and **TABLE TURNING.**

AVIATION IS IMPOSSIBLE

"It has been demonstrated by the failure of a thousand attempts that a machine, set in motion by its own resources, has not enough power to lift itself and keep itself aloft", wrote M. de Marles, in *Les cent merveilles des sciences et des arts* (Paris, 1847), concluding that aviation is consequently a hopeless enterprise.

William Thomson, Lord Kelvin, who was one of the leading physicists of the 19th century, proved mathematically that flight through the air in a heavier-than-air machine is impossible.

So the next time you hear that a statement has been proved mathematically, keep your head down: you could be decapitated by the fallacy on the runway.

There are several sorts of 'impossibility' which are mixed up in the popular mind. One is the scientific impossibility of a right angle making fewer or more than 90 degrees, for instance, or base metals being transmuted into gold. Another is the scientific possibility which has nevertheless not yet been exploited, such as (in previous ages) aviation or cinematography. Many achievements currently termed 'impossible', such as those involving elaboration of planetary exploration or computer technology, are in fact merely difficult.

B

"By the communication of general and popular Science, Vulgar Errors and Common Prejudices are constantly diminished"—SIR HUMPHRY DAVY.

LUKAS THE BABOON-BOY

Lukas, the South African baboon-boy explained in Afrikaans to eager audiences in the late 1930s and early 1940s how he had lived among the baboons. His tale was apparently accepted because he could (and did) eat cacti. A similar story of life among the baboons was told by a rival, Ndola, exposed in the *American Journal of Psychology* as 'merely a case of neglected paralysis provoking the quadrupedal posture', and seven months later Lukas' imposture was also exposed: he had in fact not lived with baboons at all, but among fellow-convicts in the Burghersdorp jail.

The credulity of the scientists can be found in the *American Journal of Psychology* (January 1940, pp. 128-33) and their honourable recantation in the same journal (July 1940, pp. 455-462).

The unfortunate Lukas was put away in an institution for the feeble-minded.

Source: Bergen Evans, *The natural history of nonsense* (London, 1947, pp. 87-88).

BACTERIA ARE HARMFUL

This is an extraordinary fallacy: it is true only of a very few species of bacteria known as pathogens, but most bacteria are quite harmless and not all parasitic bacteria cause disease. The skin and the openings of the body are crowded with harmless bacteria which seem to prevent the growth of harmful species. Some bacteria even synthesize vitamins in the intestine and thus drugs which destroy bacteria indiscriminately may do more harm than good.

If all bacteria were to be destroyed by some malignant power most other forms of life would also disappear, because throughout the course of evolution so many important duties have been taken over by microbes. For example, herbivores rely on bacteria in their digestive organs to break down plant cellulose into digestible sugars and it is because humans lack such bacteria that they cannot survive on a diet of grass.

THE **BAGPIPE** IS A SCOTTISH INSTRUMENT

An instrument of great antiquity, known to the ancient Greeks as the *askaulos* or *symphoneia*, and to the Romans as *tibia utricularis*. It is the French *cornemuse*, the Italian *cornamusa*, and the German *Sackpfeife*. The bagpipe appears on a coin of Nero's time and Nero himself is reputed (by Suetonius and Dion Chrysostomos) to have played it. Chaucer's miller performed on it: "A bagpipe well couth he blowe and sowne". The Highland bagpipe is just one of a hundred variants.

Source: George Grove, *Dictionary of music and musicians* (4th ed., London, 1940, vol. I).

BALDNESS CAN BE CURED BY RECOGNISED TREATMENTS

There is no cure for the average loss of a hundred or so hairs every day, and the condition is perfectly normal as a part of ageing, though of course loss of hair can also be a symptom of illness. Symptomatic baldness occasionally recovers of its own accord, and some loss of hair occurring as a symptom of pituitary or thyroid gland deficiency can be corrected by hormone threatment.

Baldness as such, except for the disease *alopecia areata* (in which all the hair drops out and later grows back again naturally and completely) is a strictly hereditary matter, usually (but by no means exclusively) in the male line. Logan Clendening, in *The human body* (New York, 1938), states: "The degeneration of the hair follicles on top of the head is laid down in the germ plasm to begin at a definite time in life, usually not in youth".

There are thousands of patent medicines and techniques for curing baldness even now, but not one of them can be stated to be efficacious.

Among these mistaken ideas, some of which have provided sufficient profit for a quack to make a sizeable income from the ever-gullible public, is the opinion that the common house-fly is "a counter-irritant", and "makes the hair grow if, after crushing flies, one applies them to the bald patch", according to Friedrich-Christian Lesser, in his *Théologie des insectes* (1742) translated into English as *Insecto-theology: or, a demonstration of the being and perfection of God, from a consideration of the structure and economy of insects* . . . (Edinburgh, 1799).

A BANISTER IS A HANDRAIL ON A STAIRCASE

The whole construction protecting those on an upper floor from falling is a *balustrade*. A banister is one of the bars running from the handrail to the steps. A stone balustrade's bars are more accurately termed balusters or colonets.

ADAM BARBER, AND THE EARTH IS A GYROSCOPE

The coming disaster worse than the H-Bomb (1954) by Dr Adam Barber of Washington D.C., who is a gyroscope engineer, is a book based on the theory that the Earth is a type of gyroscope. A toy gyroscope waves to and fro before it falls over, and its 'pole' sweeps out in a circle. The Earth also wobbles slightly as it spins, each wobble taking about 25,000 years. According to Dr Barber, the Earth has a 'small orbit' unknown to astronomers, which is 9,865,621,106,441,698,602 miles. When the Earth's axis makes a right angle with both the large and the small orbits at the same time, the axis will shift suddenly by 135 degrees, so that the North Pole will shift by 90 degrees. This shift, which according to Dr Barber, will take about $1\frac{1}{2}$ hours, occurs every 9,000 years. The last occasion was roughly 9,000 years ago, when Noah had the urge to make his Ark (see NOAH'S ARK) so if Dr Barber is right —which, according to the Barber Scientific Foundation he established, he most certainly is—we need to tie up a boat to our front gate, because he reasons that when the Earth's axis tilts, the seas will be 'left behind' and roar over the land, flooding everything in their path. Only the Arks will survive. Of course Dr Barber has built his own Ark to show that he can practise what he preaches, but then Dr Barber also claims to have made no fewer than seventy-five perpetual motion machines, none of which actually works.

Nobody would deny Dr Barber his illusions and delusions, but the danger of his book, which went into a second edition in 1957, is that it will inevitably be read by the lonely, the ignorant, the fearful, and the distressed, who cannot fail to be appalled and frightened by yet another irrational doomster.

FREQUENT BATHING WILL KEEP THE PORES OPEN AND PROTECT THE SKIN

The pores of the human skin do not breathe, and the skin does not excrete an appreciable amount of harmful substances from the body, so this argument for bathing frequently is fallacious. So too is the belief that bathing protects the skin. A major function of the skin is to protect the body; such poisons as mercury will not penetrate if the skin is oiled with its own secretions, but will penetrate if the natural lubricants have been washed away with warm water, or soap.

Source: Vilhjalmur Stefansson, *The standardisation of error* (London, 1928).

ADAM HAD A BEARD AT BIRTH

"The father of the human race had a beard from the first instant of his life. All men, before the Flood, had one too."

Source: Justinus Valerianus Vannetti, *Barbalogia* (Roveredo, 1760), replying to a work by Van Helmont which declared that Adam had no beard. One fallacy is, of course, that no such person as Adam ever existed. Another is that a male child could be born with a beard.

BEARS HUG THEIR VICTIMS TO DEATH

There have been very few instances of an unprovoked attack by a polar bear or grizzly bear on a human being (they avoid man whenever possible), but those attacks that are recorded give no support whatsoever to the common fallacy that bears hug or squeeze their victims. Neither do they generally eat their victims (though they will eat much else, down to insects).

Bears kill large victims with a single blow of a forepaw, which is known to be strong enough to break the neck of a large bison.

Source: Osmond P. Breland, *Animal facts and fallacies* (London, 1950).

THERE ARE SEVEN OF EVERY "CLEAN SORT OF BEAST"

According to Dr John Lightfoot, Vice-Chancellor of Cambridge University in the seventeenth century and the greatest Hebrew scholar of his time, "of clean sorts of beasts there were seven of every kind created, three couples for breeding, and the odd one for Adam's sacrifice on his fall, which God foresaw".

Lightfoot, a highly respected man, declared that "heaven and earth, centre and circumference, were created all together, in the same instant, and clouds full of water" and that "this work took place and man was created by the Trinity on October 23, 4004 B.C. at nine o'clock in the morning".

In fact the earth has probably been in existence for more than 4,000 million years. See also WE KNOW THE AGE OF THE EARTH.

Source: John Lightfoot, *The whole works*, ed. by J. R. Pitman (13 vols., London, 1822-25).

IT TAKES 44 GALLONS OF WATER TO PRODUCE A PINT OF BEER

The National Water Council of Great Britain stated the above in a leaflet distributed at the beginning of the drought of 1976. It subsequently retracted the statement, however, agreeing that the figure should have been between $3\frac{1}{2}$ and 10 pints of water, mostly used for cleaning equipment and bottles.

The same leaflet claimed that 44,000 gallons of water were used to make a single car tyre. Since these figures are widely quoted and believed, it is worth pointing out that the Council later admitted that the true figure for making a car tyre is in fact only 15 gallons.

"ALL IS FOR THE BEST IN THE BEST OF ALL POSSIBLE WORLDS"

Dr Pangloss, hanged in Lisbon by the Inquisition after a life of misery, nevertheless proclaimed that "tout est pour le mieux dans le meilleur des mondes" in Voltaire's *Candide* (1756), a novel denounced to the Council of Geneva on 2 March 1759 and publicly burned. Specifically written against the doctrine of optimism propounded in Rousseau's *Lettre sur la Providence*, Voltaire's *roman à thèse* also ridiculed the philosophy of Leibniz, Shaftesbury and Bolingbroke as regards their deterministic optimism.

Voltaire does not fall into the trap of suggesting that all is for the worst in the worst of all possible worlds, but contents himself with the observation that man's destiny is diverse and subject to complex patterns of events, most of which are beyond his control.

'BETWEEN' IS CORRECTLY USED OF TWO, AND AMONG' OF MORE THAN TWO

I suppose most of us were taught that it is wrong to say 'there was a discussion between the five of us', but the standard *Oxford English Dictionary* states that from the earliest appearance of the word it has been "extended to more than two"; Fowler concurs, as do Merriam Webster's 3rd edition and Theodore M. Bernstein in *The careful writer* (New York, 1965). Bernstein adds, "To speak of a treaty *between* nine powers would be completely proper and exact".

BIAS IN READING

Only one thing is more sad or disturbing than the serious, honest scholar's admission of his own fallacies due to unconscious bias in reading, quite different in nature from the determined bias of a religious or political bigot.

The great economic historian Sir John Clapham confessed that "Thirty years ago I read and marked Arthur Young's *Travels in France*, and taught from the marked passages. Five years ago I went through it again, to find that whenever Young spoke of a wretched Frenchman I had marked him, but that many of his references to happy or prosperous Frenchmen remained unmarked".

Even more sad and disturbing is the failure of scholars to admit to their fallacies.

Source: Edward P. Thompson, *The making of the English working class* (London, 1963, p. 210).

BIBLICAL FALLACIES

The following facts are admitted in *A new commentary on holy scripture* (1928), edited by Bishop Gore:
1. The Deluge is a legend.
2. The Pentateuch, as it stands, was not written by **MOSES** (q.v.).
3. The literal inspiration of the Bible is a theory which can only be maintained either by obstinately ignoring the established facts of science and history, or by imposing a forced and artificial interpretation upon the narratives of *Genesis*.
4. The Book of Joshua does not contain an historically accurate account of the Hebrew settlement in Canaan.
5. As regards the fall of Jericho, there is no reason to suppose that anything supernatural occurred.
6. The Jonah and the Whale story is manifestly impossible.
7. Belshazzar's Feast never happened.
8. The Tower of Babel is a legend.
9. Noah's Ark is not true.

The whole book should accompany a reading of the Bible, but the half-century since its publication has led to further difficulties which demand explanation.

If the above nine fallacies disprove the doctrine of the literal truth of the Bible as upheld by fundamentalist groups, it follows that the whole of the Bible is at least a matter for investigation and either confirmation or denial as the case may be. The best account of the conflict between Biblical scripture and a consistent scientific approach to human life and history is *A history of the warfare of science with theology in Christendom* by Andrew D. White (London, 1955).

See also AT THE **MILLENNIUM** THE MESSIAH WILL RETURN.

BIOMAGNETICS

George de la Warr's theory that it is possible to photograph thoughts and its attempted practice. It deals with matter before the matter exists, and can be studied in the late Mr de la Warr's *New worlds beyond the atom* (London, 1959). Fundamental radiations are emitted by an object, behave somewhat like a light wave, and can even be photographed. A detecting device with a rubber-covered framework and a special camera with ordinary film are needed. The trained operator rubs the rubber strip until it becomes sticky, or 'en rapport'. When the object to be photographed is rotated to its 'critical' position, the magnetic field will be stimulated with a pattern of energy, and it is possible to photograph the future kittens of a pregnant cat if the cat's molecules are properly aligned with the pre-physical energy in the growth position. De la Warr, who had laboratories in Oxford, claimed to treat and cure diseases which had not yet appeared. Another application of biomagnetics is that of mining and prospecting, though there is no more evidence for success here on an above-average scale than in any other form of divination (q.v.). See also **DOWSERS.**

BIRDS CAN FORETELL WEATHER CONDITIONS

Nobody can foretell weather conditions with 100% accuracy, not even professional meteorologists. Country folk are full of stories to 'prove' that by their actions birds are able to predict the weather. T. A. Coward, in *The migration of birds* (Cambridge, 1929) stresses that this folk belief is not "supported by any satisfactory evidence". It is also clearly open to challenge by the fact that birds in long flights often fly directly into weather that causes their death or injury.

BIRDS DIE OF COLD

Because country people find the bodies of birds frozen by hedges and fields in midwinter, they have often been inclined to fancy that the birds have died of cold. But they are frozen after death, not before, the reason for death normally being starvation due to the rapid diminution of the food supply in freezing or snowy weather. So always remember to increase your provision of food to birds during the worst weather.

Sources include: Thompson, head-keeper at Zoological Gardens during the terribly severe winter of 1894-5, reported in *Pearson's Weekly* (1 May 1897).

BIRDS GIVE MILK

This popular error arose in Vietnam when the health authorities, trying to overcome the natural antipathy of the Vietnamese to milk as a product from cows, introduced sweetened condensed milk in cans as 'birds' milk'. Milk then became acceptable and came into general use.

Source: S. and V. Leff, *Medicine fights superstition*, in *The Humanist*, September 1959.

BIRDS SLEEP WITH THEIR HEADS UNDER THEIR WINGS

A fallacy which gave rise to a popular nursery rhyme and has in turn been reinforced by the rhyme:
"The north wind doth blow,
   and we shall have snow;
And what will Cock Robin do then, poor thing?
   He'll fly to the barn,
   To keep himself warm,
And hide his head under his wing, poor thing".
A bird's method of going to sleep can be roughly described as turning its head round, putting it on its back with the beak concealed, and often in the process almost concealing the head, but never in any case so far recorded placing the head under the wings.

BIRTHDAYS OCCUR ONCE A YEAR

What an extraordinary abuse of language is the popular concept that one's birthday is an annual event! It is an *anniversary*, of course, that is the annual event, and your birthday is a day to be celebrated not by you yourself but by your lucky parents. The day that you celebrate in later years is the anniversary of your birthday, as Italian recognizes in the name *compleanno* and Spanish in *cumpleaños*, or the day on which you 'complete another year' of life.

BLACK-BEETLES ARE BLACK BEETLES

They are dark brown, not black. And while beetles form the order *Coleoptera*, black-beetles belong to the order *Orthoptera* which also includes locusts and grasshoppers.

IT IS POSSIBLE TO TRAVEL IN SPACE THROUGH 'BLACK HOLES'

Adrian Berry, in *The iron sun: crossing the universe through black holes* (London, 1977), fallaciously argues that travel through collapsars (as the Russians call 'black holes') is technically feasible. A black hole, however, is definable as a region in space from which nothing (not even light) can escape against the pull of gravity; it is probably the end of the life-cycle of a large star. Berry suggests that the traveller will arrive at another part of the universe through entering a 'black hole' but this view is contradicted by the current definition, according to which nothing (not even the optimistic traveller) can escape. In his detailed criticism of Berry's thesis, Derek Raine in *The Times Literary Supplement* for 29 July 1977 concludes that: "If this book were intended merely as commercially oriented light entertainment (or as a hoax), so be it. But what is claimed, amid learned references and explanatory appendixes, is that the light-barrier has been *shown* to be mythical. Sadly, for those who like their fantasies to be laced with a drop of reality, this claim has simply not been substantiated".

BATS AND MOLES ARE BLIND

Bats are not blind, but as they have evolved as nocturnal hunters they can see better in half-light than in the full light of day. 'Blind as a mole' is equally fallacious, since though their eyes are very small (like the eyes of other creatures that burrow underground), moles are perfectly capable of seeing.

ONE NATION'S **BLOOD** IS SUPERIOR TO ANOTHER NATION'S

"It's his Italian blood" or "his French blood" is thought by many to constitute a meaningful statement, but blood is not the seat of the passions, even if those with the same 'blood' are credited with similar innate emotional and other mental traits. The Bible equates blood with the spirit or with the place where the spirit resides and to drink blood is taboo. Aristotle's view that the menstrual blood ceases to flow during pregnancy so as to form the substance of the child's body is of course equally fallacious but was commonly believed until a century ago. No blood at all passes from mother to child during pre-natal life, nor does blood possess any of the spiritual or emotional properties attributed to it.

Source : John Cohen, *Human nature, war, and society* (London, 1946).

THE **BLOOD OF ADONIS** IS SHED EVERY SPRING IN LEBANON

Though myths can only be described as common fallacies by the most uncharitable observer (and are hence generally omitted from this book by the charitable compiler), there is a very tenacious fallacy repeated annually at Afqa, above Byblos, in Lebanon. At the Cave of Adonis, high in Mount Lebanon there every Spring, Adonis is mortally wounded by the wild boar sent by Mars, reddening Nahr Ibrahim (also known as the River of Adonis).

Actually the waters take down brown-russet haematite to the sea.

Source: Philip Ward, *Touring Lebanon* (London, 1971).

OXFORD UNIVERSITY'S COLOUR IS DARK **BLUE** AND CAMBRIDGE UNIVERSITY'S COLOUR IS LIGHT BLUE

A university has no colour. When a university or college club formally adopts certain colours, anyone who is eligible for membership and wears these colours is considered thereby to render himself liable to the payment of the club subscription. Dark blue and light blue are the colours of the *athletic clubs* of the universities of Oxford and Cambridge respectively. Thus, a graduate not

a member of one of the clubs would be ineligible to wear the colours.
Source: *University Correspondent*, 15 June 1911.

BOOMERANGS ARE USED BECAUSE THEY RETURN TO THE THROWER

The great majority of boomerangs, used predominantly by Australian aborigines in war and hunting, will not return and are not intended to do so. The returning boomerang is completely unknown in Central Australia and Northern Territory. It is used in tests of skill, and its main use is in throwing *above* flights of duck, which mistake it for a hovering hawk and consequently fly low into nets placed by the aborigines.
Source: Museum of Mankind exhibition (London), 1976.

THE BROCKEN SPECTRE

A terrifying story is told in Germany of a giant ghost seen by climbers on the Brocken Mountain. Once upon a time, a climber working his way along a precipice found himself suddenly confronted by an immense human figure which rose out of the mists towards him. In his horror he lost his footing and fell to his death. [If he had died, to whom had he told his story?]

However, the Brocken spectre is a natural phenomenon. Accompanied by one or more 'glories' (identical in appearance with the haloes customary in Italian Renaissance painting), the phenomenon is reminiscent of the description of religious episodes of the 'Assumption' and 'Ascension' types. In 1887, Henry Sharpe, quoting Claude Wilson in the *Quarterly Journal* of the Royal Meteorological Society (vol. 13, pp. 245-272), wrote "The effect was weird and beautiful in the extreme, and one could not help feeling that fifty years ago what we saw would have been ascribed to supernatural agency".

A classic description of a Brocken spectre by the Spanish scientist Antonio de Ulloa can be found in Frederic Zurcher's *Meteors, aerolites, storms and atmospheric* (New York, 1876), but the following quotation is from Ralph Abercromby's article in *Nature* (vol. 33, 8 April 1886, pp. 532-3), concerning the sunrise shadow of Adam's Peak in Sri Lanka (then called Ceylon):

"The mountain rises to a height of 7352 feet as an isolated cone projecting more than 1000 feet above the main ridge to which it belongs. The appearance which has excited so much comment is that just after sunrise the shadow of the Peak seems to rise up in front of the spectator, and then suddenly either to disappear or fall down to the earth . . . Suddenly, at 6.30 a.m., the sun peeped through a chink in the eastern sky, and we saw a shadow of the Peak projected on the land; then a little mist drove in front of the shadow, and we saw a circular rainbow of perhaps 8° or 10° diameter surrounding the shadow of the summit, and as we waved our arms we saw the shadow of our limbs moving in the mist. Two dark lines seemed to radiate from the centre of the bow, almost in a prolongation of the slopes of the Peak . . . Twice this shadow appeared and vanished as cloud obscured the sun, but the third time we saw what has apparently struck so many observers. The shadow seemed to rise up and stand in front of us in the air, with rainbow and spectral arms, and then to fall down suddenly to the earth as the bow disappeared. The cause of the whole was obvious. As a mass of vapour drove across the shadow, the condensed particles caught the shadow, and in this case were also large enough to form a bow. As the vapour blew past, the shadow fell to its natural level—the surface of the earth . . . Any idea of mirage was entirely disproved by my thermometric observations . . ."

ROBERT THE BRUCE WAS A SCOTSMAN
Robert de Bruis (1274-1329) may have been King of Scotland, but he belonged to a Norman family which landed with William the Conqueror in 1066. A good French aristocrat.

THE BUDDHISTS OF UPPER INDIA BUILT THE PYRAMIDS, STONEHENGE, etc.
Godfrey Higgins followed his remarkable *The Celtic Druids; or an attempt to shew that the Druids were the priests of Oriental colonies* . . . (London, 1829) with the two-volume *Anacalypsis* (2 vols., London, 1836).

The theme of the *magnum opus* hinges on the fallacious idea that the Buddhists of Upper India (of whom the Phoenician Canaanite Melchizedek was a priest), built most of the monuments of antiquity, including the Pyramids of Egypt, Stonehenge and Carnac. They also founded all the ancient mythologies of the world which, however they have since become corrupted, were originally one, and that one founded on principles sublime, beautiful and true.

It is quite untrue to suggest that, despite the implausibility of virtually everything that Higgins has to say, speculators on mysteries today are any less ignorant or numerous. If anything, the post-World War II reaction against applied science has led to an increased irrationalism which finds its literary outlet in books on the occult of every possible description.

See also **PYRAMIDS** and **STONEHENGE**.

BULLS ARE INFURIATED BY THE COLOUR RED

No: bulls are infuriated by a cruel posturing mercenary 'fighter' waving a cloth in front of him to the accompaniment of merciless cheering by bloodthirsty spectators. Bulls cannot distinguish red from any other colour, and *matadores* who experimentally used white capes in their antics produced an identical reaction. While visiting Palma de Mallorca in 1976 I found a poster advertising bloodless bullfights for the benefit of squeamish tourists, and Portuguese bullfights are traditionally bloodless. The colour red was probably first used partly because in strong sunlight it is the most brilliant colour, and partly because it does not show blood so clearly.

COWS WHICH EAT **BUTTERCUPS** GIVE THE YELLOWEST BUTTER

A folk fallacy found in several parts of the British Isles. Buttercups grow only on good pastureland, the surrounding grass of which is likely to improve butter (and milk) quality by giving the best quality feed to the cow. Cows will not eat the buttercups, a nauseous, bitter weed.

Source: *The Field*, 9 June 1906.

"A common error is the greater and more mischievous for being so common."—CLARENDON.

CAMELHAIR BRUSHES ARE MADE FROM THE HAIR OF CAMELS

Camelhair brushes are made for artists and architects from the hair of the tails of Russian squirrels. The hair of camels, on the other hand, was used for making carpets, tent-cloths, and for mixing with silk. But the advent of synthetic fibres has vastly reduced the use of the hair of camels, as well as that of 'camel-hair'.

CAMELS HAVE A HUMP FOR STORING WATER

Camels have a hump (or two humps in the case of a Bactrian) which does *not* have a hollow reservoir for water inside. Excess food and drink that the camel does not need at once are stored in the body as fat and other substances, to be drawn on in time of need. Water is present not only in the hump (together with the fat) but is stored also in other body tissues and in the stomach pouches, allowing the animal to survive without drinking for seven days (if working quite actively) or ten to twelve days (if inactive).

Source: Osmond P. Breland, *Animal facts and fallacies* (London, 1950).

CANARY BIRDS GAVE THEIR NAME TO THE CANARY ISLANDS

Quite the reverse! The Latin name *insula Canaria* derived from the large *canes* or dogs found there. Birds exported from these islands off the western coast of Morocco were called 'canaries' from the place they came from, not the other way round.

CAPITAL PUNISHMENT HAS BEEN ABOLISHED IN GREAT BRITAIN

This popular idea stems from the fact that the final penalty has been abolished for murder. The death penalty still applies to those convicted of high treason or piracy with violence if they are 18 years of age or more; the penalty for pregnant women is commuted to life imprisonment.

CARDANO

The Italian Girolamo Cardano (1501-1576) exemplifies the continuation of medical and popular fallacies beyond the Middle Ages. He believed that howling dogs were omens, saw on his finger an image of a bloody sword when his son was arrested for murder which disappeared when his son was executed, and said he was fond of river crabs because his mother ate them while carrying him. He was merely a doctor of his time in treating his patients on the theory of heat and cold and the four temperaments, and in purging the brain by anointing the coronal suture with ship's tar and honey.

Cardano was in fact one of the foremost doctors of his day, and avoided the most harmful of medical fallacies then current.

Cardano's *De subtilitate rerum* (1551), which gives false explanations for many phenomena, was supplemented by *De varietate rerum* (1557). Both are analysed by Rixner and Siber in their *Leben und Lehrmeinungen ber hmter Physiker am Ende des XVI und am Anfange des XVII* (vol. 2, Sulzbach, 1820). See also W. G. Waters, *Jerôme Cardan* (1898).

CASTE

Belief in caste is a racist fallacy, since caste originated not purely from class prejudice, but from colour prejudice. The Sanskrit word *varna* denotes both colour and caste, and was probably imposed by the conquering (white) Aryans on the indigenous (black) populations of India, and is yet another example of the exploitation of the weak by the strong. The Vedas have many references to colour.

A man or woman is not inferior to another because of relegation to a lower caste. See also **KARMA.**

CATGUT

is not that at all, but the fibrous layer of sheep's intestine, toughened with chromic acid. The strings of musical instruments owe nothing whatsoever to the domestic cat.

THERE WAS A REAL WOMAN CALLED **CATHERINE OF ALEXANDRIA** WHO BECAME A MARTYR DURING THE RULE OF MAXENTIUS

It is preposterous that some believers still assert that a certain Catherine of Alexandria demolished the arguments of fifty philosophers before the Emperor Maxentius (4th century), who then caused the sages to be burnt alive. Neither did she refuse to deny her faith and marry the Emperor, who caused her to be beaten and locked up in a cell, where she was fed by a dove. Nor was she tied to a wheel (the catherine-wheel of firework fame) and left unscathed when it fell to pieces. All of these and many more such tales of the Christian from Alexandria are absent from the early records of the Church, and it is now believed that she was invented by a Greek writer as the heroine of a romance.

Eusebius speaks of an unnamed woman of Alexandria to whom he attributes some of the miracles later given to Catherine and may thus be an unwitting source for part of the story.

Source: Donald Attwater, *The Penguin dictionary of saints* (Harmondsworth, 1965, pp. 209-210).

MEN WILL NEVER BE ABLE TO SEE BETTER THAN CATS AT NIGHT

Normally this is true enough, but a new 'image intensifier' is being used for nocturnal military operations, observing nocturnal animals, and intensifying X-ray photographs. It consists of a tube through which the images at night or in darkness are made brighter by electrons focussed on a phosphorescent screen, on which is built up a brighter reproduction of the original picture. Now and in the future, men will see better than owls or cats at night by means of this device.

CATS CATERWAUL WHEN MAKING LOVE

The popular notion of a boardinghouse landlady tipping a pail of cold water over noisy cats to separate them from their lovemaking activities is totally mistaken. Caterwauling is a threatening pose which may increase to a fight or decrease to an uneasy armistice, but is never, repeat *never* a matter of affection.

Nikolai Zabolotsky perpetuates this fallacy in his poem 'On the Stairs' from the collection *Stoltsi* (Leningrad, 1929), translated by Daniel Weissbort in the selection *Scrolls* (London, 1971). The poem begins

"Cats on the springy stairs,
Lifting their large countenances,
Sit like buddhas on the banisters,
Yowling, trumpeting their love".

CATS HAVE NINE LIVES

Regrettably not. They have the regulation issue of one. However, the cat's good sense, caution, and shrewdness have given it the reputation of surviving when any other animal would have perished, particularly when falling on its feet from a reasonable height.

We are indebted to Dean Inge, writing in the *Evening Standard* of 8 July 1936, for immortalizing the child's essay on cats: "The cat is a quadruped, the legs as usual being at the four corners . . . Do not tease cats, for, firstly, it is wrong to do so, and, secondly, cats have claws, which are longer than people think. Cats have nine lives, but which are seldom required in this country, because of Christianity".

JUAN DE ZABALETA'S "CELEBRATED ERRORS"

Juan de Zabaleta (1610-1670?) published in 1653 a series of thirty-four anecdotes on classical subjects from which he drew moral and religious lessons. There is a good recent edition in the "Clásicos castellanos" series (Madrid, 1972) by David Hershberg. Zabaleta's censure of the ancients was attacked by José de la Torre in *Aciertos celebrados de la antigüedad* (Saragossa, 1654), which answers Zabaleta point by point, defending the ancients.

Most of these 'errors' are not fallacies in the sense usual elsewhere in this *Dictionary*, but the first seven are included here for the guidance of the curious and in the interest of a more thorough treatment of 'error' as conceived through the ages. Logic and fact are not here involved—merely opinion.

1. The Emperor Augustus prohibited the use of the word 'Dominus' (Lord) when addressing an emperor, for it is fitting to address thus only the gods.

2. The Greek philosopher Thales fell while looking up at the stars. He was reproved by his maid, who helped him up, saying, "You cannot even see what is at your feet: how then can you hope to understand the stars?"

3. The Egyptians of the Pharaonic age lived in small houses of poor clay, yet built great tombs of marble. While living they treated themselves like the dead; the dead they treated like the living. Diodorus Siculus found much to admire in this conduct.

4. Solon and Periander were invited to a banquet with friends. After a time, noting that Solon alone said nothing, Periander murmured to a neighbour, "Solon is silent as a wise man or as a fool". Solon replied, equally quietly, "Fools are not silent at a banquet".

5. Gnaeus Metellus, a Roman, killed his wife because he found her drinking wine. The Roman judges neither punished him nor even reprimanded him, indicating by their silence a belief that the action of Metellus would deter other women from breaking the law of temperance.

6. One of a poor man's many sons left his squalid hut in Eritrea to seek his fortune and eventually arrived in Athens. Not knowing how to become rich, he entered a school by chance and, being inclined to study, remained there for several years, finally studying under Zeno. When he felt that he had learnt enough he returned home, where his father was angry beyond measure to see the youth dressed in the same rags as when he had left long before. "Where are your riches?" he demanded. "Here", said the youth, though he evidently had no possessions. The father, not realizing that the youth understood his wealth to reside in his learning, took up a stick and belaboured the boy. "Now where is your wealth?" shouted his irate father. "Here", said the boy, "—the ability to withstand a beating".

7. Sulpicius Similis was an honoured and respected Consul. He finally tired of his duties at the age of fifty-three and retired. Seven years later, on his deathbed, he ordered that his epitaph should read as follows: "Here lies Similis, who died at the age of sixty years, and only lived seven".

EVERY CENTURY HAS ITS OWN CHARACTER

Any shelf of history books has its quota of titles like *The Golden Century of Spain* or *England in the 17th Century* as though some personality rose or declined in 1600. The great French mediaevalist Marc Bloch complained in *The historian's craft* (New York, 1953), that "we tend to count in centuries: we no longer name ages after their heroes. We very prudently number them in sequence every hundred years starting from a point fixed, once and for all, at the year 1 of the Christian era [though of course the Muslim calendar begins from year 632 A.D., the year of the Flight of the Prophet Muhammad s.a.w.]. The art of the thirteenth century, the philosophy of the eighteenth, the 'stupid nineteenth': these faces in arithmetical masks haunt the pages of our books. Which of us will boast of having never fallen prey to the lures of their apparent convenience?"

A similar error has induced certain Christian scholars to divide things arbitrarily by threes; Auguste Comte (followed by Dewey in his Decimal Classification) divided human knowledge into ten [!]; and others have divided the past into six ages, according to the six days of the Biblical Creation myth.

CARNEADES ON THE FALLACY OF **CERTITUDE**

Carneades of Cyrene (c. 214-c. 129 B.C.) was the founder of the so-called Third or New Academy. With the Stoic Diogenes of Babylon and the Peripatetic Critolaus he was a member of the celebrated Athenian delegation of philosophers sent to Rome in 156-155. Though none of his writings survives, his lectures in Rome were famous in their time for their dialectical and rhetorical power as well as for their fearless moral independence, and are recorded in the *Cato Maior* of Plutarch and in the *Lucullus* and other works of Cicero.

He is the greatest systematic figure in classical scepticism, like Arcesilaus denying all possibility of certitude. His arguments lead to the withholding of judgment; he nevertheless admitted different stages of clarity in human perception, and the perception which carries conviction he entitled a 'convincing or probable presentation' (*pithanè phantasiá*; see Sextus Empiricus, *Pròs mathematikoús* ('Against the schoolmasters'), vii, 184 f.). The positive aspect of Carneades' scepticism was his theory of probability, but his negative criticism of the metaphysicians' failure to find rationality in religious beliefs made a great impression in his day. He repudiated all dogmatic doctrines such as Stoicism, and did not even spare the Epicureans as previous sceptics had done. He denied the immortality of the gods, their

allegedly superhuman qualities, pantheism, fatalism, and providence. He refused to accept any moral values as absolute, while
indicating the necessity of learning how to conduct one's life by
combining wise thought with wise action. The quotation below
is based on hearsay and is further diluted by translation; yet it
still seems to echo the quiet voice of a moderate thinker born on
the green hills of Cyrene.

"There is absolutely no criterion for truth", said Carneades.
"For reason, senses, ideas, or whatever else may exist are all
deceptive, Even if such a criterion were available, it could not be
separated from the feelings produced by sense impressions. It is
the faculty of feeling that distinguishes the living creature from
inanimate things. By means of that feeling, the living creature
becomes perceptive both of itself and of the external world. There
is no sensation or perception of anything unless the sense is irritated, agitated, or perturbed. When an object is indicated, then
the senses become irritated and somewhat disturbed. It is impossible that there be an unperturbed presentation of external things.

The subject is more or less persuaded by the image it perceives.
The strength of that persuasion depends on the disposition of the
subject and on the degree of irritation produced by the image. It
is not the distinctness of the image that constitutes its credibility.

The only way we can ever obtain certitude is by the difficult
process of examination. We cannot be satisfied with evidence that
is incomplete and only probable. Our certitude is always a pre-
carious one. Science must rely on probabilities therefore, not on
certitude".

The witty bent of Carneades' mind can be judged from his
retort to the master from whom he learnt logic, Diogenes: "If I
reason correctly, then I am satisfied; if wrong, give me back my
mina", the fee for the lectures.

Sources include: *The Oxford Classical Dictionary* (Oxford, 1949); and
Dagobert D. Runes (ed.), *Treasury of philosophy* (New York, 1955).

CHAMELEONS MATCH THEIR BACKGROUND

Most people would swear that this is the case, though few of them
have seen a chameleon. In fact, though experiments have proved
that many of these lizards can indeed change colour rapidly, there
is no evidence that the colour of their background has any but a
marginal importance, the main factors influencing colour change

being light, temperature, and the chameleon's health and feelings. (Human beings also change colour within a limited range according to their feelings, though not as violently as the terms 'purple', 'white' or 'red' would indicate).

Those keeping a chameleon are advised not to take too seriously the fallacy perpetuated by Shakespeare in *Hamlet* (III, ii, 98) that the reptile lives on air.

'CHAMOIS'-LEATHER DERIVES FROM THE CHAMOIS

Not any more. Nowadays, defying the Trades Description Act, 'chamois' has nothing to do with the Alpine creature, but derives from the flesh side of sheepskin, reduced to an even thickness with a pumice-stone and soaked in lime-water and a solution of sulphuric acid.

INHERITANCE OF ACQUIRED **CHARACTERISTICS**

A major zoological error, which persisted among many zoologists well into the 20th century, was the Lamarckian belief in the inheritance of acquired characteristics: the hypothesis that bodily or somatic changes experienced by the individual as a result of either environmental influences or his own activities would somehow be passed on to his offspring and reappear in some measure in the absence of similar influences and activities.

The theory lost impetus with the work of August Weismann (1834-1914), who advanced a view of the continuing germ-plasm as distinct from the somatoplasm, making it clear that germ-cells form a continuous line, not only between generations but also through the body of the individual in each generation.

Source: Howard M. Parshley, *Error in zoology*, in Joseph Jastrow, *The story of human error* (New York, 1936, p. 214).

THE 'CHARGE' WAS SOUNDED AT BALACLAVA

Contrary to the accepted story, the 'Charge' was never sounded at Balaclava. Nor did Lord Cardigan, once his brigade was in motion, by trumpet, voice, or signal, issue any command.

Source: Col. F. E. Whitton, in *The Nineteenth Century*, November 1926.

CHARMS

It is a fallacy to assume that the wearing of any charm (see also **AMULETS** and **TALISMANS**) can bring good fortune to the wearer, though this compound of fear and ignorance has never shown any sign of dying out in any society or in any age. The best that can be said of the error is that it bestows a spurious confidence on the superstitious owner of the charm (which can turn to panic more readily if the charm can be seen not to be 'working') and the owner then attributes success to the wearing of the charm rather than to the confidence he induced in himself by wearing it.

The mundane proof of the fallacy is that, in any given baseball or football match of importance, many players on both sides wear charms, though it is evident that both teams cannot win (especially in the event of a draw).

CHEMICAL FERTILIZERS AND PESTICIDES ARE TOO DANGEROUS AND SHOULD BE BANNED

According to Dr Norman Borlaug, 1970 Nobel Prize-winner for his work on high yield wheat strains, "the vicious hysterical propaganda campaign against the use of agricultural chemicals being promoted today by fear-provoking, irresponsible environmentalists had its genesis in Rachel Carson's best-selling book *Silent Spring* published in 1962. This poignant, powerful book presented a very incomplete, inaccurate, and oversimplified picture . . ."

In 1968, thanks to the use of chemical fertilizers, pesticides, and men like Dr Borlaug, world food production increased by 3%, while world population increased by only 2% (See *Nature*, 3 January 1970, p. 9) while in 1969, thanks to high-yield grains, India increased its food production by 5%, while its population increased by only 2.4%.

Borlaug predicted that "if agriculture is denied the use of chemical fertilizers and pesticides because of unwise legislation that is now being promoted by a powerful group of hysterical lobbyists who are provoking fear by predicting doom for the world through chemical poisoning, then the world will be doomed, not by chemical poisoning but from starvation".

Source: *The Times*, 9 November 1971.

OCCULT CHEMISTRY

In 1908 Annie Besant and Charles W. Leadbeater published a book with the above title, which treats chemistry from a theosophical point of view (see **THEOSOPHY**). And just as one would hesitate to consider a book dealing with electricity from the point of view of Islam as potentially instructive, so it must be admitted that the clairvoyant study of the structure of atoms has little to recommend it beyond the realms of curiosity. As well as being nonsense, however, the book (revised in 1919) has the unlikely distinction of also being dull.

WHITE WOMEN CAN BEAR BLACK CHILDREN

White women who marry black men cannot have truly black children: only if the genes of *both* parents are coal-black can a woman have a coal-black child.

It is incidentally almost impossible for human skin to be completely 'black'.

WEAK CHINS SIGNIFY WEAK PERSONALITIES

It is a mystery how the 'chinless wonder' myth arose to scoff at the ineffectual English upper-class dolt celebrated in the stories and novels of P. G. Wodehouse, among others.

Frederick the Great, General Wolfe, and Queen Victoria had receding chins, but nobody has yet had the temerity (or the ignorance) to call them weak characters.

This fallacy is one of the class deriving from the erroneous supposition that one can tell a person's character by looking.

IT IS MATHEMATICALLY PROVED THAT CHRISTIANITY WILL NO LONGER BE BELIEVED IN AFTER THE YEAR A.D.3150

John Craig, in his *Theologiae Christianae principia mathematica* (London, 1699), made mathematical calculations on the hypothesis that the suspicions against historical evidence increase with the square of the time elapsed so that, if Christianity had been known only orally it would have died out in A.D.800, but since its claims were written down and believed it would survive until A.D. 3150, when another Messiah would be required.

CINDERELLA WORE GLASS SLIPPERS

Of the three hundred or so early versions of this popular fairy tale (including a Chinese story of the 9th century), not one described Cinderella's slippers as made of glass, because they weren't. The mediaeval French version used by Perrault (1628-1703), author of the *Cinderella* we know today, described the slippers as 'pantoufles en vair', or slippers of white ermine. Perrault remembered the word as 'verre', or glass, and thus it has erroneously been ever since.

SQUARING THE CIRCLE

Montucla's *Histoire des récherches sur la quadrature du cercle* (Paris, 1754; 2nd ed., 1831) and Augustus de Morgan's *Budget of paradoxes* (London, 1872) are full of accounts of pseudo-mathematicians who have obtained by illegitimate means a Euclidean construction for the quadrature of the circle, or a finitely expressible value for π, and proceeded to use faulty reasoning and/or defective mathematics to establish their assertions.

When the squaring of the circle is spoken of, it is assumed that the restrictions of Euclidean geometry apply. The problem is so ancient, and has been tackled by so many leading mathematicians of every generation, that every claim to have solved it must, tentatively at least, be considered fallacious.

CIRCULAR 'PROOF'

Or *petitio principii* (Latin, 'begging the question'). This is a very common error, and can be exemplified by a statement of the theologian Barth: "That revelation is revelation can be known only by revelation" to justify his own beliefs. But the statement justifies nothing at all.

Less obviously fallacious reasoning occurs in Michael Walzer's *The revolution of the saints* (Cambridge, 1965). It is hoped to demonstrate, by an appeal to historical evidence, that a certain complex of ideas attached to Puritanism. But when Walzer discovers these ideas, he assumes that the thought of the man who expresses them is 'Puritanical' simply because he expresses them. Briefly, he assumes that Puritans were men who thought the 'XYZ' galaxy of ideas, and then proves the thesis by assuming that men who thought 'XYZ' were Puritanical.

The opposite fallacy is equally bad: that of treating an advanced proposition as a begging of the question as soon as one sees that, if established, it would establish the question.

Arnold Toynbee (in vol. 9 of *A study of history*, p. 196) wrote: "We may perhaps take it as having been already demonstrated that an historian's professed inability to discern any plot, rhythm, or predetermined pattern is no evidence that blind Samson has actually won his boasted freedom from the bondage of the 'Laws of Nature'. The presumption is indeed the opposite; for, when bonds are imperceptible to the wearer of them, they are likely to prove more difficult to shake off than when they betray their presence and reveal something of their shape and texture by clanking and galling".

In *The use of reason* (London, 1960, p. 226), E. R. Emmet argues that this is supposed to mean "Invisible bonds are hard to shake off; X cannot see any bonds; Therefore they are hard to shake off; Therefore the presumption is that they are still there".

CIVILIZATIONS HAVE ONE LIFE-CYCLE AND ONE CREATIVE CYCLE

This idea was propounded by Nikolai Yakovlevich Danilevsky (1822-1885) in *Russia and Europe: a viewpoint on the political relations between the Slavic and Germano-Romanic Worlds* (1871), Oswald Spengler (1880-1936) in *Der Untergang des Abendlandes* (Decline of the West, 1918), and Arnold Joseph Toynbee (1889-1975) in *A study of history* (11 vols., 1934-1959).

The fallacy is of course that of giving objective shape and pattern to an essentially chaotic phenomenon such as world or even national history in which events are uncontrollable, even by totalitarian methods.

Pitirim A. Sorokin, in his closely-argued *Modern historical and social philosophies* (New York, 1963), states that "the central idea of Danilevsky, Spengler, and Toynbee that each great culture or civilization has only one life-cycle and one cycle of creativity (with a minor "Indian Summer" and "second religiosity") is entirely untenable so far as real cultural systems are concerned. Even in regard to social groups it is tenable only for a small fraction of them. It is not at all tenable as applied to all social systems . . . Great cultural systems have many quantitative and qualitative ups and downs in their virtually indefinitely long life-span. Even big *social* systems like the Chinese or the Egyptian or the Hindu states and nations have had several ups and downs in their political and social history. So also have many families, religious or economic bodies, political parties and other social groups. In their "success", "creativity", "wealth", "membership" and "power", most of them have several ups and downs in their life-history instead of just one life-cycle and one period of creativity".

Sorokin supplies tables which conclusively demonstrate the fallacy of a specificity of cultural creativeness of each "civilization" or "nation" or "country" and prove that the field of creativity shifts in the course of time from religion or the fine arts to science or philosophy.

Examples of creative periods are provided from Ancient Egypt, Greece, and France. From India the examples are as follows:

Religion   c. 1000 B.C., c. 600-400 B.C., c. 272-232 B.C., c. 1-100 A.D., c. 788-860

The State (native, not foreign) and (to some extent) Economics
                c. 321-186 B.C., 78-96 A.D., 320-500, c. 606-647, 1350-1600

Philosophy   600-400 B.C., 100-500, 600-1000
Science   700-500 B.C., 400-1150 (climax c. 500-625)
Literature   400 B.C.-100 A.D., 350-750 [but note the various periods of creativity in each different language. Ph.W.]
Sculpture   c. 150 B.C., 400-725 A.D.
Architecture   1489-1706
Music   1600-1771
Painting   450-750, 1615-1800

CLAIRVOYANCE AND TELEPATHY MAY LEGALLY BE ATTEMPTED FOR GAIN

In Britain, the Fraudulent Mediums Act 1951 cites the offence of acting as a spiritualistic medium or using telepathy, clairvoyance or other similar powers with intent to deceive or when so acting using any fraudulent device when it is proved that the person so acted for reward.

The act commits the fallacy of assuming that such 'powers' exist! (Incidentally, fortune tellers are still punishable under section 4 of the Vagrancy Act of 1824).

Source: Moriarty, Police law, 22nd ed., by Sir William J. Williams (London, 1974).

CLEOPATRA WAS AN EGYPTIAN

Cleopatra (68-30 B.C.) was the eldest daughter of Ptolemy XI, the illegitimate son of Ptolemy VIII, son of Ptolemy VII. The Ptolemies were a Greek dynasty, and Cleopatra was Greek.

The granite obelisks known as Cleopatra's Needles have nothing whatsoever to do with her, but were erected at Heliopolis by

Thothmes III about 1600 B.C. The 'Cleopatra's Needle' on the Embankment in London was brought to England in 1878.

SIR WALTER RALEIGH LAID DOWN HIS CLOAK IN THE MIRE FOR ELIZABETH I

An example of a romantic idea perpetuated until it forms part of the national consciousness. The anecdote has no foundation in fact; it was invented by worthy Thomas Fuller (1608-61) and repeated by Sir Walter Scott in his popular novel *Kenilworth* (1821).

COCKERELS SING 'COCK A DOODLE DO'

They do if they sing English, but we are assured that English-singing cockerels are in a minority. French cockerels sing 'coco-rico' and German and Italian cockerels sing 'kikiriki'. Virtually every language has a different way of representing animal and bird noises, and it is a fallacy that they can or should all be represented in an identical fashion.

COCKTAILS AID DIGESTION

This fallacy is so common that no amount of proof seems to have any effect. In *Health for everyman* (1937), R. Cove-Smith categorically states that "the habit of cocktail-drinking is quite defenceless; cocktails irritate the stomach, cause a fictitious appetite and delay digestion".

COINCIDENCES ARE AMAZING

"In the eternal search for verification of the supernaturalism which engrosses so much of popular 'philosophy', nothing passes for more cogent evidence than coincidence. The marvelling over unexpected juxtapositions is at once the mark and the diversion of banal minds, and most of them do not require very remarkable happenings to constitute coincidences. Those who for lack of knowledge or imagination expect nothing out of the ordinary are always encountering the unexpected. One of the commonest of 'coincidences', as Professor Jastrow has pointed out, is the crossing of letters in the mail. It happens a thousand times a day yet thousands of men and women whip themselves into amazement every time it happens. As far as they are concerned, it is complete and final proof of the supernatural, whether it be telepathy or

Divine guidance or merely soul calling to soul. There it is, sealed, stamped, and delivered. Yet of all human happenings, what is more likely than that lovers or relatives should simultaneously decide to write to each other?" Thus Bergen Evans, in *The natural history of nonsense* (London, 1947).

But one can scarcely condemn Arthur Koestler's mind as 'banal' and he too is a believer in some magical properties of coincidence, or 'synchronicity' as he prefers to call it, following Jung, in his anecdotal *The roots of coincidence* (London, 1972). Jung kept a diary of coincidences, as did Paul Kammerer, whose faking of scientific evidence is recorded in Arthur Koestler's *Case of the midwife toad* (London, 1971). Kammerer's pathetic notebook of coincidences, as cited by Koestler in his work defending the notion of 'synchronicity' as a supernatural phenomenon within the field of 'extra-sensory perception', includes such trivia as the fact that on 4 November 1910 his brother-in-law went to a concert where he had seat no. 9 and cloakroom ticket no. 9. Kammerer's *Das Gesetz der Serie* (Stuttgart, 1919) proposes that there is a law of series in the same way that gamblers maintain that (until they lose) they are on a 'lucky streak'. He concludes that seriality is "ubiquitous and continuous in life, nature and cosmos. It is the umbilical cord that connects thought, feeling, science and art with the womb of the universe which gave birth to them". This theory leads Kammerer (and Koestler with him) to conclude that there is a reason for believing in telepathy, though no such cases have been proved *experimentally*. As an example of the credulity surrounding allegedly 'telepathic' coincidence it is sufficient to quote Renée Haynes, an ardent believer in extra-sensory perception, who quotes in her postscript to *The roots of coincidence* an article by W. J. Tarver in the *New Scientist* (24 October 1968).

Tarver, then Chairman of the Veterinarians' Union, suggested that "a gifted 10%" of dogs in boarding kennels "after being settled for a week or two become wildly excited at almost the exact moment when their owners begin the return journey from their holiday". This assumes (*a*) that the wildly-excited dogs are gifted; (*b*) that all kennels take an exact note of the time at which all their dogs become wildly excited; (*c*) all dog-owners take an exact note of the time at which they return from their holiday (when they pack their bags? board an aircraft?); (*d*) that dogs in kennels only become wildly excited at the thought of their owners; etc. But more damaging to the case of Tarver, Haynes and Koestler is the simple figure of 90% of cases which do not fit any kind of assumed pattern; one might well be justified in asking a percentage nearer to 30 before any kind of statistical inference could *reasonably* be made, with a negative percentage of around 70.

One's attitude to the coincidental and the serial must depend upon one's attitude to Koestler's rider intended to dull the sceptical intelligence: "The type of stringent controls applied to ESP experiments, and the presence of sceptical observers, would certainly not facilitate their occurrence". Koestler is thus in fact arguing: "I say this; therefore, though I cannot prove this because this is unprovable, you should believe me". This is the fallacy of authority, claiming something to be true merely because of the status of the claimant. Bergen Evans has dealt with the fallacy as follows: "Whereas the trained mind accords belief to plausible evidence only and grants a possibility solely on the basis of a sound inference from established facts, the untrained mind insists that a proposition must be true if it cannot be *dis*proved. 'You can't prove it *isn't* so!' is as good as Q.E.D. in folk logic—as though it were necessary to submit a piece of the moon to chemical analysis before you could be sure that it was not made of green cheese".

Sources include: Bergen Evans, *The natural history of nonsense* (London, 1941) and Arthur Koestler, *The roots of coincidence* (London, 1972).

COLD BATHS ARE BETTER THAN WARM OR HOT BATHS

Though commonly taught at English public schools, this theory is not accepted by any reputable doctor: "cold baths are doubtless a moral tonic", according to Peter Wingate in *The Penguin Medical Encyclopaedia*, "but are not known to do any physical good". Very hot baths on the other hand raise the body temperature and can be dangerous.

COLDS CAN BE PREVENTED BY BUILDING UP RESISTANCE

Apart from the obvious fact that a normally healthy person will be less likely to take cold than someone less healthy, there are no grounds for hoping that one could build up resistance against the common cold by such activities as strenuous exercise or 'toughening the body' by sleeping out of doors. Noah D. Fabricant indicates the absurdity of trying to stave off the cold in *The common cold* (Chicago, 1945). A Gallup poll of 1945 showed that, as a group, farmers have slightly more colds than other groups in the population.

Nobody yet knows what causes the common cold.

Source: Bergen Evans, *The natural history of nonsense* (London, 1947).

CHRISTIANS WERE THROWN TO THE LIONS AT THE COLOSSEUM, ROME

George Bernard Shaw's *Androcles and the lion* is only one of the multitude of antihistorical books, plays and films that have perpetuated this ancient error, which seems to have been due to a desire to manufacture martyrs in Rome (another case is the Catacombs fraud). No Christian was ever exposed to the lions or to any other sort of death in the Roman Colosseum.

Source: P. Delehaye, *L'amphithêatre Flavien* (1897). See also the 'Coliseum' entry in the *Catholic Encyclopaedia*.

THE COLOUR-BLIND CAN SEE ONLY GREY

This is undoubtedly true of the most extreme cases, but much more frequently the blindness applies to only one colour or two. Most colour blindness seems to apply to green, and less to red, while some of those who are colour-blind confuse green and red. The colour-blind are otherwise good at matching colours and tend to have normal vision in all else. About one man in twenty-five is colour-blind, but only about one woman in 250.

Source: F. W. Edridge-Green, *Colour-blindness and colour-perception* (London, 1891).

THE THREE PRIMARY COLOURS ARE BLUE, RED, AND YELLOW

The primary colours are violet, red, and green. The misapprehension arises through the use of 'colour' for 'pigment': they are not the same thing. There are no primary pigments, for the simple reason that pigment colours are not even nearly monochromatic. For instance, a 'red' poppy illuminated by blue light appears to be black.

A mixture of yellow and blue light does not produce a green light, whereas a mixture of yellow and blue pigments does produce

51

a green pigment. Blue and yellow light can be mixed to produce white, or fawn, or blue-grey.

Source: John Tyndall, *New fragments* (1892), p. 61.

COLUMBUS INTENDED TO LAND IN AMERICA

Columbus had no inkling of the existence of the American continent, and failed to discover *India*. "The Columbian tradition, transmitted through Columbus' son Fernando and his historian Las Casas, has given to later generations a picture of the Discoverer struggling for a new idea against entrenched unscientific conservatism. This representation of Columbus' scientific activity is certainly false; the more enlightened his critics were in the science of their day, the more firmly would they have to reject his ridiculous scientific ideas."

Source: John Leighly, *Error in geography*, in Joseph Jastrow, *The story of human error* (New York, 1936, p. 104.)

COLUMN FALLACIES

Eighteen common fallacies on columns in structural engineering were published by E. H. Salmon in *The Structural Engineer* of March and April 1924.

1. That Euler's limiting load merely implies passage from one type of stable equilibrium to another and does not involve the failure of the column.
2. That the defect in Euler's formula is the neglect of the direct compressive stress.
3. That the deflection of an ideal column is an indefinite function of the load.
4. That the Eulerian length relations have any applicability in practice.
5. That it is possible to prove the Rankin-Gordon formula theoretically.
6. That the constants in the "eccentricity" form of the Rankine-Gordon formula are the same as those in the ordinary Rankine-Gordon formula.
7. That a "straight line formula" is the simplest column formula.
8. That eccentricity of loading is the principal source of weakness in columns.
9. That the eccentricity of loading or the initial curvature are functions of the radius of gyration.
10. That the bending stress in the ordinary column perfectly

direction-fixed at the ends is equal at the middle and at the ends.

11. That for given end conditions the "free length" is a fixed proportion of the length of an ordinary column.
12. That there is a tension side in the ordinary practical column.
13. That the Considère Engesser theory gives values for the crippling load suitable for use in practical design.
14. That a column with flat ends is fixed in direction at the ends, and that its failure is brought about by the ends "swinging round".
15. That a "solid" column is stronger than a lattice-braced column.
16. That in built-up columns the moment of inertia about the two principal axes should be the same.
17. That batten plate columns are necessarily unscientific in design.
18. That the ordinary theory of columns has any applicability in practice.

COMETS ARE VOLCANOES

I am indebted to the erudite Augustus de Morgan's hilarious *Budget of paradoxes* (London, 1872) for a reference to an anonymous work, published in London about 1856, which I fear I have not seen. I content myself with its title, and de Morgan's *riposte*.

Comets considered as volcanoes, and the cause of their velocity and other phenomena thereby explained. "The title explains the book better than the book explains the title."

THE AVERAGE PERSON IS DISTINGUISHED BY COMMON SENSE

The most persistent of all fallacies is that which credits the man-in-the-street with enough intelligence and knowledge to see through the propaganda, lies, and deceitful advertisements both commercial and non-commercial that assail him every day. One way to check this is to visit your local bookshop or public library and see how many books on superstitions and pseudo-science fill the shelves in comparison with the number of titles that discuss and analyse those cults objectively.

Another way is to read sociological surveys of any group beliefs (prisoners in a jail; adolescents on a housing estate; parents at a school) such as the Lynds' *Middletown* (1925), which was based on the 'typical' small American town of Muncie, Indiana. In the daily newspaper they found that 37 display advertisements of a total of 68 were devoted to 'remedies' such as salves and soaps (see pp. 437-8). Muncie residents confessed to beliefs that a little bag of asafetida worn about the neck would prevent a child catching contagious diseases; that a worn leather shoestring around the same unfortunate child's neck would keep away croup (or cure croup if caught); that secret incantations could cure erisypelas; and that wrapping old hatbands round the mother's breast at childbirth would prevent breast infections and diseases...

We laugh at the Wise Men of Gotham, but Gotham is our home town.

AN ARCHBISHOP OF CANTERBURY WAS CONSECRATED AT THE NAG'S HEAD TAVERN IN LONDON

Roman Catholic propagandists spread the rumour that Matthew Parker, Archbishop of Canterbury from 1559 to 1576, was consecrated at the Nag's Head in Cheapside, London. The official register proves that Parker was consecrated at Lambeth.

The story arose after the sees had become vacant after the Act of Uniformity. Llandaff refused to officiate at Parker's consecration and the problem was that of obtaining consecration to preserve the 'apostolic succession' unbroken. The rumour was that a deposed bishop, one Scory, was sent for and duly officiated at the Nag's Head. Scory was indeed present at the Nag's Head for the dinner which *followed*, as was Parker.

Source: Edwin Radford, *Encyclopaedia of phrases and origins* (London, 1945, p. 86).

CONSPIRACY THEORIES OF HISTORY

Numerous fallacies have been connected with the theory that one or other group has secretly manipulated world politics for their own ends undetected until the author's own exposé was triumphantly published. The most notorious of such theories is that persistently suggesting that the world is in the hands of the Jews. The Russian tract *The secret of the Jews* (possibly drawn up by the Russian secret agent and occultist Yuliana Glinka) formed the basis for the *Protocols of the Elders of Zion* which purported to be documents proving the existence of such a conspiracy, all totally fabricated. Norman Cohn and Léon Poliakov have shown that the Nazi use of the conspiracy theory owed a great deal to anti-Jewish and anti-masonic propaganda of certain Roman Catholic writers at the turn of the century.

Johannes Rogalla von Bieberstein, in *Die These von der Verschwörung, 1776-1945* (Berne, 1977), traces a powerful conspiracy theory to a reaction against the activities in the 1770s of the Illuminati, a Bavarian secret society; to its exploitation by royalist propagandists after the French Revolution; and thence to the Roman Catholics who turned the rumour against liberals and socialists, as well as against their more familiar targets, the freemasons and Jews.

More dangerously, conspiracy theories have been utilized by most political leaders at most times to justify the existence of secret agents whose principal purpose is to stifle opposition to the leaders; whereas it is the very existence of the repressive state police/army that stimulates opposition.

THE LAW OF **CONTRADICTION**

"Nothing is both *A* and *Not-A*", states Aristotle's Third Law, which was taken to be axiomatic until the 19th century. But it is fallacious, as the following example will show.

It is 'obvious' that in the infinite sequence 1, 2, 3, 4, 5, etc. there are 'more' numbers than there are in the sequence 2, 4, 6, 8, etc., each being continued indefinitely; for the first contains all the evens 2, 4, 6, 8, . . . that broke up the second, and in addition all the odds 1, 3, 5, 7, etc., none of which occurs in the second.

But look at this:

1, 2, 3, 4, 5, 6, 7, . . .
2, 4, 6, 8, 10, 12, 14, . . .

The numbers are paired off, one-to-one, no matter how far out we go. Therefore, if we keep on going, and never stop pairing numbers, each number in the bottom row will have a unique mate in the top, for the numbers in the bottom row are got by doubling three in the top. But these rows are the sequences with which we started. The argument about the paired rows shows that there are just as many numbers in the bottom infinite row as in the top. Therefore there are just as many even numbers as there are numbers altogether, odds *and* evens. But we saw how obvious it was that there are fewer evens than numbers altogether. So Aristotle's Third Law is defied by the first sequences of numbers which we come across.

Two contradictory statements may both be true, according to Anicius Manlius Torquatus Severinus Boethius (c. 455-c. 524) in his *Introductio ad syllogismos categoricos* which was edited by J.-P. Migne in *Patrologiae cursus completus*, vol. 64 (Paris, 1860), cols. 761-832.

Boethius, better known for *De consolatione philosophiae*, argues that opposition between pairs of statements may sometimes be apparent rather than real, as in the following cases:

(1) Equivocation. 'Cato is not strong' and 'Cato is strong' may be equally correct if referring in one instance to mental and in the other to physical powers. Similarly, 'Cato killed himself at Utica' and 'Cato did not kill himself at Utica' are both true if the two historical Catos are recalled; one committed suicide at Utica, and the other did not.

(2) Univocation. 'Man walks' and 'Man does not walk' fail to contradict each other if 'man' refers in one case to mankind and in the other to a particular individual. This fallacy is more common in languages like Latin or Bahasa Indonesia which have no definite article.

(3) Different parts. 'The eye is white' and 'The eye is not white' may be equally correct even if there is only one eye in question, since one statement may refer to the pupil and the other to an eyeball: two different parts.

(4) Different relations. 'Socrates is on the left' and 'Socrates is on the right' will both be true if one stands in the appropriate relation to Socrates.

(5) Different times. 'Socrates is sitting down' and 'Socrates is not sitting down' will both be correct at different times.

(6) Different modalities. 'The egg is an animal' and 'The egg is not an animal' are both correct if one proposition refers to a potentiality and the other to an actuality.

Sources include: E. Temple Bell, *The search for truth* (London, 1935) and Charles Hamblin, *Fallacies* (London, 1970).

COPROLITES ARE THE DUNG OF DINOSAURS

Buckland, the geologist who first analysed coprolite, had already found in 1829 many types of dinosaur remains in the Lias at Lyme Regis (Devonshire, England), where coprolite material was also discovered. Jukes-Browne correctly called Buckland's association of the two finds 'an erroneous conclusion' (in *Quarterly Journal of the Geological Society*, 1875), but the damage had been done, and another common fallacy was on its way to the storehouse of folk 'knowledge'.

Coprolite is the name given commercially to phosphatic nodules, which were mined extensively in Cambridgeshire in the second half of the 19th century.

Source: Richard Grove, *The Cambridgeshire coprolite mining rush* (Cambridge, 1976), pp. 3-4.

THE **CORPSE** OF A MAN FLOATS ON ITS BACK, WHILE THAT OF A WOMAN FLOATS ON ITS FRONT

Pliny, in his *Historia naturalis*, 'explains' that this is due to the essential modesty of Nature. The fact is fallacious, the deduction is fallacious, and the whole is fallacious.

CORRELATABLE DATA ARE THEREBY CAUSAL

A common cause of belief in fallacies in the belief that correlatable data show some kind of *causal* connection. See under **STORK-MARKS** for a repudiation of this notion.

Harold A. Larrabee, in *Reliable knowledge* (Boston, 1954, p. 368), points to a near-perfect correlation between the death-rate in Hyderabad from 1911 to 1919 and fluctuations in the membership of the International Association of Machinists during the same period. The fact that nobody seriously takes such a correlation to imply causality does not prevent economists, politicians, and even trained historians from discovering causal connections in data which may simply be coincidental correlation.

To say that A caused B, one must first show that A_1 occurred before B_1; second, that there is in fact a correlation between A and B; third, one must find a presumptive agency connecting A and B. Thus, there is fairly good statistical evidence that smoking causes lung cancer; there is a proved correlation; the temporal connection exists; and the agency is presumed to be the inhalation of smoke and the deposit of carcinogens in the lung. Though the precise nature of the agency is not completely understood, the fact of its existence seems clear enough to the independent and unbiased observer.

COURTS OF LOVE EXISTED AND PRONOUNCED VERDICTS IN THE MIDDLE AGES

Books published as recently as 1937 perpetuated the error that mediaeval Courts of Love existed. Alfred Jeanroy, in *La poésie lyrique des troubadours* (2 vols., Toulouse, 1934) states that "the existence of these alleged Courts of Love must be relegated to the rank of those legends which, however attractive they may be, should none the less be banished from literary history". The legend was started by the 16th-century writer Jean de Nostredame, based on a misreading of poems by the troubadours. Gatherings of knights and their ladies frequently turned their conversation, as might be expected, to the finer points of love and courtship, but Nostredame is quite mistaken when imagining that tribunals of great ladies sat in judgment on cases involving distracted lovers. The term 'court', as understood in mediaeval France, referred to social gatherings and not to official enquiries of any kind.

A CRAB IS A RED FISH THAT WALKS BACKWARDS

The Académie Francaise read out this draft definition to the great French naturalist Cuvier, who gravely replied, "Perfect, gentlemen. But if you will give me leave, I will make one small observation in natural history. The crab is not a fish, it is not red, and it does not walk backwards. With these exceptions your definition is excellent".

The edible crab of the United States is blue, while the common crab found in Britain is brown; they are crustaceans, not fish; and they are capable of moving in any direction when on land or the seabed, but more usually move sideways.

One is only provoked to remark that, if intelligent men can make so many errors on a common observable phenomenon, how is it possible to put any trust in the opinions of theologians, philosophers, or economists whose currency is the untestable theory?

JONES ON CREDULITIES

In his work on fallacies and superstitions entitled *Credulities past and present* (London, 1880), William Jones, F.S.A., devotes ten chapters to: The sea and seamen; miners; amulets and talismans; exorcising, and the blessing of animals; birds; eggs; and luck.

Writing in the Victorian age, Jones complained (much as one might complain today): "Of what use is the exposure of the dark side of human nature—the weaknesses and follies of mankind? Were these matters of the past only, we might be contented with smiling at the ignorance and fatuity of our ancestors, but the inheritance of many strange and flimsy fancies has descended to us through long ages, and is still deeply engrafted on the popular mind in spite of the extension of wholesome intelligence".

REPORTS OF **CRIME** AND VIOLENCE IN THE MASS MEDIA DO NOT CAUSE VIOLENCE

Among the cases which refute this fallacy are:
1. As soon as a popular newspaper reported in 1872 that children were being abandoned in France, eight children were abandoned in Marseilles in a single day.
2. There were several murders by children after the Jack-the-Ripper atrocities in London.
3. The murderer Haigh copied the acid-bath methods formerly employed by George Sarrett in France, which were widely reported in the press.
4. In 1857 in New York, when a woman killed her husband, three other women did the same a few days later.

At the same time it is clear that not all violence is caused by the viewing of violent films, television programmes, or reading violent comic strips or books. It is simply that "a few abnormal minds are seriously affected by what they see and read. In 1960 a youth committed a murder while holding-up a bank on the day that another youth was hanged at Wandsworth". And such cases of blind imitation are probably so infrequent that it would be a ludicrous over-reaction to attempt to ban completely all violence in the mass media. The editors should beware of giving too much publicity to unsavoury people and doings.

Source: Christopher Hibbert, *The roots of evil* (London, 1963).

USING A **CROSS** AS SIGNATURE INDICATES ILLITERACY

For many centuries men of learning in Europe made the cross as the traditional way of *signing* their name, even though they could of course have spelt out their name had they wanted to do so. But the spelling out of the name was normally done by a witness to authenticate the sign. In the seventeenth century, certain educated people felt distaste at using the sign of the cross for secular or even mercantile purposes, and used instead their initials or some other sign recognized as their own.

Source: *Notes and Queries* 3 May 1941, p. 321.

THE BABY **CUCKOO** INTENTIONALLY KILLS ITS RIVAL YOUNG IN THE HOST NEST

No. During the first few days of its existence, the young cuckoo 'possesses closely-packed tactile organs on its back and sides, far in excess of the usual quantity'. Experiments have shown that 'when this spot is touched the young bird reacts as if it had been pricked with red-hot needles'. Thus, on touching the foster-parents' young, it becomes sensitive, burrows into the nest and arches its back rigidly to escape the painful pressure of the other young birds, thus unknowingly forcing them out of the nest. Being the largest of the young, with the largest beak and most vigorous movement to attract attention, the cuckoo would probably have survived at the expense of its foster-brethren in any case.

Source: Johann A. Loeser, *Animal behaviour* (London, 1940, p. 128).

CURSE OF THE PHARAOHS

Lord Carnarvon, who financed the excavation of the Tomb of Tut-Ankh-Amun in Egypt, died six weeks after his visit to the tomb of a mosquito bite. Howard Carter, who discovered the tomb also died—seventeen years later. The joke about the 'Curse of the Pharaohs' which took in so many people in 1922, when the tomb was first opened, was started by the Egyptologist Arthur Weigall as a hoax. It is not at all remarkable that ten people connected in some way with the Tut-Ankh-Amun expedition died within ten years. Richard Adamson, a survivor, expressed his disbelief in the curse on television in 1971.

This hoax became a fallacy because it was so tenacious in the popular mind that when a director of the Cairo Museum, Dr Mehrez, died in the early 1970s, his death was connected with the 'curse'.

D

"Defend me, therefore, common sense, say I,
From reveries so airy, from the toil
Of dropping buckets into empty wells,
And growing old in drawing nothing up."
—WILLIAM COWPER, *The Task* (Book III).

DÄNIKEN, Erich von

In books such as *Erinnerungen an die Zukunft, Zurück zu den Sternen* (both 1968) and *Aussaat und Kosmos* (1972), the German writer Erich von Däniken has proposed an illogical, unconnected but highly sensational and therefore saleable sequence of events concerning Gods, astronauts from outer space, extra-sensory perception, and an Andean cave-journey. His books, some re-written by Wilhelm Utermann, have sold over nine million copies world-wide and have been translated into more than 25 languages.

The first, *Chariots of the Gods?*, attempts to persuade the public (largely by Biblical 'interpretation') that alien beings from a distant galaxy visited our earth about 10,000 years ago, possibly after an intergalactic battle; that they created 'intelligent man' by altering the genes of monkeys 'in their image' and so created mankind who would thereafter worship them as gods because of their unfathomable technology; that many hitherto unidentified archaeological finds may be relics of the god-astronauts' visit; and that Men's sacred books are really accounts of the earthly visit of these 'gods'. Similar claims have been made by previous writers, but nobody has had the no. 1 best seller as frequently, and in so many lands, as von Däniken.

To quote *Der Spiegel*, translated in *Encounter* (August 1973, pp. 16-17), "there is no evidence, of course, either for myriads of civilised planets or for visits to the earth by alien astronauts, or for Däniken's alleged creation of human life, whether deliberate or fortuitous, by cosmic space-travellers. Däniken's realm of fancy lies in the twilight zone between the scientifically conceivable and a cowed humanity's craving for absolute certainty". Professor Wunderlich, author of *Wohin der Stier Europa trug* and a geologist, claims that Däniken has been misunderstood and is "the most important and brilliant satirist in German literature for at least a century", whereas Robert Neumann classifies him as one of those "paranoid dreamers who become, according to fate or fortune, leaders or prophets, saints, martyrs or clairvoyants".

The gold of the Gods (1972) claims to be a personal visit to caves below the eastern slopes of the Andes in Ecuador, during which he saw a menagerie of golden creatures: saurians, elephants camels, bears, monkeys, snails and crabs as well as a library written many thousand years before on thin sheets of metal "so as to remain legible in perpetuity". Däniken's chief witness to this adventure was Juan Moricz, who now claims that he did not take Däniken to the caves in Ecuador (which have incidentally been explored but without any trace of human or other habitation having been discovered) and Däniken subsequently admitted to two editors of *Der Spiegel* (Hamburg) in a taped interview at Innsbruck that he had never been to that part of Ecuador he described in his book and had merely spent six hours below ground near the town of Cuenca, 100 kilometres from the allegedly 'secret' entrance.

Reasons for the popular craze for Dänikitis, as the phenomenon has come to be known in German, have been offered by *Die Zeit* ("In an age rendered uncertain by science, people again have something to cling to: a simple doctrine") and by *Die Süddeutsche Zeitung* ("This man, who dwells on the frontiers of reality, is becoming the prophet of a 'new science' in which it is faith that counts, not proof").

Substantial refutations of Däniken's fallacies have been made by the following authorities, among others: Ernst von Khuon, in *Waren die Götter Astronauten?*; Pieter Coll, in *Geschäfte mit der Phantasie*; archaeologist Joachim Rehork, in *Faszinierende Funde*; Gerhard Gadow, in *Erinnerungen an die Wirklichkeit*; and Ronald Story, in *The space gods revealed*.

Source: *Encounter*, August 1973, pp. 8-17 and June 1977, pp. 44-46.

DEAD BODIES CAUSE PESTILENCE

The French Government, during World War I, found it necessary to issue an official communiqué stating that pestilence is not caused by dead bodies on a battlefield.

NO LIFE EXISTS IN THE **DEAD SEA**

But it does. Micro-organisms were reported to exist in the Dead Sea in *Nature*, 12 September 1936, p. 467. The old tale that 'Birds will not fly over the Dead Sea' has also been exploded by eye-witnesses.

Source: William G. Duncalf, *The Guinness book of plant facts and feats* (Enfield, 1976).

STEBBING ON THE **DEFINITION** OF FALLACIES

"The word 'fallacy' has unfortunately often been used in different senses", writes L. Susan Stebbing in *Thinking to some purpose* (Harmondsworth, 1939, pp. 156-7). "It is used sometimes as a synonym for 'error of fact', as in the statement: 'It is a fallacy to suppose that aeroplanes can be built by mass-production'. This is, in my opinion, a plainly erroneous use of the word. The speaker meant that aeroplanes cannot, in fact, be produced by methods suitable to the production of, say, motor-cars. I shall assume, without further discussion that the speaker, in using 'fallacy' in this sense, was simply showing his ignorance of the correct usage of the word. There remains to be noticed an ambiguity that is more important for our present purpose. If we say: "He is guilty of a fallacy", we sometimes mean to imply that he is guilty of a deception. The *Shorter Oxford English Dictionary* gives as a meaning of 'fallacy', now obsolete, 'deception', 'trickery'. This obsolete meaning does, I think, influence our modern usage. It would certainly be an advantage if we recognized that to accuse a person of having committed a fallacy is not to accuse him of intent to deceive. A fallacy is a violation of a logical principle; 'to fall into a fallacy' is to slip into 'an unsound form of argument', that is, to make a mistake *in reasoning*, not in what is *reasoned about*. If we mistakenly suppose that we have premisses adequate to establish our conclusion, then we are reasoning illogically and thus committing a fallacy.

If we think of a fallacy as a deception, we are too likely to take it for granted that we need to be cautious in looking out for fallacies only when other people are arguing with us. We come to suppose that a fallacy is a trick and, thus, as involving deliberate dishonesty. Thinking along these lines, we are apt to assume that where there is no dispute, and so no disputant, there is no danger of fallacies, so that honesty of intention will suffice to keep our reasoning sound. This is a profound mistake".

MACKAY ON DELUSIONS

Charles Mackay's engrossing compilation, *Extraordinary popular delusions and the madness of crowds* (London, 1852; expanded from *Memoirs of extraordinary popular delusions*, London, 1841) includes not only common fallacies such as haunted houses, alchemy, astrology, necromancy, augury, divination and omens; but also the mania for tulips (in the year 1800, the normal price in England was fifteen guineas for a single bulb); the disproportionate attention paid to the hair and the beard in political, religious, and social history (at the end of the 11th century the Pope decreed excommunication for longhaired men during their life and denial of prayer for them after death); the curious belief that slow poisoning was less offensive (especially in the 18th century in Europe, and above all in Italy); and the popular admiration of certain criminals, such as Jonathan Wild, Jack the Ripper, Vidocq, Schubry of Hungary, Schinderhannes of Germany, and Rob Roy of Scotland. In recent times one might cite the train robber Biggs and the vicious Kray brothers, exalted into mighty folk-heroes by the mass media.

Mackay, who wrote *Forty years' recollections* (1876) in autobiographical vein, observed in his preface to the 1852 edition of his book on delusions, "In reading the history of nations, we find that, like individuals, they have their whims and their peculiarities; their seasons of excitement and recklessness, when they care not what they do. We find that whole communities suddenly fix their minds upon one object, and go mad in its pursuit; that millions of people become simultaneously impressed with one delusion, and run after it, till their attention is caught by some new folly more captivating than the first. We see one nation suddenly seized, from its highest to its lowest members, with a fierce desire of military glory; another as suddenly becoming crazed upon a religious scruple; and neither of them recovering its senses until it has shed rivers of blood and sowed a harvest of groans and tears, to be reaped by its posterity. At an early age in the annals of Europe its population lost their wits about the sepulchre of Jesus, and crowded in frenzied multitudes to the Holy Land; another age went mad for fear of the devil, and offered up hundreds of thousands of victims to the delusion of witchcraft. At another time, the many became crazed on the subject of the philosopher's stone, and committed follies till then unheard of in their pursuit of it . . .".

DENTAL FALLACIES

"Clean teeth never decay" is a fallacy promulgated by at least one manufacturer of toothpaste. A clean surface is desirable, but impossible to obtain, owing to the perennial omnipresence of bacteria. However, the truism that toothpaste, dental floss, and brushing must all fail in various ways to prevent decay (they can only at best reduce the *speed* of decay) should not be taken by any youngster as an excuse to avoid brushing the teeth to remove as much as possible of accretions caused by eating and drinking. One's *general* health is a factor as important as frequent brushing in dental health.

It is frequently believed that 'primitive' peoples suffer less from tooth decay than do more 'civilized' peoples. This ignores the sugar-chewing Jamaicans, whose teeth decayed long before the white man arrived, and the Neanderthaloid 'Rhodesian' man of about 30,000 years ago was found to have decay in nearly every tooth of the upper jaw. The generalization is, however, true in the case of metropolitan white men vis-à-vis Zulus: according to V. Suk (*American Journal of Physical Anthropology*, vol. 2, 1919, pp. 351-88), at the age of 18, only 10-15% of the former have, 'perfect' teeth, while the figure among the latter is 85-94%.

An interesting fallacy, recurring in 1976 (*The Penguin medical encyclopedia*, 2nd ed., p. 433), is the old notion that "human jaws have receded in the course of evolution, and there is now barely room for the full set of permanent teeth". But there never was. Adolph H. Schutz, writing in *Current Anthropology* (vol. 7, 1966, p. 356), states that "unequivocal crowding of teeth is quite common among recent wild monkeys and apes. I have never failed to encounter cases with displaced, twisted, or impacted single or several large teeth in collections of primate skulls, and often such manifestations of unmistakable maladjustment in the size of the teeth and the jaws, resulting in crowding, are much more pronounced than in the two or three instances found in the Australopithecines".

Human teeth constitute irrefragable evidence, according to some, that Man is essentially a meat-eater, with the natural ability to rend animal flesh. Nothing could be more absurd: comparative anatomy proves the frugivorous and *not* the carnivorous origin of Man.

Cuvier states that "the natural food of man, judging from his structure, appears to consist principally of the fruits, roots, and other succulent parts of vegetables". Linnæus, Gassendi and later commentators corroborate this view. Sir Henry Thompson wrote in his *Food and feeding*: "The characters of his teeth and digestive organs indicate that during his long history of development [Man] has lived mainly on roots, seeds, nuts and fruits; in other words, he has been a vegetable feeder". A. S. E. Ackermann, in his *Popular fallacies* (4th ed., London, 1950), adds: "The assertion so often made that alcohol and animals are "sent" as food is absurd. The mere fact that we have been accustomed to eat flesh-food no more proves that animals were created for this purpose than the existence of cannibalism proves that missionaries are "sent" to the South Sea Islanders solely as an article of food, or the former existence of slavery that black men were "sent" to be slaves of the white".

Even a number of otherwise intelligent people still believe the hoary fallacy that an aching tooth should not be extracted until the "swelling" has gone down. While modern dentistry can usually avoid extraction in many circumstances, there are occasions when extraction is called for. Swelling indicates an abscess at the root of the tooth. Pus must always be evacuated and the best manner of achieving this in the case of a tooth is its removal. Unless this is done, the abscess may open and discharge, or it may break into the cellular tissue, causing general septic poisoning.

On the invention of dental 'crowns' and 'bridges', C. E. Wallis wrote in the *British Dental Journal* of 15 March 1915: "Many people have thought that the making of dental crowns and 'bridges' was introduced to mankind by our American cousins, but in various museums of ancient Greece and Rome are to be seen excellent examples of gold bridges and artificial teeth, such as were probably used by the plutocracy, if not by the aristocracy of those early days".

The best ancient dentists were the Etruscans, who made partial dentures, with gold bridge work, as early as 700 B.C. The art was lost during the Middle Ages, and Queen Elizabeth I, concerned to conceal the sinking of her face due to the loss of her front teeth, appeared in public with her mouth stuffed with fine cloth. It is not until the end of the 17th century that dentures were available to the rich again.

Sources include: M. F. Ashley Montagu and Edward Darling, *The prevalence of nonsense* (New York, 1967); and Edward de Bono (*ed.*), *Eureka!* (London, 1974).

"WHAT THE DICKENS!" DERIVES FROM CHARLES DICKENS

The common expression has nothing to do with *any* member of the Dickens family at all, but is simply a euphemism (via 'Dickson') for "What the Devil!" coined in a more squeamish age than our own.

Source: Eric Partridge, *Name into word* (London, 1949).

DIOGENES OF SINOPE LIVED IN A TUB

No reference to this legend is made in the authoritative article by K. von Fritz in the 2nd ed. of the *Oxford classical dictionary* (1970). His main principles were that happiness is attained by satisfying only one's natural needs and by satisfying them in the cheapest and easiest way. What is natural cannot be dishonourable or indecent and therefore can and should be done in public. Conventions which are contrary to these principles are unnatural and should not be observed.

Diogenes' biographer, Seneca, wrote over three hundred years after the death of Diogenes that "a man so crabbed ought to have lived in a tub like a dog". E. Cobham Brewer, in *A dictionary of phrase and fable*, corrupts this to "Diogenes. A noted Greek cynic philosopher (about B.C.412-323), who, according to Seneca, lived in a tub . . . ". A textbook example, perhaps, of the rise of a common fallacy.

BENJAMIN DISRAELI BELONGED TO THE JEWISH FAITH

Eight of the ten people I asked in Cambridge were positive of this (not that I am claiming infallibility for such an insignificant sample, but merely an indication). Lord Beaconsfield, though received into the Jewish Church, was baptized when his mother and father became members of the Church of England in 1817. The register can be seen at St Andrew's in Holborn.

DIVINATION

So far no method has been tested and proved which will predict events correctly with more than average success. This has not prevented deluded or fraudulent practices from the dawn of human history which attempt the impossible: to divine the unknown. The various types of divination may be finite, but I have never ceased to come across 'arts' previously unknown to me. John Gaule, in his *Mag-astro-mancer, or the magicall-astrologicall-diviner posed and puzzled* (London, 1652), lists stereomancy, divining by the elements; aeromancy, by the air; pyromancy, by fire; hydromancy, by water; geomancy (q.v.), by earth; theomancy, by the revelation of the Holy Spirit, Scriptures, or Word of God; demonomancy, by the aid of evil spirits; idolomancy, by idols and similar images; psychomancy, by the soul or disposition of human beings; anthropomancy, by human entrails; theriomancy, by animals; ornithomancy, by birds; ichthyomancy, by fish; botanomancy, by herbs and other plants; lithomancy, by stones; kleromancy, by lots; oneiromancy, by dreams; onomancy, by names; arithmancy, by numbers; logarithmancy, by logarithms; sternomancy, by marks from breast to belly; gastromancy, by the sound of, or marks on, the belly; omphalomancy, by the navel; cheiromancy, by the hands; podomancy, by the feet; onchyomancy, by the nails; cephaleonomancy, by asses' heads; tephromancy, by ashes; kapnomancy, by smoke; knissomancy, by the burning of incense; ceromancy, by the burning of wax; lecanomancy, by basins of water; katoptromancy, by looking-glasses; cartomancy, by writing and Valentines; macharomancy, by knives and swords; crystallomancy, by crystals; dactylomancy, by rings; koskinomancy, by sieves; axinomancy, by saws; chalcomancy, by vessels of brass or copper; spatilomancy, by skins and bones; astromancy, by stars; sciomancy, by shadows; astragalomancy, by dice; oinomancy, by wine-lees; sycomancy, by figs; tyromancy, by cheese; alphitomancy, by meal, flour, or bran; krithomancy, by corn or grain; alectryomancy (q.v.), by a cockerel; gyromancy, by circles; lampadomancy, by candles and lamps.

That is presumably more than the common reader will want to know about divination. The curious reader is referred to any of the numerous compendia which discuss some of the above fallacies, often as though there were a degree of sense or logic in them.

DOCTORS TAKE AN OATH WHEN THEY QUALIFY

In some countries this is true, but not in all. British doctors take no oath, though an unwritten code of ethics is taken for granted. The Hippocratic Oath, taken on admission to the medical school and guild on the Greek island of Cos, was sworn by 'Apollo the physician, and by Asklepios, Hygeia, and Panacea and all the gods and goddesses'. Hippocrates was born about 460 B.C. and lived to be about 100: he wrote some, though not all, of the books attributed to him, and even now represents the ideal of the medical doctor, free from magic and superstition: a humane observer and servant of the sick irrespective of their wealth or social position.

DOGS HAVE EXTRA-SENSORY PERCEPTION

Nobody and nothing has yet been proved to have extra-sensory perception, despite a great propensity on the part of many enthusiasts to prove just that. But the literature on dogs' strange abilities, every one of them based on a misunderstanding of the dog's brain so far as it has been studied so far, is almost as voluminous as that on extra-sensory abilities among human beings.

The *Odyssey* (Book XVI) was one of the first texts to invent canine clairvoyance: the dogs of the swineherd Eumaeus 'with a low whine shrank cowering to the far side of the steading' in the presence of the goddess Athene, though Telemachus couldn't see her, and Virgil and Lucan agree that dogs have this special power. They can also find their way back home by an unexplained power. Or, according to Stefansson (*The friendly Arctic*, New York, 1924), not: a lost dog 'rarely finds its way back'. His Eskimo hunter Emiu nearly lost his life in a blizzard through foolishly trusting his dogs to find their way back to camp. He had picked up this notion from white men! Eskimoes have their own irrational beliefs, but they have enough practical experience of dogs' weaknesses to doubt the white man's blind faith in their powers. Dickens perpetuated the fallacy in *Little Dorrit*, where the dog 'recognizes' Rigaud's villainy despite the gullibility of his master.

SOME PEOPLE ARE **DOUBLE-JOINTED**

No: there are no recorded cases of this. People commonly said to be 'double-jointed' have ligaments holding the end of the two articulating bones slightly looser than customary, thus permitting greater freedom in the relative movements of their parts.

DOWSERS HAVE AN ABILITY TO FIND WATER WHEREVER IT EXISTS

Dowsing or water-divining is a practice which has been recorded from a period almost as early as that when we first encounter astrology. Despite the impossibility of the forked twig in the diviner's hands responding to the non-existent 'magnetism' of water, it is true that dowsers have succeeded in locating water after trained geologists have failed to locate any. But the majority of dowsers do *not* possess any exceptional gift: they find water where the beginner would also find it. What assists them is the subconscious registration and interpretation of certain phenomena and their emergence into consciousness by means of a psychological automatism, normally twitching. The dowser has previously discovered water in terrain similar to that where he now suddenly twitches: indications include slight changes in the colour and type of vegetation or soil, visible and tactile evidence of the ground underfoot, even the smell of a wettish area, or the slight sound made by an underground stream near the surface which would be undetected by the layman. It is in the financial interest of the dowser to describe his professional expertise as a 'gift' to discourage competition from those who could with practice learn the same tricks of the trade. Dowsers are notoriously more successful in areas where water has already been found in abundance, and less so where water is known to be scarce, indicating a connection with luck. The most prevalent fallacy in amateur dowsing is to think that most underground water is confined to running streams; the dowser then follows the 'stream', even in areas well-known to be situated above a saturated and porous or semi-porous substratum, and where two 'streams' flow together, he strikes his marker into the ground. Finding water at that point only confirms his opinion, whereas he would have struck lucky at any point in the porous substratum area.

Dowsing often works, though for reasons not usually put forward by its practitioners. But see also **RADIESTHESIA.**

Sources include: W. F. Barrett and T. Besterman, *The divining rod* (London, 1926); T. Besterman, *Water divining* (London, 1938); and D. H. Rawcliffe, *Illusions and delusions of the supernatural and the occult* (New York, 1959).

DRAGONFLIES STING

The dragonfly (*Libellula*) belongs to the order *Neuroptera*: none of the *Neuroptera* stings. The dragonfly lives on flies and other insects captured on the wing, and if you are lucky enough to entice a wandering dragonfly into a room infested with mosquitoes, you will soon have an insect-free environment and a well-contented dragonfly.

Source: John Phin, *Seven follies of science* (New York, 1912, p. 210).

DRAGONS SURVIVE IN INDONESIA

David Attenborough's excellent BBC television programme "Zoo quest for a dragon" showed the 'dragon' of Komodo, an island in Eastern Indonesia, being trapped, but as Attenborough was careful to point out during the programme itself, the 'dragon' is technically just a monitor lizard: a carnivorous amphibian. A good description and illustrations can be found in David Attenborough's own book *Zoo quest for a dragon* (London, 1957).

MEN ARE BETTER DRIVERS THAN ARE WOMEN

Not true. The only ways in which the British *Transport statistics 1964-1974* (1976) show that male drivers are superior to female are "reversing into limited openings, moving away correctly and using the accelerator, clutch, brakes, gears and steering correctly". The two sexes were equally culpable in "failure to comply with road signs and traffic signals given by controllers and other road users; and failure to act correctly when meeting, overtaking or crossing the path of other traffic".

British women are superior to British men in stopping a car in an emergency, looking round properly when driving off, using the mirror, giving signals, anticipating the actions of other road users, knowledge of the Highway Code, and resisting the desire to drive too fast.

AN ABSOLUTE DROUGHT IS A PERIOD WHEN NO RAIN HAS FALLEN

No. Rain can fall in Britain to the point of 0.01 inches without affecting the term 'absolute drought'. The British definition (not accepted internationally) covers a period of 15 days, *none* of which has received as much as 0.01 inches.

A 'partial drought' is a period of at least 29 consecutive days, during which the mean daily rainfall does not exceed 0.01 inches. This definition, again, is British in origin and is not accepted internationally.

Source: W. G. Moore, *A dictionary of geography* (3rd ed., Harmondsworth, 1963).

FISHES CANNOT **DROWN**

Fish breathe by taking oxygen from the water just as animals breathe by taking oxygen from the air. So it follows that if oxygen is withdrawn from water, they must either obtain oxygen from some other source, or drown. Causes of the diminution or disappearance of the oxygen supply include the decay of a great deal of vegetation, or increased animal respiration at the bottom of certain lakes. If fish do not choose to move from areas of lakes poor in oxygen to areas richer in oxygen they perish. This happens quite frequently and regularly.

E

"Every day of my life makes me feel more and more how seldom a fact is accurately stated; how almost invariably when a story has passed through the mind of a third person it becomes very little better than a falsehood, and this, too, though the narrator may be the most truth-seeking person in existence."—NATHANIEL HAWTHORNE (in a notebook).

WE KNOW THE AGE OF THE EARTH

A selective history of wrong estimates of the Earth's age up to 1930 can be found in *Vol. 4, Bulletin 80* of the National Research Council, Washington, D.C. (1931).

Here is a short list of some views of the Earth's age which have led to wild hypotheses as to other aspects of Earth history:

Bishop Ussher	5938 years
Lord Kelvin	20-40 million years
L. Helmholtz	22 million years
G. H. Darwin	57 million years
J. Joly	80-90 million years
Joly and Clarke	100 million years
A number of geologists	2000 million years
A number of astronomers	2000-8000 million years

The National Research Council of 1931 might have been interested and surprised to find that the latest estimates (1977) include 4,700 million years, this time as a result of radio-active determination. The Universe is believed, again in 1977, to be roughly 20,000 million years old. Very roughly.

THE EARTH IS FLAT

The Earth must be flat, because it has four corners according to the Bible (Isaiah, xi, 12; Revelation, vii, 1). When the Biblical accounts were proved wrong by Galileo Galilei (1564-1642), who nevertheless continued to be persecuted by the Roman Catholic Church as a heretic, it took several centuries for the fact that the Earth is round to be absorbed by the popular Western mind.

Most flat-earthers live in Zion, Illinois, near Chicago: they are the remnants of a once-powerful sect known as the Christian Apostolic Church founded in 1895 by a Scottish faith-healer called John Alexander Dowie. Dowie was expelled in 1905 and for the next thirty years the community was ruled by the fanatic Wilbur Glenn Voliva. For years he offered $5,000 to anyone who could prove to his satisfaction that the earth is round, and travelled the world (flatways?) lecturing on his pet theme and predicting the end of the world in 1923, then 1927, then 1930, then 1935, and then 1943, but unfortunately met his own end in 1942.

The Flat Earth Society was founded around 1800 as a successor to the Zetetic Society. In 1956 its headquarters was moved from Lancaster, California, to Dover, England, the moving spirit being one William Shenton (d. 1971). The theories of the society include (a) that the Earth has *water* on the other side; (b) that the land masses are grouped around the central point, which is the North Pole; therefore (c) that the trans-Antarctic expeditions could not have happened and therefore did not; (d) that the Bible's account is of "heaven above, earth beneath, and water under the earth", therefore (a) above; and (e) that the Moon is not 2160 miles in diameter as stated by the astronomers, but only 32 miles in diameter.

Sources include: Walter Davenport, 'They call me a flathead' in *Colliers*, 14 May 1927; and Alfred Prowitt, 'Croesus at the altar' in *American Mercury*, April 1930.

THE EARTH IS HOLLOW

As if you didn't know. Cyrus Reed Teed (1839-1908) graduated from the New York Eclectic Medical College ('eclecticism' being a medical cult relying on odd herbal remedies) did not, unlike John Alexander Dowie, believe that THE EARTH IS FLAT, q.v. He agreed that it is round, but that we live on the *inside* of it rather than on the outside. This cult attracted some of those with a desire to escape back into the womb.

In *The cellular cosmogony* (1870), Teed wrote under the pseudonym 'Koresh' that the entire cosmos is like an egg. We on the Earth, as well as all the other planets, are on the inside: on the outside there is nothing. The shell is 100 miles thick and made up of seventeen layers: the inner five are geological strata, above five mineral strata, above seven metallic strata. A sun at the centre is invisible, but is reflected as our Sun (see also THE SUN IS FLAT). "To know of the Earth's concavity", writes Teed, "is to know God, while to believe in the Earth's convexity is to deny Him and all His works. All that is opposed to Koreshanity is antichrist". Teed therefore became a new Messiah and in the 1890s founded 'The New Jerusalem' at Estero, sixteen miles south of Fort Myers, Florida. He predicted Estero would become the capital of the world, and arrangements were made to accommodate eight million of the faithful. Two hundred came, but fifty years later only a dozen members of the faith kept the torch alight.

A German offshoot of the Hollow Earth Movement was the Hohlweltlehre proclaimed by Peter Bender, a pilot wounded in World War I. Durán Navarro, of Buenos Aires, was reported in *Time* (14 July 1947) to believe that gravity is really centrifugal force generated by a rotating hollow earth inhabited on the inside.

The Symmes theory of concentric spheres (Louisville, 1875) by 'Americus' Symmes is a rare pamphlet propagating the hollow earth theory. It is discussed by D. W. Hering in his *Foibles and fallacies of science* (New York, 1924) and can be read in a collection bound as *Paradoxes* in the New York Public Library.

M. B. Gardner enunciated a theory similar to that of John Cleves Symmes, except that he thought that the aurorae, marvellous light displays, are due to the radiance from a sun *inside* the hollow earth emitted through openings at the two Poles. Gardner's theory finally died when Admiral Richard Byrd flew across the North Pole without seeing an opening there. Or it would have died, but for Brinsley Le Poer Trench, whose book *Secret of the ages: UFOs from inside the earth* (London, 1976) explains, as the title indicates, that the flying saucers (q.v.) come not from beyond the Earth, but from within it.

The Society for Geocosmic Research, P.O. Box 16, Garmisch-Partenkirchen, Germany, issued in 1960 a work entitled *Why do we believe the cosmicentric theory to be right?* by P. A. Mueller-Murnau. This society also believes in a hollow earth. We live on the inside, as Cyrus Teed taught (Mr Trench says that we live on the outside), but we cannot see Australia above our heads because the sky is too bright.

The latest supporter of the still-popular hollow earth theories is Warren Smith, whose *This hollow earth* (1972) was reprinted in London in 1977.

THE CENTRE OF THE EARTH IS HOT BECAUSE IT IS AT THE CENTRE OF THE UNIVERSE

Gabrielis Frascati Brixiani, in *De aquis returbii Ticinensibus* (1575) explained that the Earth stands at the centre of the universe; consequently its centre is the centre of the universe. Both are spherical in form. The sun and planets send out rays of heat which foregather at the centre of the Earth so it is the hottest place in the universe. This farrago of error was believed by a number of scholars for a hundred years or more. Actually, the core of the Earth is molten rock and the surface is a comparatively thin crust which is broken by volcanic and other internal actions near the surface. The *Sun* is at the centre of our system and far hotter than the Earth.

THE EARTH IS STILL

Ptolemy taught, and millions believed for many centuries, that the world is still. He pointed out that if the world were whirling round, we and all other denizens of the Earth would be subjected to a continuous violent wind, and this is demonstrably not the case.

Curiously enough, and to indicate that scientific 'progress' is not always in a forward direction, Aristarchus of Samos had already realized that the Earth rotates on its axis around the sun. The heritage of Ptolemy dies hard; in fact one might ruefully observe that it does not show any signs of dying at all. Gabrielle Henriet, writing in her book *Heaven and Earth* (London, 1957), offers a 'proof' that the Earth does not rotate. The rate of the Earth's spin quoted by astronomers is about 1,000 km. per hour, so that if modern aircraft attaining this speed were to fly in the same direction as that of the rotation, they would not go forward at all, but remain suspended in mid-air. Furthermore, it would not be necessary to fly from one place to another on the same latitude: the aircraft could just take off and wait in mid-air for the destination to turn up, and then land.

Source: Patrick Moore, *Can you speak Venusian?* (London, 1976, pp. 13-15).

EARTHQUAKES CAN BE PREDICTED

Though institutes have been established with the primary or secondary purpose of predicting the time and place of earthquakes, there is no method yet available for doing so.

"Owing to the complexity of the processes involved, . . . it is by no means clear that such research is bound to lead to satisfactory methods of earthquake prediction. The Earth's rotation is affected not only by processes in the crust and mantle, where earthquakes occur, but also by the circulation of the atmosphere and by motions in the liquid metallic core, where the Earth's magnetism originates".

Source: Professor R. Hide, letter to *The Times*, 8 September 1976.

EARTHQUAKES CAN BE PREVENTED

P. Norcott, in his booklet *Bigger and better earthquakes* (Broadstairs, Kent, 1971), suggests three methods of preventing earthquakes. One is to erect huge flywheels at the Poles and start them whirling; this will keep kicking the Earth round, to keep the rate of axial spin fairly constant. Another is to build huge dams to stop the ocean waters sloshing about from one sea-basin into another; this will reduce tidal friction and thus reduce the rate at which the Earth's rotation is slowed down by the Moon's tidal influence. A third method of preventing earthquakes, states Mr Norcott, is to split the Moon in half, towing one hemisphere round to the other side of the Earth so that gravitational forces will cancel each other out.

EARWIGS ARE SO CALLED BECAUSE THEY HIDE IN HUMAN AND ANIMAL EARS

It seems that they were so called (in most languages, not only in English: cf. *auricularia, gusano del oído, perce-oreille, Ohrwurm*, etc.) because the rear wings suggest the shape of a human ear, and that this name then induced the folk-belief that they hid in human ears. That they do not in fact do so seems commonly accepted by entomologists. One reason is that the human ear contains bitter wax as a repellent against such invasions, and another is that earwigs eat vegetable matter and would have no interest in the perils of inhabiting human or animal ears.

ECONOMIC FALLACIES

There are three main categories of error in economics.
(1) Time. Many economic propositions which are governed by a

time factor do not explicitly state it. Thus, in modern dynamic economics, it is often asserted that elements in the economic system will grow at an equilibrium rate, but all that can be stated is that the rate will *tend* to move towards equilibrium.

(2) Composition. Terms are used collectively in one part of an argument and individually elsewhere. For instance, it is frequently declared that what is prudent behaviour for an individual or a single firm must be prudent for the country as a whole, but if all citizens of a nation try to save more (spend less), it does *not* follow that the total level of savings will rise: it may fall. Those who favour customs unions or free trade areas are guilty of this fallacy by ignoring the distinction between the interest of a particular country or regional grouping and that of the world as a whole.

(3) Variables. Mistakes are often made by treating variable quantities as fixed, for example the former 'Iron Law' that wages tend to sink to the level of bare subsistence. Alfred Marshall (1842-1924) did much to explode this type of fallacy, anticipating the work of the computer by introducing into economic theory a new sense of the way in which different factors are mutually dependent.

Source: Arthur Seldon and F. G. Pennance, *Everyman's dictionary of economics* (London, 1965).

ECTOPLASM

A visible 'emanation' from the body of a spiritualistic medium. One of a number of conjuring tricks performed by the so-called 'physical' mediums to convince the credulous of their powers. The mediums claim that levitation, bumps, knocks, the movement of distant objects and the production of 'ectoplasm' are due to the activity of discarnate spirits. All such 'experiments' are carried out in varying degrees of darkness and none has yet been proved genuine by disinterested investigators.

D. H. Rawcliffe, in *Illusions and delusions of the supernatural and the occult* (New York, 1959), shows that the 'spirit-substances' are seemingly "white doughy streams issuing from the mouth (sometimes regurgitated cheese-cloth), the nose and even the genitals of female mediums . . . One enterprising medium even hid her 'ectoplasm' in a hollow comb which searches previous to the séances for a long time failed to reveal".

Michael Faraday, wearying of the endless series of fraudulent 'spiritualists' and their like whom he had in a rash moment offered to test, deserves for his patience the last word:

"What a weak, credulous, incredulous, unbelieving, superstitious, bold, frightened, what a ridiculous world ours is, as far as concerns the mind of man. How full of inconsistencies, contradictions and absurdities it is".

Sources include: Michael Faraday, *Life and letters*, vol. 2 (London, 1870, p. 307).

THE GARDEN OF EDEN WAS AT THE NORTH POLE

Dilmun (on present-day Bahrain) and sites in Iran are frequently proposed as the Biblical 'Eden'. 'Edinu' was also the Sumerian name for the plain of Babylon. However, if one has to choose among the dozens of sites offered as candidates for the aboriginal home of Adam and Eve over the last few centuries, the least likely must be the North Pole. *Paradise found* (1885) is a voluminous treatise by a Methodist minister, one William F. Warren, who misuses data drawn from various scientific disciplines to prove to his own satisfaction that Adam and Eve were created in a warm, clement North Pole. The Biblical flood first submerged the North Pole, and then changed its climate to its present condition.

See also **BIBLICAL FALLACIES.**

BROWN EGGS ARE MORE NUTRITIOUS THAN WHITE

Not so. British mothers are taught so by their grandmothers and so do not question the belief. Similarly, American mothers are told by their grandmothers that white eggs are purer than brown. The colour is simply laid on by the bird for its own purposes long after the contents of the shell, and even the shell itself, are completed. The chemical composition in all eggs of the same species of bird appears to be the same.

ELEPHANTS ARE AFRAID OF MICE

Cartoonists and others have often shown an elephant cowering away from a mouse. Those who work in elephants' stalls either in zoos or in circuses have from time to time seen mice running about not far from the elephant but, far from panicking, it seems

that the elephants—mainly due to their relatively poor vision—
cannot even see the mice.
Source: Keepers at Schönbrunn Zoo and London Zoo.

ELIXIR OF LIFE

A supposed drug or essence with the capability of prolonging life
indefinitely or forever. Also known as the Philosopher's Stone.
Like the vain attempts to transmute base metals into GOLD (q.v.),
this idea may have originated in India (before 1000 B.C.). Elixirs
were also thought to heighten sexual powers. The fact that arseni-
cal poisoning inhibits putrefaction in its victims reinforced belief,
paradoxically enough, in the efficacy of the elixirs.

For the Chinese, gold was not a form of currency, but an im-
perishable substance, so the emphasis in China was always on the
making of gold as a substance to confer longevity or even immortality on the human body. The intention was to change cinnabar
(the most highly reputed of substances rich in *yang*, the active or
male principle) into lead, lead into silver, and silver into gold.
This too is impossible, as is the belief that artificial gold is a substance of such potency that the eating of food from vessels made
of it would be conducive to longevity. The human body is subject
to laws of decay and decomposition well-known to medical
science, and no drug or essence can alter those laws. Plastic surgery and the transplantation of organs are of course different
matters, completely foreign to alchemical tradition.
Sources include: F. Sherwood Taylor, *The alchemists* (London, 1952).

EMBER DAYS ARE SO-CALLED FROM THE ASHES OF REPENTANCE IN WHICH PENITENTS SIT

The four periods of fasting and prayer in the Christian Church
(one in each season) are called Ember Days from the Old English
ymbryne from their regular recurrence (*ymb*-round; *ryne*-running)
and have nothing to do with ashes or 'embers'.
Source: *Oxford English Dictionary*.

ALWAYS CONSULT THE LATEST EDITION OF ENCYCLOPAEDIAS

The layman always looks at the date of *publication* of an encyclopaedia, while the professional librarian looks to the date of the
latest source quoted in the articles' bibliographies, and the specialist scholar (who has in any case little personal need of a general

reference book for his own scholarly purposes) looks to the article's ability to take into account the *latest research*, its thoroughness, and balance.

Technical articles are usually the weak part of a general encyclopaedia, since they have gone partly out of date while the multivolume work has been going through the press. For the humanities and social sciences, it is by no means certain that later editions of an encyclopaedia should be preferred. Increasing costs of printing, binding and overheads constrain editors to reduce the length of articles and the quantity of illustrations from one edition to the next. In the case of the *Encyclopaedia Britannica*, for instance, the 11th ed. (29 vols., 1910-11), takes $12\frac{1}{2}$ pages to discuss Indian Law while the 14th ed. takes $8\frac{1}{2}$ pages, and the 1974 ed. takes up less than half a page in the *Micropaedia* (p. 332 of vol. V). Always consult an *earlier* edition for an article in the humanities, to check what has been omitted from the later edition you consulted first.

The myth of the Britannica (New York, 1964) was a valuable corrective by Harvey Einbinder to the expensive advertisements promoting that encyclopedia. However, since Einbinder wrote, listing 666 articles in the 1963 which he found faulty, out-of-date, or inaccurate, the *Britannica* has been forced to pack in even more fashionable new topics, and their standards have declined again. Other general encyclopaedias are even less comprehensive.

THERE IS MORE ENERGY IN 100 GRAMS OF FRIED BEEFSTEAK THAN IN THE EQUIVALENT WEIGHT OF WHITE SUGAR, WHOLE WHEAT FLOUR, RAW RICE OR CHEDDAR CHEESE

Quite wrong. And there is nearly *three* times as much energy in 100 grams of butter! R. A. McCance and E. M. Widdowson, in their standard work *The composition of foods* (3rd rev. ed., 1960), list the energy-properties of selected food and drink as follows (per 100 grams in each case):

Whole wheat flour	339 kcal.	raw potatoes	70
white bread	243	canned peas	86
raw rice	361	boiled cabbage	9
whole fresh milk	66	orange with peel	27
butter	793	apple	47
Cheddar cheese	425	white sugar	394
fried beefsteak	273	bitter beer (100 ml)	31
fried haddock	175	spirits (gin, whisky 70 proof, 100 ml)	222

MOST PEOPLE CAN UNDERSTAND THE ENGLISH LANGUAGE

'Most people' do not understand any one single language, though 25% of the world's population speak Chinese. English is spoken by 11% as a first language, Russian by 8.3%, Hindi by 6.3% and Spanish by 6.3%.

'EPICUREANISM' IS SYNONYMOUS WITH GLUTTONY

The word 'epicure' has come to be applied to anyone devoted to the pleasures of the table. Epicurus (341-270 B.C.) on the contrary held that philosophy consisted in the wise conduct of life, to be attained by reliance on the evidence of the senses, and by the elimination of superstition and of the belief in supernatural intervention. His ethics teach that pleasure is the only good, but by this he intimated that a perfect harmony of body and mind is to be sought in plain living, and in virtue.

Source: Sir Paul Harvey, *Oxford Companion to Classical Literature* (Oxford, 1937, entry 'Epicurus').

EPILEPTICS ARE MENTALLY DEFECTIVE

Injury to the brain in infancy can cause either epilepsy or mental defects, but there is no necessary correlation between the two. Most epileptics are normal in all other respects.

Source: Peter Wingate, *The Penguin medical encyclopedia*, 2nd ed. (Harmondsworth, 1976).

ESKIMOES LIVE IN IGLOOS

A Denver, Colorado, newspaper once erected an imitation snow house near where they kept some reindeer (at the municipal buildings) and hired an Eskimo, who had never seen that type of dwelling except in the movies, to explain to visitors that he and other reindeer herders of Alaska dwelt in that kind of house when they were at home.

By a census of the 1920s, fewer than 300 of over 14,000 Eskimoes in Greenland had ever seen an igloo!

Source: Vilhjalmur Stefansson, *The standardisation of error* (London, 1928, pp. 49, 84).

ESPERANTO IS THE EASIEST INTERNATIONAL LANGUAGE TO LEARN

Though this fallacy must to a certain extent be a matter of opinion, and could with justification be defended by Poles, there can be little doubt that Ido (reformed Esperanto as approved by Zamenhof, Polish inventor of Esperanto, himself) is easier to learn, write, speak and remember: e.g.

English: All those who saw me
Ido: Omna ti qui vidis me
Esperanto: Chiuj tiuj kiuj vidis min

ETYMOLOGICAL FALLACIES

In the words of A. Smythe Palmer—and every philologist would quickly endorse them—"there are a multitude of words which have been either altered from their true form or perverted from their proper meaning owing to popular mistakes or misunderstandings as to their derivation or kinship to other words". The *Oxford English Dictionary*, Skeat's *Etymological dictionary* and Partridge's *Origins* (4th ed., 1966) are primary reference tools, though perhaps too voluminous for those interested primarily in errors of etymology. For the latter study one might commend *Folk etymology* (1882) and *The folk and their word-lore* (1904) by A. Smythe Palmer, as regards the English language. He considers the erroneous metamorphosis of foreign words, verbal corruptions, mistaken analogies, and misinterpretations.

Etymology is a science based on the laws of language and demands a historical and comparative knowledge not only of the particular language studied, but also of those related in any relevant manner.

Fanciful sources for names are almost as widespread as they were before etymological dictionaries made them indefensible. Thus, one can still find countrymen who derive the word 'partridge' from the birds' habit of lying between the furrows of ploughed land, and so they part ridges (*Gentleman's Magazine*, February 1892). De Thaun, in his *Livre des créatures*, claimed that the same bird was called 'perdix' because it loses (*pert, perdit*) its brood. Eric Partridge, who ought to know, honestly admits that he doesn't. He merely quotes Hofmann's opinion that the Latin *perdix*, adopted from Greek, might echo the whirring wings of the rising bird.

My own favourite etymological fallacy is connected with the fallacy of the Tower of Babel, and can be found in the *Opera* (Antwerp, 1580) of the 16th-century Flemish scholar Johannes Goropius. On finding that the word 'sack' is similar in many of the languages we have since learned belong to the Indo-European linguistic group (*sakkos* in Greek, *saccus* in Latin, *sacco* in Italian, and *saco* in Spanish, etc.), Goropius concluded that, at the moment of the confusion of language, every single labourer working in the Tower of Babel remembered to carry away his sack.

EUGENICS WOULD BREED OUT SUCH TRAITS AS FEEBLE-MINDEDNESS

"It is often imagined that by preventing the breeding of feeble-minded individuals, the race might in a few generations be completely relieved of the burden of feeble-mindedness", suggested Professor A. V. Hill in a lecture at Newnham College, Cambridge, on 22 November 1930. He then went on to explode this fallacy; by eugenic control it would be possible to decrease by 11% the number of feeble-minded in the next generation.

A central difficulty (quite apart from the ethical question) is that two perfectly intelligent and normal parents may well produce a feeble-minded child.

Source: *Nature*, 3 January 1931 (Supplement).

EUNUCHS WERE FIRST INTRODUCED INTO EUROPE BY THE TURKS

The word itself is sufficient evidence to the contrary, for it derives from the Classical Greek word for an emasculated male. Eunuchs were appointed as chamberlains in ancient Greece, and frequently rose to positions of power in a great household. It is another common fallacy that their emasculation renders them less intellectual or courageous. Narses, the famous general under Justinian, was a eunuch.

The vile Vatican practice of castrating boys to prevent the natural development of the voice and hence enable them to be trained as adult soprani continued until 1878, when Pope Leo XIII finally prohibited the employment of *castrati*, long after they had been driven from the Italian musical stage by secular opinion. The unnatural practice of voluntary castration for ascetic Christian purposes is recorded as early as Origen, the eunuchs defending their action by quoting Matthew xix, 12, v. 28-30. Augustine (*De haeres*, c. 37) describes a third-century sect of eunuchs.

Eunuchs were incidentally known, long before the Greeks, to the Sumerians and Egyptians. The Turks found the century-old tradition of castration at Constantinople, and did *not* originate it.

VOLUNTARY EUTHANASIA IS OPPOSED BY DOCTORS AND PUBLIC IN BRITAIN

In 1969 the British Medical Association issued a resolution condemning voluntary euthanasia, and issued a report *The problem* of *euthanasia* (1971) opposing any recognition of euthanasia. Yet surveys of doctors conducted by National Opinion Polls in 1964 and 1965 showed that nearly half said they had been requested by incurably ill patients to give euthanasia, that more than three quarters admitted that some doctors do grant such requests, and that more than one-third said they would themselves be prepared to do so if voluntary euthanasia were legal.

A National Opinion Polls survey in September 1976, published the following month, showed that the public was even more in favour of voluntary euthanasia than was the medical profession. In 1969 Mass Observation's national survey found that 51% favoured euthanasia and 28% opposed it. In 1976 the proportions were 69% in favour to 17% against (the rest saying 'don't know').

Source: *New Humanist*, September-October 1967, p. 107.

EVERY SCHOOLBOY KNOWS THAT . . .

Macaulay occasionally wrote disparagingly of fellow-historians that some facts were known to 'every schoolboy', but he himself must have been aware of the fact that even in his day, when there were fewer facts to remember, very few facts were common knowledge among all schoolboys even of the sixth form. "Every schoolboy knows . . . who strangled Atahualpa", he wrote. He himself spelt the name of the Inca ruler Atahuallpa incorrectly, but had certainly taken the trouble to verify the name of the strangler for the purposes of his essay. The phrase more often signifies "some scholars have forgotten, or omitted sufficiently to stress, the fact that . . ."

WE CAN KNOW EVERYTHING

Ernest Renan wrote in 1863 to Berthelot: "Who knows but that man may succeed in learning the last word about matter, the laws of life, the laws of the atom? . . . He who shall possess such science will verily be the master of the universe . . ."

The contrary has since proved to be the case: that discoveries constantly upset previously-held 'certitudes' so that less and less is truly *known* about more and more.

EVOLUTION THEORY IS NOW ACCEPTED BY BRITISH VOTERS

Charles Darwin's *Origin of species* (London, 1859) explained in general terms the theory of natural selection which has been modified through knowledge of the mechanism of inheritance, of genes, and of mutations. "It was not until 1930", writes Isaac Asimov in vol. 2 of his *Guide to science* (New York, 1972), "that the English statistician and geneticist Ronald Aylmer Fisher succeeded in showing that Mendelian genetics provided the necessary mechanism for evolution by natural selection. Only then did evolutionary theory gain its modern guise. Nevertheless, Darwin's basic conception of evolution by natural selection has stood firm, and indeed the evolutionary idea has been extended to every field of science—physical, biological and social".

But *The psychology of Conservatism* (1973) by Glenn Wilson and others demonstrated that only 40% of Liberal voters believed in evolution theory in the early 70s (a century after the theory had become a scientific commonplace); only 37% of Conservative voters believed in evolution theory; while the figure for Labour Party voters was as low as 25%.

THE EXCEPTION PROVES THE RULE

Five 'senses' of this nonsense are cited by Margaret Nicholson in *A dictionary of American-English usage* (New York, 1957), which is avowedly very heavily dependent on Fowler's *Modern English usage*.
1. The original simple legal sense;
2. The secondary, rather complicated, scientific sense;
3. The loose, rhetorical sense;
4. The jocular nonsense;
5. The serious nonsense.

But even the first of these is undermined if we return to the origin of the Latin phrase: *exceptio probat regulam*, which does not mean what it appears to mean at all, but 'the exception *tests* the rule'. That is, the apparent exception affords the opportunity of testing the universality of the rule, since if the apparent exception is genuine, the rule is false, whereas if the exception is not genuine, at least we have discovered that the 'exception' is false. In his *Etymological dictionary* (1921), Weekley suggests that the phrase is an abbreviation of a phrase *exceptio probat regulam in casibus non exceptis*, meaning 'the exception proves the rule in cases not excepted'.

EXPERTS ARE INVARIABLY CORRECT

'Experts', a modern term for those professionally acknowledged to be competent in their field(s), are usually reliable about what they have empirically found to be the case. Where they are often completely unreliable is in the prophecy of what is feasible. Sir Humphry Davy, despite his eminence, laughed at the suggestion that London might some day be lit by gas. Learned men categorically denied Stephenson's claim that a railway locomotive could travel as fast as 12 miles an hour. In *Der Neue Geisterglaube* (1882, p. 261), W. Schneider reported a case in which a scholar asserted the impossibility of a steamship's ever being able to cross the Atlantic Ocean.

Connoisseurs will love to hear the oracular statement by Lord Rutherford, as reported in the *Evening News* of 11 September 1933: "The energy produced by the breaking down of the atom is a very poor kind of thing. Anyone who expects a source of power from the transformation of these atoms is talking moonshine, but it is enormously interesting to scientists". See also *Nature* for 16 September 1933, p. 433.

EXTRAPOLATION FROM MISLEADING DATA

All data is misleading when extrapolated in a certain way, without due regard to common sense or research into variable factors involved. Mark Twain loved to deflate pompous nonsense, as the following passage from *Life on the Mississippi* (New York, 1917, pp. 155-6) demonstrates.

"The Mississippi between Cairo and New Orleans was twelve hundred and fifteen miles long 176 years ago. It was eleven hundred and eighty after the cut-off of 1722. It was one thousand and forty after the American Bend cut-off. It has lost sixty-seven miles since. Consequently, its length is only nine hundred and seventy-three miles at present.

Now, if I wanted to be one of those ponderous scientific people, and "let on" to prove what had occurred in the remote past by what had occurred in late years, what an opportunity is here! Geology never had such a chance, nor such exact data to argue from! Nor "development of species", either!

Glacial epochs are great things, but they are vague-vague. Please observe: In the space of one hundred and seventy-six years the lower Mississippi has shortened itself two hundred and forty-two miles. That is an average of a trifle over one mile and a third per year. Therefore, any calm person, who is not blind or idiotic, can see that in the Old Oölitic Silurian period, just one million years ago next November, the lower Mississippi River was upward of one million three hundred thousand miles long, and stuck out over the Gulf of Mexico like a fishing-rod. And by the same token any person can see that seven hundred and forty-two years from now the Lower Mississippi will be only a mile and three-quarters long, and Cairo and New Orleans will have joined their streets together, and be plodding comfortably along under a single mayor and mutual board of aldermen."

Mark Twain's gibe at 'science' is as fallacious as his conclusions, of course, but the joke at the expense of those who exploit statistical data for their own ends is as true today as it was when his book first appeared in 1883.

THE EYE CAN BE REMOVED BY SURGEONS, WASHED, AND REPLACED

In a letter to *The Daily Telegraph* (26 June 1911), Sir E. Ray Lankester found it necessary to repudiate this fantastic notion, which continues apparently to be widely believed. "The eyeball cannot (as many people erroneously believe) without destruction, be moved forward or 'laid on the cheek', since such a movement would tear the muscles attached to it, and also the optic nerve".

The Daily Mail (7 April 1927) was again compelled to devote an article to this fallacy: "The popular myth that ophthalmic surgeons remove eyes, scrape or treat them, and replace them was exploded yesterday when the Royal Westminster Ophthalmic Hospital gave a demonstration of its methods and apparatus. Although frequently spoken of, and although people can always be met who believe they have been the subject of such an operation, it never has been done, said one of the hospital's leading surgeons".

Eye transplants are, of course, another matter.

EYES ARE RUINED BY FINE NEEDLEWORK

A number of common errors are connected with allegedly excessive use of the eyes, whether in needlework, microscopic study or watchmending. J. D. Rolleston, in the *British Journal of Ophthalmology* (November 1942) drew attention to the fallacies that operation for cataract should be delayed until the moment is judged correct; that eyes should be bandaged in acute inflammatory conditions; and that the loss of one eye necessarily involves impairment of the other's visual ability.

F

"The faintest of all human passions is the love of truth."
—A. E. HOUSMAN.

FAIRIES AND FAIRY RINGS

Fairy rings, to dispose first of them, are caused by a circular-seeding fungus which, by its annual decay, renders the soil unfit for a new crop of fungus but increases the fertility of the ground. There consequently appears a gradually increasing circle of grass which is greener than the surrounding turf. The traditional explanation, harmless enough to those who don't mind misleading ignorant children into a lifetime of superstitition by the primrose path of faery, is that such rings spring up where fairies habitually dance, or grow above a subterranean fairy village. E. and M. A. Radford's *Encyclopedia of superstitions* (London, 1961) observes that if anyone ran nine times round such a ring on the night of the full moon, he would hear the fairies laughing and talking below. Walter P. Wright, in *An illustrated encyclopedia of gardening* (London, 1932) advocates not running round the ring but destroying it "by syringing with a pound of sulphate of iron dissolved in three gallons of water". It is not recorded what the fairies thought of Walter Wright.

European and other folklores are saturated in fairy myths, from the 'men of peace' or *daoine sithe* of the Scottish Highlands to the Greek woodland spirits and the Scandinavian elves. The industrious Puck of Shakespeare's *A midsummer night's dream* is only one of the most famous fairies of English lore. A belief in fairies is as old as the hills themselves, for it dates to animist days long before Christianity overtook country 'wisdom'. It seems that the earliest stage of a religious system has been ignorant awe of the elements and natural phenomena such as trees and animals. Much or all of nature is believed to possess individual spirits capable of feeling, reason and volition. The animists (35% of an intensively-missionaried province of South Sulawesi remain animists according to Darby Greenfield, *Indonesia: Bali and the East*, New York, 1976) believe in the existence of spirits in streams, the wind, wood and iron, and carve fetishes to retain their magic power. This nature worship entered European romanticism as pantheism, and retains an integral if embarrassing hold on many people who would otherwise claim to be above such primitive beliefs, despite the absence of the slightest shred of evidence that spirits of any fairy kind exist.

Joseph Jastrow, in *Wish and wisdom* (New York, 1935), retells the belief of Sir Arthur Conan Doyle in fairies; this the inventor of Sherlock and Mycroft Holmes justified by 'fairy photographs' showing two girls with 'fairies'. Elsie, aged 16, and Frances, aged 10, were taken back to the scene of their alleged fairy encounter four years later under test conditions, which proved completely negative. Conan Doyle also believed in 'spirit photographs' (q.v.), in which 'extra' faces appear 'in a cloud of ectoplasm'. Dr W. F. Prince, Research Officer for the American Society for Psychical Research, patiently explained time and again the detailed methods by which these photographs had been fraudulently manipulated. Conan Doyle, who published a *History of spiritualism* in 1926, refused to accept the evidence, having founded a Society for the Study of Supernormal Photographs.

'FALL' IS THE AMERICAN WORD FOR 'AUTUMN'

There is nothing American about the use of 'Fall' for the third season of the year other than its current use in the United States; both 'Fall' and 'Autumn' have a long European ancestry: the latter from the Latin 'autumnus' (possibly from Etruscan?), and the former from the Old English 'feallan', akin to the Old Frisian 'falla'.

'Fall' in this sense can be found in the works of Raleigh, Drayton, and other writers of the Elizabethan period.

Source: Eric Partridge, *Origins* (4th ed., London, 1966).

FAMINE IS LOGICALLY BOUND TO OCCUR

William and Paul Paddock, in their *Famine 1975!* (Boston, 1967), carefully demonstrated the inevitability of widespread famine in or before the year 1975. How they did this was by taking singly all the devices and tactics proposed to forestall famine (agricultural innovations, land reform, government bounties and controls, population-control devices such as the IUD, sterilization and the pill) and by proving that each panacea individually is quite inadequate to solve the problem, and consequently famine was bound to occur. One does not need hindsight (similar presagers of doom have cropped up every decade since the eighteenth century) to see that they were guilty of assuming that famine was *logically bound to occur*, simply because *logically it could occur*. Since most of the measures were applied, at roughly the same time, famine was averted, and human intelligence (with rapidly increasing technological capability) can be relied upon to minimize most of the threats that do and will threaten modern man.

FASCISM IS DEAD IN ITALY

Following the death of Benito Mussolini, and particularly in view of the gathering strength of the Communist Party since World War II, it is tempting to believe those who dismiss the neo-fascists in Italy as of no account (and see also the fallacy **FASCISM IS DEAD IN WEST GERMANY**).

The following table, drawn from official statistics, shows the voting strength of the Italian fascist party (MSI) in post-war general elections:

Year	Votes for the MSI	% of total vote
1948	526,670	2%
1953	1,580,293	5.8%
1958	1,407,718	4.8%
1963	1,569,815	5.1%
1968	1,414,764	4.4%

FASCISM IS DEAD IN WEST GERMANY

According to the Bundesamt für Verfassungsschütz's official figures up to 1 October 1966, only 22% of the age-group in the Nationaldemokratische Partei Deutschlands (NPD) was over 60 (compared with that age-group's total percentage 20% in the Federal Republic), whereas 29% was aged 46-60 (27% of the total population were in that age-group), 27% aged 31-45 (25%), and 22% aged 16-30 (28%). In 1966, therefore, nearly half of the fascist party's total membership consisted of people under the age of 46. In round figures, actual party membership in 1966 stood at the 25,000 mark, and was rising quickly.

As regards the voting strength of the neo-fascists, the 1965 elections in West Germany brought the fascist party 664,193 votes, equivalent to 2% of the votes cast; this strength was more than doubled in 1969, when the party polled 1,422,010 votes (4.3 % of the total), but drastically reduced in 1972 (last figures available) to 207,465 votes (0.6 % of the total). See also the fallacy **FASCISM IS DEAD IN ITALY.**

Sources include: Heinrich Fraenkel, *Neo-Nazism — cause or effect?* in *The Humanist*, February 1967 and official statistics.

THERE IS MORE FAT IN 100 ML. OF WHOLE FRESH MILK THAN IN THE EQUIVALENT WEIGHT OF FRIED HADDOCK

There is less. The fat content of some common foods can be seen in the following table from McCance and Widdowson's *The composition of foods* (3rd rev. ed., 1960):

whole fresh milk	3.7 g per 100	raw potatoes	trace
raw rice	1.0	canned peas	trace
white bread	1.4	boiled cabbage	trace
whole wheat flour	2.5	orange with peel	trace
butter	85.1	apple	trace
cheddar cheese	34.5	white sugar	nil
fried beefsteak	20.4	bitter beer	trace
fried haddock	8.3	spirits (gin,	
		whisky 70 proof)	nil

FATIMA MIRACLE

The alleged miracle was that at Fatima in Portugal on 13 October 1917 the Sun left its place in the firmament, fell from side to side, plunged zigzagging on the crowd below, and sent out an increasing heat.

The Roman Catholic crowd of 70,000 swore to a man, woman and child that that is what actually occurred, as did Pope Pius XII from the Vatican gardens in Rome, but nobody else outside Fatima saw or heard anything unusual on that day.

The most common explanation for the purpose of the prophecy is political: the Virgin allegedly gave three Portuguese peasant children the message that Russia would be converted to Catholicism, presumably after a great war which would need massive psychological preparation.

FIRE-WALKERS HAVE OCCULT POWERS TO PROTECT THEM FROM HARM

Nobody has occult powers to protect him from harm, unless one counts self-discipline, concentration, and self-confidence as occult powers. A major report on the subject by G. B. Brown, *Three experimental fire-walks*, appeared as Bulletin IV of the University of London Council for Psychical Investigation (1938), and found that the fire-walk is not a trick, for the walker's feet are bare and chemically unprepared. However, those who habitually perform the fire-walk normally walk barefoot, and so tend to have thick calloused skin on the soles of their feet which greatly reduces the risk of severe burning.

Hindu and Buddhist priests have traditionally performed fire-walking to impress laymen in South Asia. Dr Carlo Fonseka, at the 26th annual session of the Ceylon Association for the Advancement of Science (1971?) gave demonstrations with burning logs varying in temperature from 300°C to 450°C. The traditional fire-walkers took ten steps across the logs in a matter of three seconds, their immunity from serious injury being partly due to their steadiness and lightness, but principally to the brevity of contact. This was proved when Dr Fonseka challenged the walkers to walk over fire for up to thirty seconds without burning themselves. Not one could be persuaded to do so.

Sources include: D. H. Rawcliffe, *Illusions and delusions of the supernatural and the occult* (New York, 1959, pp. 291-6).

FISH AND PLANT LIFE IN THE WORLD'S SEAS IS DYING

The well-known underwater diver and author Jacques-Yves Cousteau has claimed more than once that "the vitality of the seas, in terms of fish and plant life, has declined some 50 per cent in the past 20 years".

However, in 1970 the U.N.Food and Agriculture Organization reported an *increase* in the world fish catch of 10%.

Source: *The Times*, 3 January 1972, p. 17.

FISH ARE ESPECIALLY GOOD FOR THE BRAIN

This fallacy, propagated in dozens of Bertie Wooster stories and novels by P. G. Wodehouse (on whom otherwise be blessing), appears ultimately to derive from the views of the German philosopher Friedrich Büchner (1824-1899), that "without phosphorus there is no thought"; of the French chemist Jean Dumas (1800-1884) that "fish are a rich source of phosphorus"; and finally of the Swiss naturalist Jean Louis Agassiz (1807-1873) that "fish are good for the brain".

This assumption ignores the fact that phosphorus occurs in many foods other than fish, and the further fact that other foods are equally good for the brain.

"There is no foundation whatever for this view", stated Sir Henry Thompson in *Food and feeding*, and Dr Charles Hill ('The Radio Doctor') declared that "as for brain food, there are no foods for the brain except work".

FISH CAN FLY

Not one of the hundred or so species of 'flying fish' can actually fly in the commonly accepted sense. They do, however, have enlarged pectoral fins which enable them to glide just above the sea's surface at a maximum of ten miles an hour for a maximum of two hundred yards. They usually glide to escape predators such as dolphins.

FLOGGING IS A DETERRENT TO CRIME OR VIOLENCE

So much prejudice exists, mainly on the side of the above idea, that I propose to set out the evidence obtained by a U.K. Government Departmental Committee in 1948. Until September 1948 flogging could be imposed for robbery with violence and armed robbery. All corporal punishment was abolished as from that date except for attacks by prisoners on prison officers.

Convicted of subsequent serious crime:
Flogged   55%   Not flogged   43.9%
Convicted of subsequent serious crime with violence:
Flogged   10.6%   Not flogged   5.4%
Convicted of subsequent crime of violence:
Flogged   13.4%   Not flogged   12.4%

Since this view is known to be true only of a certain time and place, it is instructive to go back to the 1880s in England. During the terror inspired in the public by the violent crimes of the Liverpool High Rig gang, the gutter press agitated for flogging as an effective deterrent. Mr Justice Day ordered flogging. During the next three years, 1887-9, there were 176 cases of robbery with violence in Liverpool, but three years later the number had risen to 198.

It is not certain, on the other hand, that flogging is not a deterrent in other countries, and at other times. But it seems to be as much at odds with the ideal of gentle human behaviour as the Biblical revenge motto, "An eye for an eye, and a tooth for a tooth". Until flogging is proved deterrent to malefactors, its use seems unjustifiable even on severely practical grounds.

THERE WAS A **FLOOD**, OR DELUGE, AS DESCRIBED IN THE BIBLE

The geological record indicates that there have been epochs when the Earth's surface now covered by land was covered by water and *vice versa*, not once, but repeatedly. Climates have changed more than once, both gradually and less gradually. Flooding of the Earth's surface has thus occurred in certain areas at frequent intervals and in other areas less frequently, but there is no scientifically recorded deluge of the type described in the Bible.

Yet a college textbook, *The new geology* (1923) by the Seventh Day Adventist George McCready Price, born in Canada in 1870, teaches that the entire Creation took place a few thousand years before Christ, in six literal days exactly as described in *Genesis*. Fossils (q.v.) are simply the records of antediluvian flora and fauna buried by the convulsion of the Flood. "The Grand Canyon of the Colorado", he could write in all seriousness, "may not be very much older than the Pyramids of Egypt". As a geologist, Price led his scientific gifts along the prejudiced paths of his religion, and had a vested interest in professing the truth of the Old Testament narrative. While no serious scientist troubled to refute Price's anti-evolutionary books, the Catholic writer George Barry O'Toole summarized Price's opinions in *The case against evolution* (1925) and Price was praised in the 1932 edition of Arnold Lunn's *Flight from reason*.

There was brief academic respectability for the notion of an actual 'Flood' in 1929 when Leonard Woolley, excavating the great royal cemetery at Ur of the Chaldees (reputed to be Abraham's native city) wrote: "Taking into consideration all the facts, there could be no doubt that the flood of which we had thus found the only possible evidence was the flood of Sumerian history and legend, the flood on which is based the story of Noah". This after finding in a deep pit sunk into the ancient ruins a stratum of more than eight feet of clean clay. Woolley estimated that the disaster which caused his layer of silt evidence affected an area four hundred miles long by about one hundred miles wide.

He did not think to make a control test at any other of the ancient cities in the same valley, otherwise he would have concluded (as we now know from later investigation) that the layer of silt was localized, and occurs at no other site of similar age.

FLOODING DUE TO DIVINE RETRIBUTION

The Bishop of Metz declared in 1846 that the flooding of the Loire was due to the excesses of the press and the failure to observe Sunday as a day of rest.

The difficulty is that the French did not observe Sunday as a day of rest when the Loire did not flood, and the excesses of the press have grown steadily more obvious, without the concomitant flooding.

Source: Guy Bechtel *and* Jean-Claude Carrière, *Dictionnaire de la bêtise et des erreurs de jugement* (Paris, 1965, p. 231).

FLYING SAUCERS EXIST!

Yes, apparently they do, but some at least, if not all, of those observed in the U.S.A., are really skyhook balloons used for cosmic-ray research, whereas an unfortunate crank literature early arose to identify them with vehicles sent from outer space. Frank Scully, in *Behind the flying saucers* (Chicago, 1951) categorically stated that the saucers were piloted by inhabitants of Venus who were exact duplicates of earthmen except that they were three feet tall. But then at least Scully confessed (in *True* magazine, September 1952) that his book had been a hoax from beginning to end.

After Orson Welles' notorious broadcast of H. G. Wells' *The war of the worlds* in 1938, which was mistaken for a genuine report of invasion from outer space, dozens of Americans frantically telephoned news that they had not only seen the Martians, but some had even felt the heat-rays.

The first reports of flying saucers occurred in 1947, when Arnold, a Boise (Idaho) pilot flying over the Cascade Mountains of Washington, reported nine circular objects in diagonal chain formation moving at high speed and slightly smaller than a DC-4 which happened to be in the sky at the same time. Then the usual flood of similar 'sightings', some of them probably hoaxing or imaginary, filled the U.S. newspapers, until in 1951 the Office of Naval Research published a report showing how their balloons, in effect giant plastic bags a hundred feet in diameter, could reach a height of 100,000 feet and travel with jetstream winds at more than 200 miles an hour. Furthermore, at a distance the balloon takes on the appearance of a saucer.

After the publication of the official report, sightings of 'flying saucers' decreased, but a mass hysteria movement based on fear and ignorance makes good news, and the media were reluctant to let this story alone.

Arnold himself persisted with his assertions in a blaze of publicity, including an article 'I *did* see the Flying Disks' in Raymond Palmer's magazine *Fate* (Spring, 1948), and a fifty-cent pamphlet entitled *The flying saucer as I saw it*. The magazine *Life* (7 April 1952) printed an argument in favour of the extra-terrestrial origin of flying saucers after the official report, and large numbers of crank books prove the durability of human folly against all the available evidence. One such is by the mystic, scholar, and novelist Gerald Heard: *Is another world watching?* (New York, 1951), in which the intruders are said to come to Earth from Mars. They are super-bees about two inches long with an intelligence much higher than Man's.

George Adamski is one of the most celebrated flying-saucer writers, having published *Flying saucers have landed* (with D. Leslie, London, 1953), *Inside the flying saucers* (New York, 1955), and *Flying saucers farewell* (New York, 1961). Several years before the Moon was visited by men, he was able to state authoritatively that vegetation, trees, animals and human beings lived on the Moon, just out of sight of the Earth, in the temperate section. He obtained this information from an inhabitant of Saturn whom he had met in a café and who subsequently (in 1955) took him for a ride in a flying saucer which was able to hover only a few thousand miles from the Moon.

With Earthmen like these, who needs enemies from outer space? See also **AETHERIUS SOCIETY.**

Sources include: Martin Gardner, *Fads and fallacies in the name of science* (New York, 1957), pp. 55-68.

PHIN'S FOLLIES OF SCIENCE

John Phin contrasts to the 'seven wonders of the world' the 'seven follies of science', barring as fraudulent astrology and magic:

1. The quadrature of the circle; or, as it is called familiarly, squaring the circle.
2. The duplication of the cube.
3. The trisection of an angle.
4. Perpetual motion.
5. The transmutation of the metals.
6. The fixation of mercury.
7. The elixir of life.

Source: John Phin, *Seven follies of science* (New York, 1912).

FOOD FROM A DENTED OR OPENED CAN SHOULD NOT BE EATEN

Food in damaged cans will only be contaminated if germs have entered through a split in the tin. Otherwise, food from opened tins is no more susceptible to infection than is fresh food. The cans themselves cannot cause poisoning.

THE LIFE OF FOOD-GATHERERS IS HARSH AND RELENTLESS

It depends what your standards are. Presumably Australian aborigines would consider the traffic in Sydney harsh and relentless compared with their quiet and happily communal existence. If one is judging by the hours of work that one has to work, the contrast is even more obvious. The Bushmen of the Kalahari Desert in southern Africa work a 12-19 hour week to gather food for their subsistence, and spend the rest of the time in leisure activities, while the Hadza people of Tanzania spend less than two hours a day in their search for adequate food.

GOD CREATED FOSSILS

God created nothing, Himself being a creation of the fertile mind of fearful men and women. Fossils are the remains of animals and plants belonging to previous geological epochs and found in the appropriate strata of the earth. By comparing fossils found in certain strata, it is possible to date those strata more closely than was hitherto possible.

However, before palaeontology became a recognized body of knowledge, fantasies on the origin of fossils were varied and numerous. Fundamentalists who believe that *Genesis* is a literal account of the Creation settle for the notion that they are the relics of plants and animals destroyed during the Great Deluge. Solemn scientific 'corroboration' of this fallacy appeared as recently as 1726 in Johann Scheuchzer's work *Homo diluvii testis*. Scheuchzer described and illustrated articulated skeletons from certain mid-Cenozoic lake beds at Oeningen, Switzerland, declaring them to be human remains preserved since Noah's Flood. When Cuvier restudied one of the best of Scheuchzer's specimens and found the skeletons to be only the remains of giant salamanders, he referred them to the genus *Andrias* and amusingly named the species *scheuchzeri*! Two reptilian vertebrae were described by the unlucky Scheuchzer as "relics of that accursed race that perished with the Flood" and his illustrations appeared in the so-called 'Copper' Bible of 1731.

Johann Beringer, a teacher at Würzburg, was an ardent collector of fossils but completely misunderstood them and when his students 'planted' carvings of animals on a soft shale outcrop where he habitually sought fossils, Beringer was so far led astray that he amassed a large collection of counterfeit insects, flowers and frogs. After publishing this hoax material as *Lithographia würceburgensis* (1726) he found Hebrew letters and even his own name carved on similar 'fossils' and in his humiliation tried to buy up the whole edition of the book. The work consequently increased enormously in price, and after Beringer's death his family cashed in on the hoax by reprinting the book and making a huge profit. It was about the year 1800 that the organic nature of fossils came to be generally appreciated, though there are still groups of religious fanatics who repudiate the scientific explanation.

Sects such as the Plymouth Brethren even now pour scorn on the idea of fossils as a genuine proof of organic evolution. In 1857 they supported the naturalist Philip Henry Gosse, whose *Omphalos* (London, 1857) was accurately if unfilially described by his son Sir Edmund Gosse as "this curious, this obstinate, this fanatic volume". P. H. Gosse stated that, while the fossils *seemed* to imply organic evolution, God might so have arranged them at the Creation in order to damn nineteenth-century sceptics! 'God' might move in a mysterious way, his wonders to perform, but we might be forgiven for thinking that this way was more mysterious than most.

Zakaria bin Muhammad, in his Arabic-language *Wonders of nature*, suggested that fossils were animals petrified by steam emerging from the ground, according to Erik Nordenskiöld in *History of biology* (New York, 1928).

Sources include: Carl O. Dunbar, *Historical geology* (New York, 1949), pp. 48-50.

THE FOX AND THE FLEAS

We read the *Fables* of Aesop knowing them to be invented, but thousands of animal stories are sworn to be true and read by generation upon generation of the gullible. The *Saturday Evening Post* of 5 August 1944 reported on p. 166 that a fox in southern Illinois had got rid of its fleas by backing into a pond while holding a tuft of wool in its mouth. The fleas 'hastily crawled up through his fur and took refuge in the wool', which the cunning fox released once he was completely submerged, thus ridding himself of the unwanted guests.

One's faith in the allegedly-firsthand report is slightly dented by finding the same story in John Swan's *Speculum mundi* (2nd ed., Cambridge, 1643, p. 443). Swan says he got the story from the *Historia* (1555) of Olaus Magnus. Bergen Evans, recounting this pack of rubbish in *The natural history of nonsense* (London, 1947, p. 65), adds 'Olaus doesn't say where he got it'.

'FRANKENSTEIN' WAS A MONSTER

By analogy, possibly, with Bram Stoker's fictional Count Dracula, Mary Wollstonecraft Shelley's *Frankenstein* (1818) is often believed to be a story of an eponymous monster, but Frankenstein was an imaginary student of medicine in Geneva who learnt the secret of imparting life to inanimate matter and, after constructing the semblance of a human being from bones gathered in charnel-houses, gives it life. The creature inspires all who view it with fear and loathing, and it comes to feel only hatred for its creator. It kills Frankenstein's brother, his bride, Frankenstein and finally itself.

FRECKLES CAN BE REMOVED BY LEMON JUICE

"*Nothing* will remove freckles", write Ashley Montagu and Edward Darling in *The prevalence of nonsense* (New York, 1967). "At least, nothing will remove freckles *only*. There are preparations which will remove the skin, if that's what you want. Then the freckles disappear".

Freckles are a series of small areas of pigmentation usually evoked by exposure to the chemically active ultraviolet rays of the sun, but since most of these pigment cells do not reach the dead surface layer forming the outermost portion of the skin, no substance applied to the surface of the skin can have any effect on those cells which lie deeper.

Preparations sold to remove freckles are, so far, all believed fraudulent and can cause injury to the skin.

WARM WATER FREEZES SOONER THAN COLD

A fallacy which even caught out the illustrious Francis Bacon (*Novum organum*, 1620). The reverse is the case.

There is an interesting exception which is not widely appreciated. Water which has been boiled and then cooled to the same temperature as the cold fresh water will freeze just ahead of the other, probably because the boiling process drives off the carbonic acid gas and air, and deposits any calcium carbonate previously in solution.

I suppose that, as boys, many of us remember pouring boiling water on a snowy hillside to make a slide, but the true purpose of that is to make for a smooth surface once the snow has frozen again.

FREEZING KILLS ALL FORMS OF INSECT LIFE

Micro-organisms cannot be killed by the intensest natural cold, so the old fallacy that if you put meat in a refrigerator or freezer you will thereby kill off any bacteria present should be scotched at once. What you have done is merely to freeze them: once they are thawed out they are free to infect you again. Daddy-long-legs' grubs frozen experimentally at Kew Gardens survived on thawing.

Interestingly, some fish die before freezing temperature is reached, while others can be frozen yet survive. Instances are recorded of dogs swallowing frozen fish whole, only to experience intense discomfort when the fish were thawed by the warmth of the dogs' stomach. Fish swallowed in this way are usually regurgitated.

The Alaskan blackfish remains frozen for several months in the winter, and seems none the worse when thawed out by the warmth of spring.

FROGS FALL FROM THE SKY

Robert Plot's important, ambitious *The natural history of Staffordshire* (Oxford, 1686) is one of the many books in dozens of languages responsible for this fallacy. In Michael Paffard's view, the man responsible for hoaxing Plot was Walter Chetwynd of Ingestre Hall, who also offered his guest, then Keeper of the Ashmolean

Museum, 'potted otter' which Plot found to be "indistinguishable from venison, which it probably was". Chetwynd described to the credulous but enthusiastic Plot how frogs had showered down from the sky and were afterwards found in very great numbers even upon the leads of the stately gatehouse at Ingestre. Plot concludes that sometimes "the Spawn or Seed of Frogs may be either blowne from the tops of Mountains, or drawn up with the Vapours out of uliginous places, and be brought to perfection in the Clouds, and discharged thence in Showers", though he prefers to think frogs more often "produced on the surface of the Earth . . . by a Fermentation excited in the Dust".

This of course provoked other fantastic tales of frogs, such as the live frog allegedly encased in the solid stone of the pinnacle of Statfold church steeple. He did not find it incredible that a creature "of so slender a dyet" should remain in such a situation "without meat or air" for some hundreds of years.

It rains frogs, of course, because after rainfall frogs suddenly emerge. But conversely, frogs never emerge in dry weather if they can avoid it because they can only survive if their skin is moist, so they are bound to live near damp places, such as rainbarrels or stagnant. So, when it appears to 'rain frogs', in fact the frogs (or ageing tadpoles) were there all the time, but unperceived.

Charles Fort, in his amusing *The book of the damned* (New York, 1919) records the 'raining' not only of frogs, calves, and milk, but also mentions popular press accounts of raining fish, fungi, stones (some of them inscribed), protoplasm, hatchets, masks, and ceremonial regalia. Most of the fish fall on India, if one judges by the preponderance of newspaper reports. See also LIFE CAN BE CREATED BY THE ACTION OF SUNLIGHT ON MUD.

Source: Michael Paffard, *Robert Plot: a county historian* in *History Today*, February 1970, pp. 112-7.

G

"Great truths find no resting place in the heart of the people so, all mankind living in error, how may I teach them even if I know the way myself? If I know that I cannot instruct successfully, the attempt will be another error. It is consequently better to desist from the attempt. But, if I make no effort, who then will do it?" - CHUANG TZU

ROMAN 'GAUL' WAS MODERN FRANCE

It was in fact much more extensive, including the Low Countries, Switzerland, and parts of northern Italy, in addition to continental France. Allcroft and Plaistowe, in their edition of Caesar's *Gallic War*, Book I, write: "In the time of Caesar the Gauls occupied roughly the whole of that part of Europe which lies west of the Rhine and north of the Pyrenees, together with much of Switzerland, and that part of the Italian peninsula which lies to the north of the rivers Rubicon and Macra (thence called Gallia Cisalpina). They had once overrun the land as far as the Tiber, and had routed the Etruscans and settled in the Po Valley; but in the year 218 B.C. the Romans had planted the colonies of Placentia and Cremona as the symbol and safeguard of the final reduction or expulsion of these Cisalpine Gauls."

GAUTAMA'S LIST OF FALLACIES

The *Nyāyasūtras* of Gautama, a 2nd-century Indian writer also called Aksapāda, have been edited, and translated from the Sanskrit, by Gangānātha Jhā (2 vols., Poona, 1939).

His list of five types of fallacy, usually accompanied by the commentary of Vātsyāyana (who is perhaps better known as the 5th-6th century author of the *Kama sutra*) formed the basis of subsequent Indian lists, much as Aristotle's list (see **LOGICAL FALLACIES**) formed the basis of Western lists.

(1) The erratic or inconclusive reason. Thus, 'Sound is eternal because it is intangible', whereas some intangible things are eternal while others are not.

(2) The contradictory reason. Thus, Yoga doctrine states both that 'The world ceases from manifestation, because it is non-eternal' and that 'The world continues to exist, because it canno-be utterly destroyed'. These cannot both be unacceptable, bet cause they are mutually exclusive; if one is right (which is not certain), then the other must be wrong.

(3) The neutralized reason. Instead of leading to a decision about an argument, a reason may lead to an inconclusive answer, or be repetitious of the thesis itself. Thus, 'Sound is non-eternal because we do not find in it the properties of the eternal thing' is a statement that offers no conclusion.

(4) The unknown or unproven reason. Thus, 'Shadow is a substance, because it has motion' is guilty of this fallacy because it is not known whether a shadow has motion.

(5) The inopportune reason. Thus, if thesis and reason refer to *different* times, a paradox will arise not unlike that of Achilles and the tortoise, wherein it is argued that Achilles will never catch up a yard on the tortoise because before he can catch up a yard he must catch up 35 inches then 34 inches, and so on *ad infinitum*. [In a variant, Boethius argues that 'Socrates is sitting down' and 'Socrates is not sitting down' may both be true but at different times.]

GELLER, URI

A phenomenon of mass gullibility of the 1970s, the Israeli conjuror Uri Geller is widely believed to possess certain 'extrasensory' perceptions which enable him to bend metal spoons, break metal forks, stop watches, and draw facsimiles of sealed drawings. Otherwise intelligent television viewers are persuaded that he possesses 'psychokinetic abilities', 'supranormal faculties of the mind' or 'paranormal magnetic power'.

The various fallacies have been patiently exposed by another conjuror, James Randi, who has travelled the world behind Geller doing the same tricks by means of his training in 'magic', and has written a famous exposé, *The magic of Uri Geller* (London, 1976) to contradict claims made in Uri Geller's *My story* (London, 1976).

As early as the December 1973 issue of the International Brotherhood of Magicians (British Ring's) magazine *The Budget*, conjurors were debating the two classic dilemmas arising from performances such as those by Geller: (*a*) is he morally justified in prolonging the hoaxing of the mass media and the general public? and (*b*) does the conjurors' ethical code demand that conjurors keep silent?

The consensus was that he should be backed up. As one conjuror wrote, "I address those of our membership who might find themselves tempted to prove or disprove the various theories which abound at this time. Remember the ethics expected of us—it is so easy to fall into the ever-open trap".

Naturally, failure on the part of those members of society most immediately able to refute Geller's allegedly paranormal powers to do so has only permitted the fallacy of 'extra-sensory perception' to gain a deeper hold on the receptive human imagination.

Sources: Barbara Smoker's article in *New Humanist* (February, 1974) and Christopher Evans' article in the same journal (July/August 1976).

GEMATRIA

Numerology in the mystical Kabbala of Judaism. It is as fallacious as numerology within other religious systems or outside religious systems. Each letter of the Hebrew alphabet represents a numerical value, so that *aleph* is 1, *bet* 2, and so on to *shin* 300 and *taf* 400.

In *The joys of Yiddish* (New York, 1968), Leo Rosten gives the following example of illogical reasoning from the strange world of gematria: "Simon the Just used to say, 'Upon three things the world is based: upon the *Torah*, upon worship, and upon the practice of loving kindness' (*Sayings of the Fathers*, 1:2). So, *Torah*, numerical value of 611; *Avodah* (worship), value of 87; *Gemilut chasadim* (deeds of loving kindness), value of 611. From this we are supposed to learn the co-equality of *Torah* and practising loving kindness! Moreover, if Israel observes the obligations assumed when it accepted the Lord 'to be your God' (value, 611), then 'His Kingdom will come' (611)!.

GENERALIZATION AS A FALLACY

I am indebted to Carl Bridenbaugh, author of *Mitre and sceptre* (New York, 1962) for the following splendid fallacy due to false generalization conceived by the Congregationalist clergyman Rev. Ezra Stiles in 1760, projecting the following denominational demography of New England:

Year A.D.	Episcopa- lians	Friends	Baptists	Congrega- tionalists
1760	12,600	16,000	22,000	440,000
1785	23,200	32,000	44,000	880,000
1810	46,400	64,000	88,000	1,760,000
1835	92,800	128,000	176,000	3,520,000
1860	185,600	256,000	352,000	7 Millions

(Luckily he did not estimate for the following century.)

Incidentally, the number of *churches* increased quite substantially from 465 in 1750 to 1,706 in 1850. But the number of Congregationalists is thought to have increased in a much smaller ratio than this: see Edwin S. Gaustad's *Historical atlas of religion in America* (New York, 1962).

Such generalized projections should be treated very carefully, since by their nature they are unable to take account of future variables.

A dangerous type of generalization, which is alas all too common, is the stereotyping of national characteristics, often even by eminent historians. This is Henry Steele Commager, in *The American mind* (New Haven, 1950), falsely attributing to all Americans a single set of ideas or tendencies:

"The American was incurably optimistic . . . He had little sense of the past . . . He preached the gospel of hard work . . . The sense of equality permeated the American's life and thought . . . The American was good natured, generous, hospitable, and sociable . . . Carelessness was perhaps the most pervasive and persistent quality in the American . . . The American was at once intelligent and conservative, independent and reliable . . . The American was romantic and sentimental . . ."

Commager is strictly incorrect in all of these opinions, since they are postulated of 'the American' instead of 'an American'. The former is a figure of speech of the kind condemned by G. K. Chesterton in *Heretics* (London, 1905): "the universal modern talk about young nations and new nations; about America being young, about New Zealand being new. The whole thing is a trick of words . . . Of course we may use the metaphor of youth about America or the colonies, if we use it strictly as implying recent origin. But if we use it (as we do use it) as implying vigour or vivacity, or crudity, or inexperience, or hope, or a long life before them, or any of the romantic attributes of youth, then it is surely as clear as daylight that we are duped by a stale figure of speech".

MEN OF GENIUS ARE ALWAYS SMALL

Cesare Lombroso, in his *The man of genius* (London, 1891) affirms that the greatest conquerors, generals, artists, theologians, lawyers and politicians have all been small men. The only exceptions, according to Lombroso, are Volta, Petrarch, Helmholtz, D'Azeglio, Foscolo, Monti, Mirabeau, Bismarck, the Dumas, Schopenhauer, Lamartine, Voltaire, Peter the Great, Carlyle, Washington, Flaubert, Turgenev, Kropotkin, Tennyson, Whitman . . .

[And as many more as you need to list in order to prove Lombroso's confident assertion a fallacy]. See also **GENERALIZATION AS A FALLACY**.

GEOMANCY

The *Shorter Oxford English Dictionary* defines this term as 'The art of divination by means of lines and figures, formed originally by throwing earth on some surface, and later by jotting down on paper dots at random'.

Émile Grillot de Givry, in his *Picture museum of sorcery, magic and alchemy* (New York, 1963, p. 301), offers a slightly different definition: "Geomancy is divination by earth; it was also known as the Art of the Little Dots, which was formerly confused with cartomancy [divination by playing cards. Ph.W.]. It consisted in throwing a handful of earth on the ground and examining the figure thereby formed, or even in marking dots at random on a sheet of paper and interpreting their position". The origin of this fallacy was the more general error that each of the four 'elements' (actually the notion of these elements has been proved wrong) had its own mode of divination, or foretelling the future. Pyromancy was divination by fire (if pounded peas caught fire quickly the augury was in some obscure manner considered 'good'); hydromancy was divination by water; and aeromancy was divination by examining the variations and different phenomena of the air in a manner not easily grasped.

This all seems harmless enough until one realizes how much 'geomancy' and similar activities are being pursued at this very minute. The Institute of Geomantic Research was recently founded in the Cambridge area and counts among its publications a quarterly journal (vol. 1, no. 1, 1976) and the so-called 'Nuthampstead Zodiac', a map of parts of Herts., Essex, and Cambridgeshire which claims that signs of the zodiac have been built by man, a claim made also for the Pendle area of Lancashire and the Glastonbury area. The Institute, operating from 142 Pheasant Rise, Bar Hill, Cambridge, obtained sixty members during its first year; within its scope are terrestrial geometry, aligned sites, ley-lines, and the geometry of sacred buildings. Their *Geomancy of Cambridge* is claimed to include 'startling information' about King's College Chapel and other sacred sites in the city.

Belief in the mystic powers of the zodiac and all related fallacies are held because the believer has been unable to make the mental leap from the superstition of astrology (q.v.) to the science of astronomy. It would be a pity for the young to be deluded into thinking that there were some truth in geomancy.

Sources include: Dan Jackson, article 'The zealous hunters of the zodiac' in *Cambridge Evening News*, 10 December 1976, p. 15.

GHOSTS

The perpetuation of fear in succeeding generations of the young in most human societies derives partly from the fear and ignorance of the adults, and partly from the universal adult need to control the young by all means at their disposal.

Most tales of apparitions in psychical research history date from the period before 1900, when superstition and belief in the supernatural were stronger than they are now. Those unusually nervous (such as children, or lonely women) had only to think about ghosts for an unusual sound or sight to induce the belief that spectres were at hand. Romantic literature of the 19th century throughout Europe encouraged a belief in magic and ghosts which was an exacerbation of the fears of hell-fire nurtured by priests and parsons in the Middle Ages, before, and after.

The simple mind is capable of great illusion. Suggestion and autosuggestion are always stronger than scepticism among the young, the rural, and the otherwise impressionable. The works which have enjoyed the longest and greatest repute among those interested in reports of ghosts (which are connected with the fallacy of life beyond death, a self-evident impossibility) are *Phantasms of the living* (2 vols., London, 1886), by E. Gurney, F. W. H. Myers, and Frank Podmore; and Myers' *Human personality and its survival of bodily death* (2 vols., London, 1903). These works, written from a viewpoint of total commitment to both the idea of bodily survival after death and the existence of ghosts, were nevertheless unable to admit more than a small number of "fairly conclusive cases", repudiating the vast majority as spurious. Yet neither book publishes any contemporary written evidence, and E. Parish, analyzing them both in *Hallucinations and illusions* (London, 1897, p. 104), concluded that a large percentage of reported cases contained unmistakable evidence of a dream state of consciousness. D. H. Rawcliffe, in *Illusions and delusions of the supernatural and the occult* (New York, 1959), declares that "a purported telepathic, clairvoyant or prophetic experience must more or less correspond to some external event to render it veridical; and the only admissible evidence in such cases is an account of the experience written down, or otherwise recorded—*before* the external event takes place—in a diary, a letter, or other document". Needless to say, there are no cases which obey the minimal scientific requirement of proof.

For the benefit of those still frightened of the dark, of 'inexplicable' noises, and of shapes and shadows, THERE IS NO SUCH THING AS A GHOST!

GIANTS

In *Atlantis and the giants* (London, 1957), Denis Saurat proceeds from a single phrase in the Bible ('There were giants in the Earth in those days' from the story of Noah, *Genesis* 6:4), to concoct a theory according to which a moon gradually approaching the earth would tend to produce giants, since it would counteract the earth's gravitational force. A great civilization of giants arose at Tiahuanaco, near Lake Titicaca in the Andes, and their ships travelled across the globe. Saurat thus explains certain resemblances in human culture all over the earth: the megaliths of Stonehenge (q.v.) and Malekula, legends of Greece and Mexico.

Saurat, a disciple of Hörbiger and the World-Ice Theory (q.v.), performs the fanatic's usual trick of seeing resemblances but failing to observe discrepancies, a fault in men's thinking which derives partly from a desire to create neatness and pattern from what is essentially coincidental and chaotic. It would be much more striking and inexplicable if *no* correlation could be found between human artefact and myth in different societies.

A later, equally uncritical account, this time of alleged giants inhabiting present-day Earth, *There are giants in the Earth* (New York, 1974) by Michael Grumley, glosses over the fact that no actual example of such a giant has ever been produced for scientific investigation, dead or alive. As Grumley himself confesses (p. 8); "Expeditions, organized by such strange academic bedfellows as Prince Peter of Greece and the late Texas oil magnate Tom Slick, have come up with a sizable amount of data on the habits and appearance of the elusive 'snowman', yet never with the furry gentleman himself".

See also **SASQUATCH** and **YETI**.

THE **GIRAFFE** OF COURSE HAS MORE CERVICAL VERTEBRAE THAN ANY OTHER MAMMAL

Because of its long neck, the giraffe is the subject of this observation by most visitors to zoos or wildlife parks. So just check on your next visit to a science museum: like man, the whale, and all other mammals, the giraffe has seven cervical vertebrae.

BLUE **GLASS**

Between 1870 and 1880 America and Europe were engulfed in a wave of enthusiasm for blue glass and blue light. Blue and violet rays were thought to be especially good for certain ailments. In 1861 General A. J. Pleasonton experimented with blue rays in a grapery, which was covered and encased by sashes of glass of which every eighth row of panes was, as he supposed, violet in colour. He had good results, reported in *Blue and sun-lights, their influence upon life, disease,etc.*, a paper read in 1871 to the Philadelphia Society for Promoting Agriculture. "I investigated the matter, and found that the glass was a dark mazarin blue—owing its colour to a preparation of cobalt which had been fused with the material composing the glass". Pleasonton's ideas on blue glass were eagerly taken up, and a wealthy Baltimorean suffering from chronic rheumatism was to be seen on sunny days, driving in a phaeton of which the cover was a canopy of blue glass.

Dr Seth Dancoast of Philadelphia published a work called *Blue and red light; or light and its rays as medicine* "not only to prove that the gentle Blue ray has curative properties for some disorders, and the strong, Red ray for others, but to demonstrate just why they, and not the Green or the Yellow, must be employed, and how they act, and then explain the best methods of employing them".

VENETIAN **GLASS** IS MADE IN VENICE

The particular sand needed for Venetian glass is not found in Venice, but in Murano—an island in the lagoon easily accessible by regular *vaporetto*—and that is where 'Venetian' glass has always been made. The glassblowers are still active on Murano, and a visit to them, with the fine early church on neighbouring Torcello, is an integral part of any holiday in the Veneto.

BILLY-GOATS PROTECT INHABITANTS OF A HOUSE FROM THE PLAGUE

Ambroise Paré (1517-1590), in his *Oeuvres*, wrote: "The breath of the billy-goat fills the place it inhabits, thus preventing the plague-bearing air from entering". The notion is totally false.

THE EXISTENCE OF GOD CAN BE PROVED GEOMETRICALLY

This interesting fallacy was propounded in all seriousness by Richard Jack in his *Mathematical principles of theology; or, the existence of God geometrically demonstrated* (London, 1747). Jack, author of a textbook on the *Elements of conic sections* (Edinburgh, 1742) which can be seen in Edinburgh University Library, failed (or did not wish) to recognize that his symbols are not geometrical but logical, and consequently liable to demolition by the usual rules of logic. His notion is not unique: he probably copied it from Jean-Baptiste Morin's *Quod Deus sit* (Paris, 1636), which is to be found on the shelves of the Bibliothèque Nationale.

NO-ONE HAS EVER REFUTED THE PROOFS OF GOD'S EXISTENCE

Immanuel Kant, in his *Kritik der reinen Vernunft* (1781; *The critique of pure reason*), made the classical refutation of the three traditional 'proofs' of God's existence, namely, the ontological, the cosmological, and the teleological.

The *ontological proof* attempts to establish the existence of God simply from the fact that we can conceive of an idea of God. Kant replies, "To attempt to extract from a purely arbitrary idea, the existence of an object corresponding to it, is a quite unnatural procedure and a mere innovation of scholastic subtlety".

The *cosmological proof* takes as its point of departure the fact that something exists, and purports to prove from this that an absolutely necessary, perfect being exists. As a proof, it presupposes the ontological proof. If the latter is invalid, so too is the

112

former; while if the ontological proof is valid, the cosmological proof is superfluous.

The *teleological proof* with the physico-theological proof, starts from a specific view about the nature and order of that which exists, stating some such view as 'the world displays such immeasurable order, variety, purposiveness, and beauty' that we must postulate a perfect being as the author of this order. Its weakest point is perhaps the initial premiss, unproven, that the world *does* exhibit order, and evidence of a purpose or design, of the highest excellence. It also involves both of the other proofs, so that if either or both of those are rejected, the whole evidence is rejected. The 'harmonious' and 'beautiful' arrangement of the heavenly bodies otherwise attributable to God's direct intervention is now known to be a product of the blind working of certain natural laws.

Source: H. J. McCloskey, *Kant's refutation of the proofs of God's existence* in *The Rationalist Annual*, 1963, pp. 78-90.

BASE METALS CAN BE TRANSMUTED INTO GOLD

In his magisterial *Science and civilisation in China* (vol. 5, part II, Cambridge, 1976), Dr Joseph Needham (writing with Lu Gwei-Djen) has proposed the terms 'aurifaction' to denote the idea of transmuting base metals into gold, which was known to be impossible at least a thousand years before the composition of the Hellenistic works which influenced first Islamic and then Christian 'adepts'; and 'aurifiction' to describe the well-known recipes for faking gold known as early as the Hellenistic technical papyri. Needham suggests that earlier historians P. E. M. Berthelot and E. O. von Lippmann were mistaken in thinking that metalworkers practising aurifiction finally duped themselves into believing that aurifaction was possible.

Needham thinks that the social barriers which ruled out contacts between the metalworkers and scholars perpetuated the myth of transmutation, for the metalworkers knew that their fakes could not pass the cupellation test, while the scholars bypassed the cupellation test because they were ignorant of its existence or because their definitions of gold assigned the metal and its imitations to a single class.

Thousands of years have passed since the first 'alchemists' attempted the impossible achievements of transmuting base metals into gold and mixing an elixir of eternal life (see **ELIXIR OF**

LIFE), and as neither task has been fulfilled, we must put another two human aspirations into the category of common fallacies.

It is usual to consider alchemy an essential rung on the ladder which leads up to modern chemistry, and while there is no doubt that scholars and craftsmen were led to discover more of the chemical world in their lust for gold, knowledge, and eternal youth than they would otherwise have done, this half-truth conceals the important question of the scientific attitude, which so sharply divides the scientist from the mere adventurer. As P. M. Rattansi observed in *The Times Literary Supplement* (12 November 1976), alchemy "is a difficult study because the adepts wrapped up their wonted secrets in obscure symbols to conceal them from the un-initiated. Robert Boyle in the seventeenth century pointed out that such mystification had robbed the 'chymists' of the gain in scientific understanding which a vast knowledge of materials, chemical reactions, and laboratory reactions had brought within their reach".

Sources include: F. Sherwood Taylor, *The alchemists* (London, 1952).

GOLD PAINT IS MADE OF GOLD

There is no more gold in 'gold' paint than there is in mosaic 'gold'. The glittering in both is due to stannic sulphide, a golden-yellow crystalline compound of one atom of tin combined with two atoms of sulphur. It is obtained by heating tin amalgam, sulphur, and ammonium chloride in a retort.

GRAVITY IS A FORCE PULLING OBJECTS BACK TO EARTH

The Gravity Research Foundation was founded in 1948 with the specific purpose of discovering a type of 'gravity screen' which will 'cut off gravity' in the same way that a sheet of steel cuts off a light beam. However, Einstein showed that gravity is not a 'force' as had been imagined earlier, but a warping of the space-time continuum. One of the Foundation's mistaken endeavours is to measure the effect of changing relations of the sun and moon on human beings; another belief is that weight (i.e. gravity) has a greater effect on temperament than body-type has, so that the discovery of a gravity screen could change a person's weight and thus alter his temperament.

114

When theories like these are offered, serious scientists are yet again in danger of losing their gravity.

Source: Martin Gardner, *Fads and fallacies in the name of science* (New York, 1957, pp. 80-100).

GROLIER WAS A BOOKBINDER

Because Grolier bindings are greatly prized in the antiquarian book market, laymen think that Grolier himself was the binder, whereas he was of course a book collector.

Source: Henry B. Wheatley, *Literary blunders* (London, 1893, p. 18).

ALL CHILDREN SUFFER FROM GROWING PAINS

There is nothing normal about growing pains, though I always understood there was as a child. These pains are not an inevitable concomitant of growing up, but are caused (usually in the legs and back) by physical strain or exhaustion, disease of the bones, or a manifestation of rheumatism. Growing pains are not often serious, but they should not be dismissed if they persist.

Source: J. A. C. Brown, *Pears medical encyclopaedia* (London, 1967).

DR GUILLOTIN INVENTED THE GUILLOTINE

An understandable mistake, but he merely encouraged the machine's use in the interest of a painless death. It was invented by a German mechanic called Schmidt under the direction of Dr Antonin Louise, and was thus known first as a 'Louison' or 'Louisette'.

Neither was Guillotin the first victim of the machine—that was the highwayman Pelletier (25 April 1792). Guillotin outlived the Revolution by twenty years, dying at the age of 76 on 26 May 1814.

H

"He who has heard the same thing told by 12,000 eye-witnesses has only 12,000 probabilities, which are equal to one strong probability, which is far from certainty."—VOLTAIRE.

CUTTING OR SHAVING HAIR AFFECTS ITS SPEED OF GROWTH

Cutting hair has no effect at all on its growth. Shaving is believed to thicken hair because newly-shaved stubble feels rough.

Source: Peter Wingate, *The Penguin medical encyclopedia* (2nd ed., Harmondsworth, 1976).

HAIR CAN TURN WHITE NATURALLY OVERNIGHT

Normally through fear, horror, or terror, goes the well-authenticated story in the cases reported by *Time*: 2 March 1942 (C. Yates McDaniel, after witnessing 'the collapse of Singapore at close hand'); 31 May 1943 (Ernie Pyle, whose hair merely turned grey during the African campaign); 14 August 1944 (Air Marshal Coningham); and 4 September 1944 (Jimmie Hines, but over a period of three years, in Sing Sing).

However, this is ridiculous in the light of due natural processes, and all recorded cases of 'overnight' bleaching are either exaggerated, or due to bleaching or the sudden removal of artificial colour. In their *Diseases of the skin*, R. L. Sutton and R. L. Sutton, Jr. write, "Sudden, overnight blanching, reliably reported, is doubtless the result of the removal of cosmetic coloration or the application of a bleach. Physiological and anatomical facts are incompatible with the possibility of actual, nonartificial, instant blanching".

HAIR ON MEN'S BODIES IS A SIGN OF STRENGTH

This curious fallacy probably derives from the Biblical story of Samson and his hair. Ordinary daily observation by doctors shows

116

no correlation whatsoever between the amount of hair on a man's body and his actual or potential strength.

A man with hair on his chest is commonly thought to be uncommonly strong, 'like a gorilla'. The gorilla has hair on his belly, his back, his shoulders, arms and legs, but none on his chest.

Source: R. M. Yerkes and Ada W. Yerkes, *The great apes* (New Haven, Conn., 1929).

HAY FEVER

The following fallacies are discussed by August Astor Thomen in *Doctors don't believe it* (New York, 1935, pp. 155-160): That hay fever is contagious; that it is caused by goldenrod; that it occurs chiefly in so-called nervous people; that it is a disease of the eyes or nose; that there is such an ailment as "nose cold"; that the term 'hay fever' is an accurate one; that it is a trivial matter; that it is spontaneously cured after seven years; that it is contracted as a result of the patient having lived in, or visited, a certain place; that it occurs most often in educated people; that diet is a factor in its causation; that it is caused by proximity to weeds, grasses, and trees when they are in bloom; that all are equally susceptible to it; that it cannot be cured; and that it can be cured by a nasal operation.

THE HUMAN HEART IS SITUATED ON THE LEFT OF THE THORAX

It is situated in the *centre*, immediately behind the breastbone and between the lungs; only the point is directed towards the left. If a line were to be drawn down the centre of the chest to divide the heart into two parts, the slightly larger part would be found on the right side. This may dispose of a few strip cartoons or Hollywood movies which show the bullet 'to the heart' oozing blood only on the left. Or it may not.

THE HEART IS THE SEAT OF THE MIND

This Aristotelean fallacy, which accompanied so much that was sound in the origins of anatomy and embryology propounded by the Stagirite, was dispelled by Herophilus (3rd century B.C.), an anatomist whose works have been lost except as quoted by Galen in the second century A.D.

THE 'HEART OF MIDLOTHIAN' IS EDINBURGH

Sir Walter Scott's novel *The Heart of Midlothian* (1818) indicated by that name the Tolbooth prison, demolished in 1817, near the Municipal Chambers in Edinburgh, and not the city itself as is usually supposed.

HEBREW WAS THE ORIGINAL LANGUAGE OF MANKIND

B. Atkinson, in *The triumph of truth, or a popular lecture on the origin of languages* (Melbourne, 1857) asserts: "Hebrew was the primary stock whence all languages were derived" and that Sanskrit is "a dialect of the Hebrew". Sanskrit philology really began with the foundation of the Asiatic Society at Calcutta in 1784. The early Sanskrit scholars disposed of the pietistic myth that Hebrew preceded Sanskrit as well as the myth of the multiplication of languages at the Tower of Babel.

Yet Atkinson's fallacious opinion was widely held, and as late as 1859 the Presbyterian Dr John Cumming spoke of Hebrew from his London pulpit as "that magnificent tongue—that mother-tongue, from which all others are but distant and debilitated progenies".

HELL IS AN ARTICLE OF FAITH AMONG ENGLISH CHRISTIANS

"Belief in eternal hell fire was an essential item of Christian belief until pretty recent times. In this country, as you know, it ceased to be an essential item because of a decision of the Privy Council, and from that decision the Archbishop of Canterbury and the Archbishop of York dissented; but in this country our religion is settled by Act of Parliament, and therefore the Privy Council was able to over-ride their Graces, and hell was no longer necessary to a Christian".

Sources: Bertrand Russell, *Why I am not a Christian* (London, 1927); and *The Times*, 9 February 1864, p. 11.

HIPPOPOTAMI SWEAT BLOOD

From Biblical times to at least the nineteenth century (and who knows, beyond?), it has been popularly believed that the hippopotamus sweats blood. The view has been encouraged by popular magazines and by circus exhibitors.

What actually happens is that the hippo's skin secretes a reddish, oily liquid in warm weather. This makes the skin more resistant to water and possibly protects it from the air. This liquid is not blood, even if it looks like blood from a (safe) distance.

Source: Osmond P. Breland, *Animal facts and fallacies* (London, 1950).

HISTORICAL FALLACIES

These are numerous, and have been divided into three main types: fallacies of *inquiry*, including fallacies of question-framing, of factual verification, and of factual significance; fallacies of *explanation*, including those of generalization, narration, causation, motivation, composition, and false analogy; and fallacies of *argument*, including those of semantic distortion and substantive distraction. As David Hume ruefully asked, "When we run over libraries persuaded of these principles, what havoc must we make?"

D. H. Fischer has also identified five main types of fallacist's fallacy:

1. An argument which is structurally fallacious in some respect is therefore structurally false in all respects.

2. An argument which is structurally false in some respect, or even in every respect, is therefore substantively false in its conclusion.

3. The appearance of a fallacy in an argument is an external sign of its author's depravity.

4. Sound thinking is merely thinking which is not fallacious.

5. Fallacies exist independent of particular purposes and assumptions.

Source: David Hackett Fischer, *Historians' fallacies: toward a logic of historical thought* (New York, 1970).

HISTORY IS THE SAME AS POETRY

The English historian A. L. Rowse thinks so, and in *The use of history* (London, 1946-55) has written that "History is a great deal closer to poetry than is generally realised; in truth, I think, it is in essence the same".

Aristotle taught that history is particularized poetry (an equally startling proposition to the *modern* historian such as those contemporary with, or taught by, Rowse) and events should be selected in historical writing significant both for their function and their aesthetic quality. But the two standards are incompatible and, as Darrett B. Rutman and other critics of Rowse have pointed out, "details are often murky and sometimes inaccurate; biased judgments and dubious points of history are frequently put forward as established fact".

This comment by an American critic is not intended to disparage Dr Rowse personally or generally; it is merely taken as an instance to substantiate the fallaciousness of regarding two disciplines (history and poetry, or geography and drama) as 'in essence the same' and to illustrate the possible consequences of so regarding them.

Source: D. B. Rutman in *William and Mary Quarterly* (3rd ser., vol. XVIII, 1961, p. 134) reviewing Rowse's *The Elizabethans and America* (New York, 1959).

HISTORY REPEATS ITSELF

No: this is quite impossible, despite the protestations of thousands of amateur (and even a few professional) historians to the contrary. The passage of time changes a nation and its places; change to places and people affects all factors taken singly or collectively (from government to sanitation), and nothing can be repeated identically. John Duncan Mackie was guilty of perpetrating this fallacy in *A history of Scotland* (2nd ed., Baltimore, 1966, p. 141): "history had repeated itself exactly . . . the year 1286 was come again [in 1542]" and G. A. Williamson, editing Eusebius' *The history of the Church from Christ to Constantine* (Harmondsworth, 1965, p. 10) falsely claimed that "No one can read Eusebius's account of how the cathedral of Tyre, with all its elaborate symbolism, rose from the ashes, without thinking of Coventry. Truly that generation and this are one". Not only is it unlikely that the inhabitants of Sur (ancient Tyre) in Lebanon and Coventry are even aware of each others' existence; it is an affront to intelligent readers to ask them to believe that all the surrounding circumstances of early Christianity and mid-20th century bomb warfare have any but the remotest resemblance.

HOLIST FALLACIES

The holist fallacy is the mistaken idea that a historian should select significant details from a sense of the whole thing. Though plausible at first glance, this would prevent a historian from knowing anything until he knows everything, which is both absurd and impossible.

The weakness of holism is best exemplified by the attack on Hegel's *Philosophy of history* in Bertrand Russell's *History of western philosophy* (London, 1945), pp. 743 and 745.

"The view of Hegel and of many other philosophers", writes Russell, is that the character of any portion of the universe is so profoundly affected by its relations to the other parts and to the whole, that no true statement can be made about any part except to assign its place in the whole. Thus there can be only one true statement; there is no truth except the whole truth . . . Now this is all very well, but it is open to an initial objection. If the above argument were sound, how could knowledge ever begin? I know numbers of propositions of the form "A is the father of B", but I do not know the whole universe. If all knowledge were knowledge of the universe as a whole there would be no knowledge. This is enough to make us suspect a mistake somewhere".

Hegel's work is so riddled with fallacies that D. H. Fischer, author of *Historians' fallacies* (New York, 1970), states that most of the fallacies in his book could be illustrated by [Hegel's] arguments. "All metahistorians, by definition, are guilty of this mistake—Toynbee, Spengler, Sorokin, Marx, Comte, Kant, Condorcet, Vico—and others who have tried to discover *the* "meaning" of *the* "past".

"HOME, SWEET HOME" IS A BRITISH SONG

The words are by the American John Howard Payne, and the music by Sir Henry Bishop taken from a Sicilian air. The song was first heard in the opera *The maid of Milan*, first produced at Covent Garden in 1823.

HOMOEOPATHY

A cult purporting to be of medical significance. It was invented by Samuel Christian Hahnemann and first adumbrated in his *The Organon* (1810). The name of the cult is contrasted with *allopathy*, a term coined by Hahnemann to describe the treatment of disease by drugs having effects opposite to the symptoms, in other words, orthodox medicine.

Homoeopathy depends on the inaccurate belief that an overdose of quinine (for the treatment of malaria) causes symptoms like those of malaria. He therefore argued that small doses of a drug cure symptoms like those that larger doses would cause. Homoeopathic drugs are diluted by trituration with milk sugar. A 1:10 mixture is finely ground and a fresh 1:10 mixture with sugar is made of the resultant powder. At the 30th such dilution or 'potency' there is one part of drug to 10^{30} parts of milk sugar, so that it is only by something like a miracle if the patient gets even a single molecule of the drug. Hahnemann's other teachings included the statement that seven-eighths of all chronic diseases are variations of psora, commonly known as the itch.

The cult spread rapidly across Europe in the 1820s, reached England and America in the 1840s, when it was the subject of Oliver Wendell Holmes' *Homeopathy and kindred delusions* (1842) and by 1900 there were twenty-two homoeopathic 'colleges' in the U.S.A. Now there are no specifically homoeopathic colleges though New York Medical College and the Hahnemann Medical College in Philadelphia still offer graduate courses in the subject. Misleadingly, some excellent doctors call themselves 'homoeopathic' to indicate their lack of faith in all drugs; this attitude is healthily sceptical, but rare. The cult's leading journal is *The Journal of the American Institute of Homeopathy*. See also NATUROPATHY.

Sources: Peter Wingate, *The Penguin medical encyclopedia* (2nd ed., Harmondsworth, 1976); and Martin Gardner, *Fads and fallacies in the name of science* (New York, 1957).

"THE FALLACIES OF HOPE" A FALLACY?

The great English painter J. M. W. Turner (1775-1851) quoted verses from his epic poem 'The fallacies of hope', though Martin Butlin, in his catalogue entries for the 1974-5 Tate Gallery exhibition (London, 1974, p. 57), says in one place that the poem was "almost certainly never a complete entity", and in another that the poem is "almost certainly non-existent". This confusion means that it might be fallacious to consider the existence of 'The fallacies of hope' merely a fallacy.

I have traced an anonymous poem (author not known in Halkett & Laing) entitled *The fallacies of hope* in both the British Library and Cambridge University Library. It was published by C. Chapple (London, 1832) and consists of 92 pages, p. 14 containing some Turnerian imagery. Thackeray, writing in *Fraser's Magazine* (quoted in Finberg's standard biography of Turner), was in no doubt that Turner was the author of a published *Fal-*

lacies of hope, though I am still wholly unconvinced that the one I have discovered is Turner's.

HUMAN LIFE IS IMPOSSIBLE WITHOUT THE HORSE

"Without the horse, there could have been no culture; our cities would have remained unpaved; there could have been no civilisation, even life would have been impossible".

This theory commits the fallacy of exaggeration.

Source: Urbain Gohier, *Pour être sages* (Paris, 1914).

A GALLOPING HORSE ALWAYS HAS AT LEAST ONE HOOF ON THE GROUND

It is astounding that the fallacy should have survived the demonstration of about 1878 by the photographer Eadweard Muybridge (1830-1904, an Englishman who emigrated to the U.S.A. in 1852) which actually culminated in a book, called *Animal locomotion* (11 vols., Philadelphia, 1887). Every so often the newspapers publish photographs which again demonstrate this well-known fact. The difficulty is that the tiny fraction of a second when all four feet are off the ground cannot be detected by the human eye unaided.

Source: Peter Pollack, *The picture history of photography* (London, 1963, p. 225.)

DRINKING HOT TEA COOLS THE BODY

A very widespread fallacy, which was exploded by Dr Leonard Williams, in the London *Evening Standard* of 25 May 1922, among others. It derives from the relative coolness we feel shortly after *raising* the temperature by drinking hot tea. The drinking of hot tea during a heat wave might in fact cause heat stroke if one were already very near to heat stroke. Drink cold water (but not too much or too quickly) in a heat wave. Cold water absorbs heat as we drink it, as its temperature has to be raised in our system from say 60°F to 98.5°F, our blood temperature. Thus, the drinking of a half a pint of cold water at 60°F absorbs 24 British thermal units, a usefully large amount of heat.

IN BRITAIN HUMAN RIGHTS BEGIN AT BIRTH

The Congenital Disabilities Act 1976 invested the human foetus with sufficient status in law to sue if it is born alive but damaged.

This is quite a significant piece of legislation, because it is estimated that around a thousand children are born handicapped in the U.K. each week. The causes include radiation, drugs, diseases during pregnancy, pollution, and the genetic shortcomings of the parents. Parents will now take greater care, it is hoped, of the unborn child.

I

"If our aim is never to succumb to falsehood, it would be prudent for us to abstain from using language altogether. Our behaviour might still be hesitant or misguided but it is only with the use of language that truth and error, certainty and uncertainty, come fully upon the scene."—A. J. AYER, *The problem of knowledge* (Harmondsworth, 1956, p. 52).

ICE IS WHITE OR TRANSPARENT, LIKE WATER

"The colour of ice, like that of water, is blue, and the colour is deep and intense in proportion to the thickness of clear ice or water through which the light passes. There is a great deal of persistent error about the blue colour of water. A good many people insist that it is due to the reflected blue colour of the sky. It is easy to prove that this is not so since the clear water of seas and lakes is seen to be blue when the sky is completely overcast".

Source: Sir E. Ray Lankester, *Science from an easy chair* (London, 1913, p. 46).

I CHING

An ancient Chinese system of divination (see also **OMENS** and **DIVINATION**). The 'system' consists of eight 'trigrams', or blocks of short or long lines in various combinations, forming sixty-four hexagrams which can be deployed in 11,520 different situations, including the psychological, social, and cosmic. A sacred text corresponds to each hexagram.

However, there is no conceivable manner in which random sets of hexagrams (or anything else for that matter) can be said truly to teach one anything about past, present or future situations. The revered *I Ching*, like its western counterparts in palmistry or astrology, is merely a vain attempt on the part of ignorant men to control their destiny; its pernicious aspect is that acceptance of deterministic readings might (and demonstrably does) so easily lead to resignation and apathy.

The *I Ching* (or Book of Changes) as translated by James Legge has been excellently edited by Ch'u Chai with Winberg Chai (New York, 1964) with a number of traditional appendices.

FRANCIS BACON'S IDOLA

Bacon dealt with fallacies in many of his works, not always consistently. The definitive statement of his views is to be found in the *Novum organon* as edited (with notes) by T. Fowler (Oxford, 1878), an editor who usefully compares the *idola* of Francis Bacon with the *offendicula* (q.v.) of Roger Bacon.

The *eidolon* in Plato is the transient image of a real thing (*Republic*, vii, 516A) and Bacon uses the word to denote the false notion of a thing, or an erroneous manner of regarding it. Bacon identifies four types of *eidolon* or *idolon*, two ineradicable from the human mind, a third creeping almost undetectably into the mind, and a fourth imposed from outside the mind.

The first category consists of *idola tribus*, or 'idols of the tribe', that is to say those fallacies which are accepted by the whole of humanity or at any rate by a large segment of it.

Bacon illustrates this tendency with the following errors: that of assuming a greater order, purpose or regularity in nature than there actually is; the tendency to generalize from a small number of cases; the belief that man is the measure of the universe; and the tendency to support an assumption by quoting affirmative instances and omitting all negative instances.

The *idola specus*, or 'idols of the cave', are errors incidental to the peculiar mental or bodily constitution of each individual, so that his view of things is distorted by his individual circumstances. Errors of this type include the disposition to regard as perfect only what is new or only what is old. Bacon warns every student of nature to "take this as a rule, that whatever his mind seizes and dwells upon with particular satisfaction is to be held in suspicion".

Idola fori, or 'idols of the market-place', are the fallacies arising from the influence exercised over mind by mere words. Some words are names for non-existent things which are supposed to exist because they possess a name. Others are names abstracted from a few objects and applied recklessly to all that has the faintest connection or analogy with these objects, thereby causing widespread and lasting confusion.

Idola theatri, or 'idols of the theatre', are fallacious modes of thinking which result from received systems of philosophy and from erroneous methods of demonstration. Bacon takes as an example the 'sophistical' philosophy of Aristotle which forces nature into abstract schemata and explains by definitions; the 'empirical' philosophers whom he attacks for jumping to conclusions from experiments which are too few in number and too limited in extent; and the 'superstitious' philosophers who corrupt philosophy by the introduction of theological and poetic notions.

SULLY ON ILLUSIONS

In *Illusions: a psychological study* (London, 1881), James Sully devotes twelve chapters to: the study of illusions; the classification of illusions; illusions of perception (four chapters); dreams; illusions of introspection; other quasi-presentative illusions: errors of insight; illusions of memory; illusions of belief; results.

On the connection between fallacy and illusion, Sully states: "No sharp line can be drawn between much of what, on the surface, looks like immediate knowledge, and consciously derived or inferred knowledge. On its objective side, reasoning may be roughly defined as a conscious transition of mind from certain facts or relations of facts to other facts or relations recognized as similar. According to this definition a fallacy would be a hasty, unwarranted transition to new cases not identical with the old . . . Illusion becomes identified at bottom with fallacious inference".

THE HUMAN SOUL IS IMMORTAL

Nothing that we know is *immortal*; some things just last longer than others, but there is no guarantee at all that the universe itself is immortal. One of the most fallacious 'proofs' of the immortality of the human soul was made by the British physicists Balfour Stewart and Peter Guthrie Tait. The following paraphrase of a characteristic extract from their *The unseen universe* (1875), a bestseller of popular science in the late 1870s and 1880s, has been made by E. Temple Bell.

"Matter is made up of molecules (size A), which are vortex-rings composed of luminiferous ether. The luminiferous ether itself is made up of much smaller molecules (size B), which are vortex-rings in a second or sub-ether. Call these smaller molecules and the sub-ether in which they are embedded the Unseen Universe.

The human soul exists in the Unseen Universe. It is made up of the smaller molecules (size B). In life it permeates the body like a subtile gas. The thoughts we think in life are accompanied by vibrating motions of the molecules (size A) of the brain. These motions undulate through the material universe. But, by the conservation of energy, part of these motions will be absorbed by the molecules (size B) of the soul. Therefore the soul has memory. On the dissolution of the body the soul with its memory intact becomes a free agent in the sub-ether. The physical possibility of the immortality of the soul is thus demonstrated".

As E. Temple Bell writes, in *The search for truth* (London, 1935): "Had these daring theorizers taken the trouble to doubt their *assumptions* about the atoms they might have proceeded with less enthusiasm to their truly remarkable *proof . . . Pick the assumptions to pieces till the stuff they are made of is exposed to plain view* —this is the cardinal rule for understanding the basis of our beliefs".

IT IS ILLEGAL TO **IMPERSONATE** A LIVING MEMBER OF THE ROYAL FAMILY ON THE BRITISH STAGE

Oddly enough this idea persists years after the restrictions were lifted (1968). Queen Elizabeth the Queen Mother was legally impersonated by Amanda Reiss in Royce Ryton's *Crown matrimonial* which opened at London's Haymarket Theatre on 19 October 1972.

SLAPPING THE STOMACH IS A CURE FOR INDIGESTION

"Several years ago a medical man in New York attained so high a reputation for the cure of dyspepsia that he had no difficulty in obtaining a fee of five hundred dollars for each case he undertook, payable in advance. His patients were bound by solemn oath not to reveal his mode of treatment; but after his death scores of them considered themselves freed from the obligation and published the secret, which mainly consisted in slapping the stomach," etc.

The symptoms of dyspepsia can be relieved by a wide range of drugs, but *not* by slapping the stomach.

Source: George Black, *The doctor at home* (p. 441), quoted in L. P. Jacks, *Among the idolmakers* (London, 1912, p. 127).

THE POPE OF THE ROMAN CATHOLIC CHURCH CLAIMS TO BE INFALLIBLE

Roman Catholics weary of repeating that this has never been the case. The statement of infallibility was first made at the Vatican Council of 1870, but refers only to occasions when the Pope speaks *ex cathedra*, that is from the Chair of St. Peter (metaphorically, of course; the chair on which he sits is several centuries later). In fact, there has so far been no occasion when he has proclaimed *ex cathedra*, so there has been no case in which the claim has been reasserted since 1870. Another fallacy is that infallibility began to operate only in 1870: it was predated to St. Peter himself. Laymen who point to the corruption and wickedness of certain popes are guilty of another fallacy: the Pope does not claim to be *impeccable*.

Source: Catholic Truth Society, London.

INFLUENZA IS A NEW DISEASE

The pandemic of 1918-9 killed some twenty million, most of them as a result of pneumonia or other complications, and it was perhaps the scale of that pandemic that persuaded most people that the disease is a product of the 20th century. Influenza (Italian, 'influence') was given its present name in 1741, but had been known earlier under other names, such as *grippe*.

As early as 1797, in *Medical and vulgar errors refuted*, John Jones ridiculed the fallacy that "the influenze . . . is a very dangerous distemper, and a new one; never known in this country till a few years ago". "It is neither a new nor a dangerous distemper", snorted the good Dr Jones.

Source: Charles Creighton, *History of epidemics in Britain* (vol. 2, Cambridge, 1894, p. 304).

ASSOCIATION WITH THE INSANE LEADS TO INSANITY

"Another popular fallacy, often confidently asserted in the press, is the pernicious effect of association with the insane. According to this theory, those who nurse and attend the alienated must in time become unbalanced. There is no evidence for this belief. Doctors and nurses attached to mental hospitals are specially trained, and their insight into the abnormal mind is, if anything, a protection against contagion".

Source: Dr George Somerville, in *New Health* (October 1929).

INTELLIGENCE IS A MATTER OF RACIAL SUPERIORITY

"Racial differences in measured intelligence . . . remain neither proven nor disproved. There are differences, but like stature, they do not necessarily indicate the maximum level of capacity in the absence of standard or controlled conditions. To the confirmed believer in racial differences in intelligence, we can simply say that the more nearly two groups are matched in educational level, family background, opportunity, and security, the closer they agree on averaged I.Q. scores. To the dedicated equalitarian, the believer in no race differences, the disparate levels in the currently best-matched negro-white comparisons remain to be refuted . . . A very reasonable guess is that races are comparable in the sum and total of what we call "intelligence", but differ in many interesting details. As with the automatic response patterns that so neatly differentiate one individual from the other, race differences may exist in form-discrimination, color-sense, tonal-memory, mechanical-reasoning, abstract-reasoning and with other special (rather than general) aspects of intelligence. This supposition, moreover, is directly susceptible to testing."

Source: Stanley Garn, *Human races* (Springfield, Ill., 1961).

(N.B. M. F. Ashley Montagu has described results from alpha tests of the U.S. Army in World War I which found that negroes from some Northern states scored higher in one kind of intelligence than whites from some Southern states. See his paper 'Intelligence of northern negroes and southern whites in the First World War' in *American Journal of Psychology*, vol. 68 (1945), pp. 161-88).

YOU CAN GUESS A PERSON'S INTELLIGENCE BY LOOKING AT HIM

A very deep-seated fallacy, at least among Europeans, who can often be heard to whisper that someone 'looks stupid' or 'is obviously clever'. It begins from the need of teachers, businessmen, psychologists, and others, to attempt to assess interviewed subjects quickly and with a minimum of background data. *Nature* (October 1918) reported the results of an investigation by R. Pinter to test the above generally-held belief by showing photographs of twelve children known to vary in intelligence from the feeble-minded to the brilliant to four groups of people. These groups were teachers, psychologists, physicians, and a miscellaneous selection of people from all walks of life. The best guessers were the psychologists, but even their score was insufficiently high to justify confidence in their ability.

So much for the complacency of the next friend who tells you that his "first impressions of a stranger are always confirmed".

SMALLER FORMS OF LIFE CONTAIN NO INTERNAL ORGANS

This was universally believed until Marcello Malpighi's dissection of the silkworm in about 1675. Malpighi used the recently-developed microscope to discover an anatomy in the silkworm no less complex than that of the larger animals.

THE AURORA ISLANDS LIE SOUTHEAST OF THE FALKLAND ISLANDS

The islands, first discovered by the *Aurora* in 1762, reported again by the *Princess*, Captain Manuel de Oyarvido, in 1790, and by other vessels at various dates including the Spanish surveying vessel *Atrevida* in 1794, and recorded on all charts of the South Atlantic until the nineteenth century, do not exist.

Neither do Saxemberg Island, 600 miles NW of Tristan da Cunha; the Belcher Islands 'in Hudson Bay'; S. Brandan's Isle to the west of the Azores; or Mayda, shown in the middle of the Bay of Biscay on a map published in Chicago as recently as 1906.

It is by no means a simple case of an island's temporarily rising above the surface of the sea and then returning below, or a vast ice floe such as that recorded by the Norwegian whaler *Odd I* in 1927 off the South Shetlands. These are pure inventions, repeated uncritically by succeeding generations. Admiralty charts still mark some islands 'E.D' (existence doubtful) or 'P.D.' (position doubtful).

Source: Rupert T. Gould, *Oddities* (2nd ed., London, 1944).

ITALIAN IS THE FIRST LANGUAGE OF ITALIANS

'Italian' is actually Tuscan, which has spread since the time of Dante (1265-1321) to become the *lingua franca* of the whole of Italy, of newspapers, radio, television and books. But, to quote *Romagnol: Language and Literature* (New York, 1972) by D. B.

Gregor: "Italians are bilingual, and Italian is their second language. Each man's mother-tongue is the speech of the region in which he was born; and how big that region is, and what its frontiers are, depends on historical events and geographical features . . . Romagna is one such region, and Romagnol one such *patois* elevated to literary dialect". If the criterion of a language is that it should have produced important works of literature, then Romagnol for example again has to be taken into consideration for *Pulon Matt* (Cambridge, 1976), translated with facing text by D. B. Gregor from a burlesque 16th-century epic on the scale of Ariosto's *Orlando furioso*. Sardinian, Friulan, Neapolitan, and Sicilian are other major Italian regional languages with important literatures.

J

"J'ai tant médit de la vie que, souhaitant enfin lui rendre justice, je ne tombe sur aucun mot qui ne sonne faux" (I have meditated on life so long that, hoping to do it justice at last, I encounter not one word that does not ring false).—EMIL CIORAN, *Le mauvais démiurge* (Paris, 1969).

'JACK' IS SHORT FOR 'JOHN'

'Jack' is on the contrary short for 'Jacobus' (Latin for 'James') through the Old French 'Jaques' (modern French 'Jacques'). It has curiously enough come to be the commonest pet form of 'John', though the correct pet form 'Johnny' has its periods of ascendancy over the wrong word.

JERICHO'S (LATE BRONZE AGE) WALLS CAME TUMBLING DOWN

It must be true: it's in the Bible. John Garstang, who excavated at Jericho in the 1930s, announced that he had found the city's Late Bronze Age walls, which he ascribed to the time of Joshua, following Biblical tradition. The inner wall was discovered "to have fallen together with the remains of buildings upon it". Furthermore, the city had been destroyed by fire, "precisely in the manner described in the Book of Joshua". Garstang asserted beyond all doubt that "the destruction . . . corresponds in all material particulars with the Biblical narrative".

And so all laymen were taught, and believed, until Kathleen Kenyon returned to Jericho (or *Ariha* as it is known locally) in the 1950s with more scientifically-controlled techniques and a more open mind. She found that the fortifications dated by Garstang to the time of Joshua were a thousand years earlier in date.

Source: James B. Pritchard, *Seeds from stony ground*, in *Radio Times*, 15-21 January 1977.

THE ENGLISH WERE ORIGINALLY JEWS

According to the *Pall Mall Gazette* of 3 April 1894, the founders of the English nation [among others] were descended from the lost tribes of Israel, *Saxon* being clearly a corruption of *Isaac's son*.

This fallacy is both historical (being unsupported by any written or archaeological evidence of any kind) and etymological (the word *Saxon* being apparently, according to Partridge, derived from Old English *seax*, a knife or dagger, and hence denoting men of the [long] knife).

Unexpected support for this preposterous fallacy can be found in Roger Lambelin's *Le règne d'Israël chez les Anglo-Saxons* (1921): "It is agreed that only two of the twelve tribes of Israel, returned from captivity in Babylon, lived in Palestine at the time of Christ's birth. The others had emigrated to the north-west of Europe and were established in the British Isles".

There is still in existence (see the *Guardian directory of pressure groups*, 1976) the Society for Proclaiming Britain is Israel, with the stated dogma of "the identity of the Celto-Anglo-Saxon peoples with the Israel of the Old Testament as distinct from Judah".

THE MAID OF ORLEANS WAS CALLED JOAN OF ARC OR JEANNE D'ARC

She is now, but it is a fallacy to think that she came from a village called Arc, because there simply isn't one near her home town of Domrémy. Littré confirms that the name was spelt Darc on all contemporary documents, and that she was the daughter of a farmer, Jacques Darc. She was not canonized until 1920.

JOSEPH WORE A COAT OF MANY COLOURS

Much more picturesque than the truth, but the *Cambridge Bible* editors kindly divest us of yet another appalling mistranslation. Joseph, according to the original Hebrew, wore 'a long garment with sleeves'. But as there is no reliable support for the tales of Joseph, regrettably even that emendation seems to do little service.

Source: *Cambridge Bible* (*Genesis*, p. 351, n.3).

JOSEPH OF ARIMATHEA CAME FROM GAUL TO CHRISTIANIZE BRITAIN

Nothing early is recorded of this person, who is believed to have lived during the 1st century, other than the Gospel account. Legendary tales began to circulate of him in the 4th century but it was not until the 13th that it is asserted that the apostle Philip sent Joseph to Britain, where he is alleged to have founded the first British church, at Glastonbury. His connections with the romance of the Holy Grail and with King Arthur (q.v.) have obtained wide credence, even in the 20th century, but they are totally devoid of any historical foundation.

Source: J. Armitage Robinson, *Two Glastonbury legends* (1926).

A JUGGERNAUT IS A HUGE VEHICLE, SUCH AS AN ARTICULATED LORRY

'Juggernaut' is merely the anglicized form of Jagannath, (Hindi, 'Lord of the World') an idol of Krishna at Orissa in India. The English sense stems from the entirely erroneous belief that devotees of Krishna threw themselves beneath the wheels of the idol as it was carried in procession at the annual festival on a huge carriage.

Source: Eric Partridge, *Origins* (4th ed., London, 1966).

BUTCHERS ARE EXEMPT FROM JURY SERVICE

Jane Green, contributing to *Notes and Queries* (29 January 1938), explored this ancient fallacy, which was believed by Fuller, Locke, Butler, Swift, Lamb, and Hazlitt. She described it as 'quite mythical', at any period of English law. It may have arisen from the fact that physicians or surgeons actually practising are exempt, and from the opinion that butchers can be grouped with them on the analogy that, since they are so accustomed to seeing animal flesh cut, they are hence devoid of human feelings!

K

"Knowledge being to be had only of visible and certain truth, error is not a fault of our knowledge, but a mistake of our judgment, giving assent to that which is not true."—JOHN LOCKE, *Essay concerning human understanding* (1690), Book IV, Ch. XX.

KARMA

A Hindu belief as ineradicable as **CASTE** (q.v.), and equally objectionable for its fallacious assumption of superiority on the part of one group over others. One of the Hindu scriptures states: "As the dweller in the body experiences in the body childhood, youth, and old age, so he passes on to another body. The steadfast one grieves not thereat".

In Christianity this fallacy is known as **REINCARNATION** (q.v.). In Islamic mysticism (Sufism), there is a saying "I died from the mineral and became a plant. I died from the plant and became an animal. I died from the animal and became a man. Wherefore then should I fear? When did I grow less by dying?"

The difficulty in accepting any of these yearnings for immortality, new life, or even godhead in the case of al-Hallaj, the mystic who claimed "Anā 'l-haqq" ("I am the Truth") and was judicially executed for blasphemy, is that no scientist in the relevant fields of medicine, genetics, or biology will agree that in any meaningful sense one body can die and the 'spirit' (in fact the life) can pass to another body, whether that of the same species, or a different species.

KEPLER BELIEVED IN ASTROLOGY

The great German astronomer Johannes Kepler (1571-1630), whose three laws of planetary motion provided the basis for some of Newton's work, was occasionally persuaded to cast horoscopes, but did so purely to keep himself alive, and not because he believed in them. In sending his *Ephemerides* to Professor Gerlach, he wrote that they were nothing but worthless conjectures, but he was obliged to compile them, or he would have starved. "Ye overwise philosophers", he exclaimed in his *Tertius interveniens,* "ye censure this daughter of astronomy beyond her desserts! Know ye not that she must support her mother by her charms? The scanty reward of an astronomer would not provide him with bread, if men did not entertain hopes of reading the future in the heavens".

Source: Charles Mackay, *Extraordinary popular delusions and the madness of crowds* (London, 1852).

THERE IS A CONNECTION BETWEEN KING ARTHUR AND CERTAIN PUBS

In *The Black Horsemen: English inns and King Arthur* (London, 1971), S. G. Wildman propounded a fantastic theory that there is a connection between English inns called 'The Black Horse' and the activities of the real or mythical tribal chieftain Artorius or Arthur commonly known as 'King' Arthur.

Wildman concludes without a shred of evidence that the plotting on the map of the inns known today as 'The Black Horse' would show the areas where 'Arthur' fought against the invading Saxons. One of the difficulties in accepting this idea is that anyone can call his inn 'The Black Horse' without the prior approval of either King Arthur or Mr Wildman, and does. Other difficulties can be supplied by the reader, to whom they may readily occur.

L

"A lie travels round the world while Truth is putting on her boots."—CHARLES HADDON SPURGEON, *Saltcellars* (1885).

CHARLES LAMB'S FALLACIES

One of the *Last essays of Elia* (London, 1833) is on popular fallacies, which Charles Lamb lists as follows: that a bully is always a coward; that ill-gotten gain never prospers; that a man must not laugh at his own jest; that such a one shows his breeding—that it is easy to perceive he is no gentleman; that the poor copy the vices of the rich; that enough is as good as a feast; that of two disputants the warmer is generally in the wrong; that verbal allusions are not wit, because they will not bear a translation; that the worst puns are the best; that handsome is as handsome does; that we must not look a gift-horse in the mouth; that home is home though it is never so homely; that you must love me and love my dog; that we should rise with the lark; that we should lie down with the lamb; and, that a sulky temper is a misfortune.

GINGER WAS SOLD AT 'THE LAND OF GREEN GINGER' IN HULL

Hull people still maintain that their square known as The Land of Green Ginger was where ginger was landed and sold in open market. A perpetual fallacy, which never dies.

Sir Willoughby Hickman, a parliamentary candidate for Hull in 1685, wrote in an extant letter that the stage coach took him from the waterside to the George Inn 'at the corner of the land of Moses Greenhinger'. And the land of Greenhinger thus became transmuted into 'The Land of Green Ginger'.

Source: Edwin Radford, *Encyclopaedia of phrases and origins* (London, 1945, p. 70).

AN INTERNATIONAL LANGUAGE CAN BE LEARNT AND SPOKEN BY ALL PEOPLE ON EARTH

It is one thing to learn another nation's language in an effort to understand more about that nation; another thing to learn an artificial language to communicate in that language with someone of a different native tongue; but it is a fallacy to assume that the universal propagation of any single living or artificial language is feasible.

For one thing, there are so many thousands of different tongues, many with their own literatures and unique characteristics, that few men of culture or common sense would agree to unify all these cultural vehicles into a single amorphous mass (it would in any case disintegrate at once into units, probably slightly different from the earlier components). For another, on political and religious grounds no national or cult leader would agree to impose an alien language on his subjects. Arabic is the God-given language of the *Qur'an*, according to Arabs, and no other language can rival it in religious power and profundity. The hundreds of millions of Chinese could not all be taught a non-Chinese language, even if it were politically possible or desirable to allow such a thing: the Chinese culture depends for its continuity on the Chinese tongue.

THE NUMEROUS LANGUAGES OF WEST AFRICA HAD A MINUTE RANGE AND WERE UNRELATED TO EACH OTHER

The full extract from Arnold Toynbee's *Mankind and mother Earth* (Oxford, 1976) is: "In the tropical forests of West Africa, before these were opened up by invaders from outside the region, there used to be numerous languages, apparently unrelated to each other, in close juxtaposition. The range of each of these languages was minute. The inhabitants of two villages that were separated from each other by only a few miles of forest might be unable to communicate with each other by word of mouth. Their lingua franca was dumb-show. The vocal languages that are now widely current in West Africa have come in from outside . . ."

Thomas Hodgkin, in the *Times Literary Supplement* (19 November 1976), describes the extract as "A mist of ancient errors. The forest was not "opened up by invaders from outside the region". If we follow Greenberg, there are three main language families in West Africa of which one, Niger-Congo, is the most important and widespread. Though there has been some linguistic fragmentation, here as elsewhere in the world, the major language groups count their members in millions. Travellers' tales about dumbshow communication have been shown to be largely legend. All, or almost all, West African languages—major and minor—have developed within the region".

If one of the most respected historians of our time can concoct such a tissue of errors and legends, what chance has even the best-read layman to understand the sequence of selected events presented in the text-books as 'history'? Hodgkin concludes his review by observing that: "Absorbed in his dialectic of civilizations, [Toynbee] forgot, or perhaps never sufficiently considered, Marx's useful maxim (though having a "high respect for Marx and Engels's intellectual powers" he confessed to being "ill-read in them") in *The Holy Family*: History does nothing; it possesses no immense wealth; it wages no battles. It is *man*, real living man who does all that, who possesses and fights. 'History' is not, as it were, a person apart, using man as a means to achieve its own aims; history is nothing but the activity of man pursuing his aims".

To which one might also reasonably add, "History, as it is normally understood, might more accurately be termed 'human history' to put into perspective its insignificant span of time compared with geological history and, in particular, astronomical time.

LAWSONOMY

"The knowledge of Life and everything pertaining thereto" is the definition given to this allegedly parallel system of world knowledge by Alfred William Lawson, Supreme Head and First Knowledgian of the University of Lawsonomy, Des Moines, Iowa. Lawson's doctrines appear in the self-published *Lawsonomy* (3 vols., 1935-9), *Manlife* (1923), and *Penetrability* (1939) and over fifty other publications.

The fallacy that applies to all such claimants to universal knowledge and understanding is simply that after a lifetime of study, meditation, learning and thought one is still very far from grasping the principles of a wide range of arts and sciences. Such humility is foreign to Lawson's nature. He wrote anonymously in the 'blurb' of *Manlife*, "In comparison to Lawson's Law of Penetrability and Zig-Zag-and-Swirl movement, Newton's law of gravitation is but a primer lesson, and the lessons of Copernicus and Galileo are but infinitesimal grains of knowledge". A certain Cy Q. Faunce ('sycophancy'=flattery?), whose name has not yet been established as pseudonymous, called Lawson "the greatest tree of wisdom ever nurtured by the human race".

It is not sufficient to draw up a map of human knowledge; it is first necessary in all modesty to indicate the deficiencies of the map of knowledge painstakingly acquired by civilization over the millennia. This Lawson does not trouble to do, saying "The basic principles of physics were unknown until established by Lawson". Those who have troubled to examine Lawson's books do not deny that there may be elements of truth in most of them dotted about if one is clever or imaginative enough to disentangle them in the welter of neologisms and vague assertions which are often unsupported by experimental data. What is denied is that, as a system, Lawsonomy has any validity in the light of traditional physics. Lawson repudiates the concept of 'energy', hypothesizing a cosmos with neither energy nor empty space but substances of varying density. Substances of heavy density move towards substances of lighter density through the operation of suction and pressure, two key oft-recurring terms in Lawsonomy. Another common term is zig-zag-and swirl, defined as "movement in which any formation moves in a multiple direction according to the movements of many increasingly greater formations, each depending upon the greater formation for direction and upon varying changes caused by counteracting influences of suction and pressure ot different proportions". This is a complicated way of saying that no object in the universe moves in a simple straight line or simple curve because it partakes of a number of motions which end up by causing it to follow an uneven path, though not of course necessarily either zig-zag or swirl. Among his many odd theories are the idea that the North Pole has an opening which sucks into the Earth substances supplied by the sun and by gases from meteors; and another that the South Pole is the Earth's anus, discharging gases. In the human brain there are mental organizers ('menorgs') or tiny living creatures building and operating the mental instruments within the cells of the mental system, and these strange creatures are Good. They are opposed by the mental disorganizers ('disorgs') which are vermin that destroy the cells and instruments carefully built by the menorgs. This fantasy makes good science fiction, but nobody should be required to believe it.

His Direct Credits Society was founded after the Great Crash in the interests of economic reform. In his book *Direct credits for everybody* (1931) he proposed to abolish the gold standard and to issue valueless money and interest on debts. This aspect of his system attracted tens of thousands of followers at the height of America's financial insecurity. Lawson sold his University in 1954 after an investigation for tax-dodging, and it is now a shopping centre.

The power of the man to attract adherents to one facet of his system or another can be assessed by the illustrations in such books as *Fifty speeches* (1941) and *Lawson's mighty sermons* (1948). In *A new species* (1944) he predicts the gradual evolution of a super race developing from mankind capable of communicating by telepathy which is, as he explains, another example of the universal principle of suction and pressure.

Sources include: Lawson's own books and Martin Gardner, *Fads and fallacies in the name of science* (New York, 1957, pp. 69-79).

"GREAT LEADERS ALWAYS KNOW WHERE THEY ARE GOING"

One of the great fallacies in historiography is to assume that because events occurred in a certain manner and at a certain time, they were bound to do so. Historical determinism is as fallacious as every other kind of determinism, yet many historians seem incapable of avoiding it in their own work.

J. L. I. Fennell's *Ivan the Great of Moscow* (New York, 1962) includes the following passage: "Ivan III, more clearly than any of his predecessors or followers on the grand princely throne of Moscow, knew precisely where he was going. He knew his goal, the means at his disposal, the obstacles to be encountered. He never over-estimated his own strength or underestimated that of his enemies. His cold reasoning told him just how far he could abuse the freedom of his subjects and tamper with the sanctity of religious institutions. He never fought a war for the sake of fighting, sought a friendship from altruism, or disgraced a subject through spite. All the deeds of this dedicated, hard-headed ruler and shrewd diplomat were directed toward one goal only".

Yet 336 pages later Fennell confesses: "Almost nothing is known of his personal qualities or of his private life" and one suspects that Ivan (1440-1505) had no great idea what he was going to do or how he could achieve his aims but, like most rulers before or since, simply did the best he could to retain maximum power for as long as possible.

LEAD PENCILS CONTAIN LEAD

The 'lead' in pencils is a compound of graphite and clay or occasionally plumbago. The name was given to it in the sixteenth century when the contents were commonly believed to be lead, but were not even then.

THE LEANING TOWER OF PISA WAS DELIBERATELY BUILT TO LEAN

It is a bell-tower, begun in 1174, which was built on too small a base and too shallow a foundation and subsided in one direction. It continues to stand because a vertical line drawn through its centre of gravity passes through the base. The fact that the tower leans testifies not to the ingenuity of a designer or builder, but to the builder's incompetence.

THE TORCH OF WESTERN LEARNING WAS PASSED ON BY MONKS

Quite the reverse. Western learning (that is to say Greek and Roman culture) were lost to all intents and purposes in the mediaeval period, and it was the Arabs who maintained the tradition, as De Lacy O'Leary shows in *How Greek science passed to the Arabs* (London, 1949).

The fallacious picture most people have of industrious monks copying and recopying the classics should be totally rejected. Those few scriptoria (studies or libraries where such copying was done) which did exist confined their reproduction to purely religious texts, but these scriptoria were few and far between. Compayré, in his *History of paedagogy* (1903), points out that at the height of the thirteenth century not one of the thousands of monks in the famous Swiss Abbey of St. Gall was able to read or write.

LEMMINGS COMMIT SUICIDE

The lemming, a small rodent inhabiting the central mountain chain of Norway and Sweden, is popularly believed (if one can call the *Encyclopedia Britannica*, 14th ed., vol. 13, p. 905, a source and distillation of popular belief) to 'descend . . . in countless multitudes and proceed in a straight line until they reach the sea, into which they plunge and are drowned'. The reason for this lunacy is stated to be that their march 'is a survival from the old times when there was dry land over the Baltic and North Seas'.

But lemmings have more sense than those who write on their communal suicide for of course it has never happened. They do breed in larger numbers in certain years, and then if the food supply in the mountains is low, they do descend in varying numbers. They can and do swim streams, and it is probable that some reach the ocean and imagine that it is another small stream, get out of their depth, and drown. But the cosmic death wish is a fallacy, as is the regularity with which they are said to emerge from the mountains, as is their multiplicity. Most lemmings stay in the mountains. Not one has been known to commit suicide. John Masefield (in *The Lemmings*) declared that the fatal urge comes on them once in a hundred years, whereas Breland, in *Animal facts and fallacies* (London, 1950, pp. 62-3), claims that their feeding grounds become overpopulated roughly every three or four years.

LEMURIA

'Lemuria' is a hypothetical landmass invented by a zoologist, P. L. Sclater, in the 19th century to account for the geographical distribution of the lemur, which he placed in the Indian Ocean. The theosophists, who had taken up the popular myth of Atlantis (q.v.) from Plato's *Critias* and *Timaeus*, now supported the myth of Lemuria. Madame H. P. Blavatsky, founder of Theosophy (q.v.), decided that five 'root races' have so far appeared on Earth, and two more are to come. Each root race has seven 'sub-races' and each sub-race has seven 'branch-races'. Such speculations have of course more to do with numerology than with anthropology.

'Lemurians' were the third root race. They were ape-like giants who gradually evolved into something like modern man, but Lemuria was engulfed in a great convulsion shortly after a sub-race had migrated to Atlantis, where they began the fourth root race.

Rudolf Steiner asserts in *Atlantis and Lemuria* (1913) that the Lemurians were unable to reason or calculate, living chiefly by instinct and communicating by telepathy. They lifted enormous weights by exercising great will power.

The British, who gave the world *Jabberwocky* and *The Lord of the Rings*, also gave the world James Churchward, who attained the rank of colonel with the Bengal Lancers and, while in India, claimed to have been permitted by a temple priest to see (and with the priest's help, to decipher) a collection of Lemurian tablets which Churchward then published and described in four hilarious 'Mu' books which are so full of geological and archaeological howlers and anachronisms that even fellow Lemurian 'scholars' have regarded them as a deliberate hoax. Lemuria, or 'Mu' as Churchward called the island, was the original Garden of Eden (see **EDEN**) where man was created 200 thousand years ago. However, Churchward's particular Lemuria was situated in the *Pacific* Ocean, not the Indian (tallying with Madame Blavatsky's opinion), and its level of civilization was not that of the cave-dwellers of Steiner or the giants of Blavatsky, but highly superior to all existing societies. All human races come from Mu, whose most powerful colony lies buried below the Gobi Desert. The Aryans are the closest (though still degenerate) descendants of the mighty men of Mu, which Churchward saw as the first and leading instance of the way in which Aryans dominate coloured races. Churchward began to write in 1870, at the time of the great occult revival, but his books were not published until much later: *The lost continent of Mu* (New York, 1926), *The children of Mu* (New York, 1931), *The sacred symbols of Mu* (New York, 1933), and *Cosmic forces of Mu* (New York, 1934). The reader's scepticism concerning the 'lost language' of Mu, called 'Naacal' by Churchward, may be heightened by the fact that his tablets were never published, nobody ever saw them, and he failed even to identify the monastery or temple where he 'found' them.

Yet in 1936 a Lemurian Fellowship was founded in Chicago to promote the study of Mu. The writings, by a 'reincarnated Lemurian', were published by Lemurian Book Industries in Milwaukee, and promised new 'super-cities' to be built in Southern California.

Sources include: L. Sprague de Camp, *Lost continents* (New York, 1970).

THERE ARE NO CHILDREN OF TWO LESBIAN PARENTS

The seemingly impossible has now occurred as a result of artificial insemination of one of the lesbian partners, and at the moment of writing three AID babies have been born to lesbian couples. All three babies are boys.

Source: Carolyn Faulder, *Women who prefer women* in *Good Housekeeping*, July 1976, p. 150.

LEYS AND TUMPS

The old straight track (1925) by the Hereford businessman Alfred Watkins took 'leys' (straight tracks allegedly associated with prehistoric mounds or 'tumps') to be roads of prehistoric man in England. In *The view over Atlantis* (1969), John Michell stated his opinion that unidentified flying objects (UFOs) are associated with places where leys are supposed to intersect, one example being Cradle Hill, near Warminster, and suggests that these leys were 'lines of power' analogous, as he says, to Chinese 'dragon paths', lines associated with *fung shui*, the ancient earth energies. Leys link up S. Michael's Mount in Cornwall with Glastonbury and Stonehenge, and all Britain is intersected with these 'paths', which were associated with a higher ancient civilization than archaeologists have so far identified. Michell's ideas are presented as serious science, despite the fact that he regards Britain as Plato's Atlantis (see **ATLANTIS**).

Michell's later book, *City of revelation*, subtitled *on the proportion and symbolic numbers of the cosmic temple* (London, 1972), deals with the notion that the mythical Golden Age did in fact exist and that information on it is concealed encoded in many early buildings, including Stonehenge (q.v.).

While no archaeologist would argue with the existence of the tracks and mounds over which enthusiasts pore with measuring devices, they would very definitely argue that there is absolutely no justification whatsoever for *connecting* a wide variety of these phenomena in any mystical sense. Interpretation of the *meaning* of artefacts presupposes the view (seemingly quite fallacious) that artefacts should have a meaning independent of their practical use. Woodhenge may well have been a ritual centre, for instance, but that does not entitle anyone to speculate with real authority on the nature of the ritual in question.

ONE CANNOT LIE AND TELL THE TRUTH SIMULTANEOUSLY

The lie or falsehood is a particular sensitive area of fallacy-theory, by which I refer to the importance of paradox in such statements as the demonstration that a man may lie and tell the truth at the same time by asserting that he is lying (in the 3rd-century *Lives of eminent philosophers* by Diogenes Laertius, translated by R. D. Hicks for the Loeb Classical Library, London, 1925).

If the reader still thinks that an argument *cannot* be valid if the

146

conclusion contradicts a premiss, ponder this example from Charles Hamblin's *Fallacies* (London, 1970):

Epimenides was telling the truth when he said 'I am lying'.

Therefore, Epimenides was lying when he said 'I am lying'.

If this is still not sufficiently sophisticated to convince you, consider this apparently correct paradox:

No class is a member of itself.

Therefore (since it follows that the class of classes that are not members of themselves is not a member of itself, and from this that the class of classes that are not members of themselves *is* a member of itself), at least one class is a member of itself.

LIGHTNING NEVER STRIKES TWICE IN THE SAME SPOT

The fear of lightning felt by primitive peoples, animals, and children has led, like the fear of the unknown that has encouraged the spread of religion, to a whole host of mistaken notions which lie more in the realms of folklore and superstition than in the field of the popular fallacy. Perhaps the commonest fallacy is that lightning never strikes twice in the same place. However, the mast on the top of the Empire State Building was struck 68 times in the first ten years of its existence. Human beings are not very good conductors, but are struck roughly ten times as frequently as the laws of chance would indicate for the space they occupy.

Lightning is not a zig-zag in shape. The many photographs now available show that the old theory is wrong, and that lightning is most frequently in the form of a river, with tributaries; ball lightning, recorded but rare, is attested in *Nature* (June 1919, p. 284).

Among the fallacies exposed by Sir H. Spencer Jones, the then Astronomer Royal, in the *Daily Mail* of 16 September 1936, were the notions that if mirrors, scissors, knives or other bright objects, are covered (or curtains are drawn) the risk of lightning's striking is reduced.

THE THIRD EYE AND OTHER WORKS BY LOBSANG RAMPA ARE BY A TIBETAN LAMA

The third eye (London, 1956), allegedly by a Tibetan lama of high rank, caused a sensation on its publication.

When its author was discovered to be an Englishman living in Dublin, Cyril Henry Hoskin, the book's authenticity was impugned. The author maintained however that he *was* a Tibetan lama merely inhabiting the body of Hoskin, who had kindly agreed to vacate it for that purpose. As a result of this assurance, 'Lobsang Rampa' continues to write best-sellers: *Beyond the Tenth, Cave of Ancients, Chapters of Life, The Rampa story, Feeding the flame, Living with the lama, Saffron robe,* and *Wisdom of the Ancients.*

LOGICAL FALLACIES

Until recently it has been usual to classify fallacies with Aristotle into the thirteen types listed in his *Peri ton sophistikon elenchon,* known in Latin as *De sophisticis elenchis,* and in English as *Sophistical refutaions.* A few of the more independent thinkers have challenged Aristotle, among them Pierre de la Ramée in *Aristotelicae animadversiones* (Paris, 1543; facsimile ed. with introduction by W. Risse, Stuttgart, 1964), who refused to consider fallacies as a proper subject for logic on the ground that the study of *correct* reasoning is enough to clarify fallacies, but one of Ramée's own disciples, Heizo Buscher, published a work on fallacies: *De ratione solvendi sophismata solide et perspicue ex P. Rami logica deducta et explicata, libri duo* (3rd ed., Wittenberg, 1594).

Both Bacon and Locke produced rivals to the Aristotelian theory of fallacies, but the succeeding centuries managed to confuse the later theories with the earlier and thus made little progress. Mathematical logicians such as Boole took no interest in the realm of fallacies, and the only major book on the subject which does not merely regurgitate Aristotle, or at least use him as the basis for belief or reaction is *Fallacies* (London, 1970), by C. L. Hamblin, Professor of Philosophy in the University of New South Wales.

Because the kinds of error that men may fall into are unlimited, it has been argued that there can be no exhaustive classification of fallacies. As H. W. B. Joseph writes in his *Introduction to logic* (1906): "Truth may have its norms, but error is infinite in its aberrations, and they cannot be digested in any classification". M. R. Cohen and Ernest Nagel, in their *An introduction to logic and scientific method* (London, 1934) agree that "it would be impossible to enumerate all the abuses of logical principles occurring in the diverse matters in which men are interested".

Nevertheless, there is a relatively small number of commonly-found fallacy-types, which Aristotle divided into two major categories: those dependent on language and those outside language.

Fallacies Dependent on Language

(1) Equivocation, or ambiguity of terms. J. A. Oesterle's example in his *Logic: the art of defining and reasoning* (Englewood Cliffs, N.J., 1952; 2nd ed., 1963) is: "Whatever is immaterial is unimportant; whatever is spiritual is immaterial; therefore, whatever is spiritual is unimportant". This is fallacious because of the punning use of 'immaterial'.

(2) Amphiboly, or the ambiguity of grammatical structure. Examples are frequent, due to carelessness or haste in composition, or to poetic cunning, as in "The Duke yet lives that Henry shall depose" (Shakespeare, *King Henry VI*, Part II, Act I, sc. iv).

(3) Composition, and its contrary, Division. It is a fallacy of composition to argue that because each footballer selected for a national team can play well, the team will therefore play well as a whole. It is a fallacy of division to argue that because the Italians are a demonstrative people, every individual Italian is a demonstrative person.

(4) Accent, or the perversion of meaning in a phrase or sentence by false emphasis in speaking or writing. Originally, as the name 'accent' shows, the fallacy arose simply through mistaken Greek pronunciation (though Greek had no *written* accents when Aristotle wrote). A slightly garbled example in Latin cited by Pope John XX or XXI, also known as Petrus Hispanus (1210/20-77) is "Omnis populus est arbor; gens est populus; ergo gens est arbor", which depends on the word 'populus' meaning both 'poplar' and 'people': "Every poplar is a tree; a nation is a people; therefore a nation is a tree".

(5) Figure of speech, or the confusion of two words apparently of the same grammatical type or origin, but actually different. The classic instance is John Stuart Mill's *figura dictionis* in his *Utilitarianism* (ch. 4, p. 32), where he writes: "The only proof capable of being given that an object is visible, is that people actually see it. The only proof that a sound is audible, is that people hear it; and so of the other sources of our experience. In like manner, I apprehend, the sole evidence it is possible to produce that anything is desirable, is that people do actually desire it". Mill's error is to think that the ending '-able' in 'desirable' is to be equated with the '-ible' in 'visible', but this is wrong, since something 'visible' is something that can be seen, whereas in the common acceptance something 'desirable' is something *worthy* of desire, not something that *can* be desired.

Fallacies Dependent on Thought (not on Language)

(1) Accident, or the confusion of an essential difference or resemblance with inessentials. It consists in applying a general rule to a particular case whose 'accidental' circumstances render the rule inapplicable.

An instance of the fallacy of accident might be: Nehru is different from Gandhi; Nehru is a man; therefore, Gandhi is different from man.

(2) *A dicto secundum quid ad dictum simpliciter*, and its converse, which are really a variant of the fallacy of accident. Arguing from the universal to the particular, one might say (fallaciously) that what is bought in the market is eaten; raw meat is bought in the market; therefore raw meat is eaten. Arguing from the particular to the universal, one might say (equally fallaciously) that taking drugs to ease pain is beneficial, therefore taking drugs is always beneficial.

(3) *Petitio principii*, or 'begging the question' is the fallacy of reasoning in a circle, or assuming that which is to be proved. Thus, early astronomers stated that the sun must be moving *because* the Earth was standing still. J. S. Mill pointed out that all *valid* reasoning is bound to commit this fallacy, since all proof ultimately rests on assumptions which are not derived from others but are justified by the set of consequences which are deduced from them. (But then Hume and others argued that every argument *a dicto secundum quid* must be fallacious, since it is impossible to enumerate *all* conceivable particular cases one intends to govern by a general rule).

(4) *Consequens*, or the fallacy of assuming that because a conclusion is reached by invalid arguments it is necessarily false. Thus, if the weather is foggy, the flight will be delayed; the flight is delayed; therefore, the weather is foggy. Or, if the weather is not foggy, the flight will not be delayed.

(5) Many questions, a fallacy depending on receiving an answer 'yes' or 'no' to a question which is more complex than the answer could reveal. Thus, the simple answer cannot be given to the question 'Have you stopped beating your wife?'

(6) *Ignoratio elenchi*, or ignoring the conclusion to be proved or disproved. This is the fallacy of offering a misleading or irrelevant conclusion. One such fallacy is that of the person making an assertion who places the burden of disproof on his opponent, whereas it is incumbent on the former to offer proof. Thus, in a

court of law the trial is opened by the case for the prosecution, and the evidence for the charge or claim must be proved before a conviction can be obtained. If the charge implies the defendant's presence at a given place and time, the defendant may then prove the negative (as in the case of an alibi) by showing that he was actually somewhere else at the time.

This is a most significant fallacy, for it includes various devices used by the unscrupulous to back up worthless arguments. Some of these devices are the *argumentum ud hominem* (which attacks a case by defaming those who hold it); *ad populum* (which excites the feelings of one's listeners to prevent them from forming a balanced judgment); *ad ignorantiam* (which trades on the ignorance of those addressed, often by using high-flown words); and *ad verecundiam* (which appeals to authority and usage, rather than to reason.

(7) *Non causa pro causa*, or the *reductio ad absurdum*. This fallacy derives from the wilful use of absurd but unstated arguments from an innocuous statement to an absurd conclusion. One should guard against it by ensuring that all propositions in one's premisses are stated and not merely inferred. A common type of *non causa* fallacy is the superstition: "the captain of the winning team at Wembley wore a rabbit's foot, therefore rabbit's feet are lucky", since it is usual that all twenty-two players will have some superstition or other, but that the losers will not blame their defeat on inefficacious talismans.

The logical fallacies were described in the 19th century by, among others, Jeremy Bentham, whose *Book of fallacies* (London, 1824) has been revised and edited by Harold A. Larrabee (Baltimore, 1952). Sydney Smith (1771-1845) reviewed the book wittily by giving an example of each fallacy in turn in his celebrated *Noodle's oration* (*Edinburgh Review*, vol. 42, 1825, pp. 367-89).

Sources include: Charles Leonard Hamblin, *Fallacies* (London, 1970).

THE REIGN OF LOUIS XIV CAN BE DIVIDED INTO TWO PARTS

Michelet divided the reign of Louis XIV into two periods: 'avant la fistule' and 'après la fistule' separated by the appearance of a painful anal fistula on the bottom of the monarch.

It was a good idea, but fallacious, as all such arbitrary divisions of time are (see EVERY **CENTURY** HAS ITS OWN CHARAC-

TER). G. J. Renier has noted, in *History: its purpose and method* (New York, 1965) that this hypothesis is disproved "through the study of the diary kept by the physicians of the Grand Monarque. This manuscript, which was published in the nineteenth century, reveals that the health of Louis had been extremely bad for many years before a *fistula analis* was diagnosed, and that this new illness was not an exceptional phenomenon in the career of this coarse contemner of hygiene and sensible living".

LOURDES

The first fallacy of Lourdes is the supposed miraculous vision of a woman standing in an opening in a rock to a peasant girl, Bernadette Soubirous, eleven times between February and April 1858. The woman is alleged to have said 'I am the Immaculate Conception'. The 'vision' was clearly one of the hallucinations which are common in puberty.

The second fallacy concerns the 'miraculous' cures claimed for pilgrims and other sick visitors to Lourdes since the quarryman Louis Bouriette claimed that sight had been restored to his right eye following application to it of water from the rock spring. The number of these visitors reported for 1948 was 2.2 million pilgrims and 15,800 sick; the following year it was 3 million pilgrims and 20,000 sick.

Discounting the first fallacy as a typical visual hallucination or the appearance of a physical woman hitherto unknown to Bernadette, emphasis falls on the second. The great majority of visitors to Lourdes are pilgrims with nothing to cure; some of the sick recover quite naturally, so it is the residue which bear inspection.

A. Castiglioni, in *Adventures of the mind* (London, 1947) describes how the Lourdes organizers operate: "The patient is not allowed to dispense with preliminaries. He must not straightway touch the relic or drink the healing waters of the sacred spring. There is a probationary period, a propitiatory novena. There are long waits at the gateway of the temple during which the sufferer listens to sermons and repeats prayers. Above all, during these periods of probation, the sick hear a great deal about miraculous cures, and have an opportunity of looking at the numberless votive offerings. In a word, their entry into the temple is a slow one, and their minds are prepared by a special incubation".

Suggestion is consequently heightened by autosuggestion, and occasional hysteria in the patient of course heightens his (or more frequently her) suggestibility.

To give the proponents of the existence of 'miraculous' cures beyond the level of suggestion and autosuggestion the best possible chance of proving their case, Dr D. J. West in *Eleven Lourdes miracles* (London, 1957) selected the best cases. All cases before 1946 were rejected because it was only in that year that the present procedures for authoritative ecclesiastical scrutiny and pronouncements were set up. The new procedures are threefold: the Medical Bureau at Lourdes itself; an international medical commission in Paris; and finally a mixed medical and ecclesiastical Canonical Commission appointed by the Archbishop of the patient's own diocese. At that point the Archbishop makes his authoritative pronouncement that a cure has been effected by the miraculous intervention of the Virgin Mary. In ten years, only eleven 'cures' have passed the triple test. However, 'miracles' of the traditional type have not occurred; that is to say, "there are no cases of lost eyes or amputated legs sprouting anew". The miracle therefore refers to an accelerated rate of recovery.

Dr West analyses these cures meticulously and concludes that "in no case was the evidence really satisfactory, and in certain cases the evidence suggested a perfectly natural alternative explanation".

If this view of a medical researcher applies to the best possible cases of 'miraculous cures', what then is the unbiased reader to make of all the other countless 'miracles' reported throughout the last two thousand years?

DUNCAN LUNAN AND THE SPACE-PROBE FROM EPSILON BOÖTIES

In *Man and the stars* (London, 1974, published in the U.S.A. as *Interstellar contact*), the Scotsman Duncan Lunan has argued that an automatic space-probe is encircling the Earth on behalf of a star formerly known as Izar, in the constellation of the Herdsman, and now known as Epsilon Boöties. The star is about 600 million miles from Earth (equivalent to about 103 light-years). Mr Lunan's conclusion is based on unrepeated tests of 1927-9 in the course of which some delays were found in receiving the echoes of some radio signals sent out from Earth, and on the theory that the delay times are a code which, worked out, indicates Epsilon Boöties as the transmission point.

It would be an act of charity to find some word of comfort to those about to embark on the thankless task of reading *Man and the stars,* but I can find none: the intending reader is recommended instead to read a good introductory textbook on astronomy. So is Mr Lunan.

LUNATICS ARE AFFECTED BY CHANGES IN THE MOON (Latin: *luna*)

We recall *Othello* (Act V, scene ii):
> *"It is the very error of the Moon;*
> *She comes more nearer Earth than she was wont,*
> *And makes men mad"*

but it was already a common error among the Greeks that there was a connection between the changing moon and the periodically insane, that is to say, those who enjoy lucid intervals. Plutarch should not, therefore, have been puzzled by aristocratic Roman matrons who carried moon-amulets on their shoes to attract the lunacy-bearing moon-spirit so that it might enter the crescent charm and not its wearer.

Simple observation has helped to diminish the effect of this fallacy, though as always those who choose not to observe, and then to correlate their data with their assumptions, will continue to cherish the latter rather than the former.

LYSENKOISM

Trofim D. Lysenko was the Soviet Union's leading authority on heredity and evolution. With Lamarck, the pre-Darwinian French scientist, Lysenko believed that evolution worked through the inheritance of traits which organisms acquired in response to their surroundings, as in the case of the giraffe's long neck. Giraffes stretched their neck to eat leaves which were beyond the reach of lesser animals, and because this trait was effective, giraffes with longer and longer necks were born. Darwin accepted this fact, but suggested that it was more important that the giraffes with shorter necks died out, thus proving the survival of the fittest. Evolution theory (q.v.) has now rejected Lamarckianism, but it was official party policy in the USSR and in two articles on Lysenkoism for the *Saturday Review* (4 and 11 December 1948), the Nobel Prize-winning geneticist H. J. Muller described what had happened to Lysenko's opponents: "In 1933 or thereabouts, the geneticists Chetverikoff, Ferry, and Ephroimson were all, on separate occasions, banished to Siberia, and Levitsky to a labor camp in the European Arctic . . . from 1936 on Soviet geneticists of all ranks lived a life of terror . . . Ironically, the great majority of the geneticists who have been purged were thoroughly loyal politically; many were even ardent crusaders for the Soviet system and leadership as the writer well knows through personal contact with them".

Muller continues to explain that the Lysenkoist view "implies a mystical Aristotelian 'perfecting principle', a kind of foresight, in the basic make-up of living things, despite the fact that it claims in the same breath not to be 'idealistic' at all".

The fallacy of regarding Lamarckianism as a kind of dogma inherently sound and not to be tested experimentally and discarded if found wanting is compounded by the fallacy of elevating a scientific hypothesis to the status of a political truism, when the two ideas are entirely distinct. Racist dogmas were similarly at the back of German fascism.

M

"The man who wishes to educate himself must first learn how to doubt, for it is the doubting mind that will arrive at the truth."—ARISTOTLE.

MACKINTOSH INVENTED A WATERPROOF CAPE

It is peculiar that everyone gets this wrong, for the Scottish chemist Charles *Macintosh* (1766-1843) appears under his correct name in the *Dictionary of national biography* and elsewhere. His waterproof cape was patented in 1823, shortly after which his name was facetiously corrupted to 'mucking-togs' by Thomas Ingoldsby, whose "vulgar little boy" at Margate was seen "with a carpet-swab and mucking-togs and a hat turned up with green".

'MAD AS A HATTER' REFERS TO MADNESS OR HATTERS

Lewis Carroll with his penchant for linguistic games presumably knew perfectly well that his 'Mad Hatter' meant 'a venomous adder', but since his readers may have been misled by Tenniel's drawings, it should be pointed out that 'mad' meant 'venomous' and 'hatter' is a corruption of 'adder', or viper, so that the phrase 'mad as an atter' originally meant 'as venomous as a viper'.

MALARIA IS CAUSED BY BAD AIR

The origin of the word is Italian, 'mal aria' meaning 'bad air', since it was observed that those exposed to night air in certain lowlying parts of Italy were liable to contract the disease.

Shakespeare propagated the fallacy in *The Tempest* (II, ii, 1-3)
"All the infections that the sun sucks up
From bogs, fens, flats, on Prosper fall, and make him
by inch-meal a disease!"

It was Sir Ronald Ross who first identified the cause of malaria as micro-organisms injected into human blood by the bite of the anopheles mosquito. This type of mosquito breeds in stagnant water, which should be filled in wherever possible; where this is not possible, the body should be covered up as far as possible by clothes during the day and by mosquito nets round the bed at night, as well as by the use of fine wire-gauze over windows and extra doors.

Source: Sir Ronald Ross, *Memoirs: with a full account of the great malaria problem* (1923) and review (by W. G. King) in *Nature*, 7 July 1923.

MANNA MACHINES WERE USED BY THE ANCIENT ISRAELITES

Erich von Däniken (q.v.) cites in all seriousness in his outrageously mistitled *According to the evidence* (London, 1977) a *New Scientist* article, 'Deus est machina?' by George Sassoon and Rodney Dale, which revealed their discovery that the ancient Israelites possessed a machine manufacturing manna, which is described in *Exodus* 16:31 as "like coriander seed, white; and the taste of it was like that of wafers made with honey". The machine comprised a male and a female part, and an algal culture was grown in it at the rate of 1.5 cubic metres a day. "After the capture of Jericho", relate the authors, "the machine, now a holy object, was kept at Shiloh (I *Samuel*, 4:3). Later, it was captured by the Philistines, who hastily returned it after it killed many of them, and inflicted a plague of 'emerods' upon the survivors" [who, the Jewish historian Josephus recorded] "also suffered from diarrhoea because of it".

King David erected a tent for the machine, and his son Solomon built a Temple in Jerusalem for it. Sassoon and Dale state that the machine was destroyed when Nebuchadnezzar plundered the Temple. Däniken has consequently revised his original opinion that the first Jewish Temple sheltered the Ark of the Covenant which was neither more nor less than a transmitter and receiver by which the god-astronauts and Moses kept in touch.

The only problem is that the article on the Manna machine appeared in the issue of the *New Scientist* published on 1 April 1976, and was intended by the Deputy Editor (Technology) as a clever, amusing April Fool's joke. The point was quickly seen by a reader in Haifa, whose letter (6 May 1976) includes the following clarification: "Judaism, for all its kabbalistic overtones, is essentially a delicatessen cult and may explain the Jewish longing to return to the recipes of yesterday. These longings are embodied in many of our folkloristic manifestations, such as "My Yiddishe Manna" which, during Nabataean times, was mixed with plant seeds and was known in the trade as "Pistil Packing Manna".

The idea of the manna machine is however not a hoax; in *Encounter* (August, 1977), Rodney Dale defended the hypothesis as serious and announced a forthcoming study based on it: *The Manna of the Lord.* The hypothesis is demolished in the same issue by Hyam Maccoby, who concludes that "after one has taken up all the literary and mystical allusions, there are no parts left from which to build a machine". Nicholas Valery, Deputy Editor (Technology) of the *New Scientist*, who was largely responsible for perpetrating the April Fool's joke on his readers, prevailed on Dale and Sassoon to add "This raises as many problems as it solves, and we would prefer not to propound such a hypothesis today". Valery adds, "of course, if Messrs Dale and Sassoon actually believe in this hypothesis, then that's an entirely different matter and their own business".

Sources include: Helmut Gumnior, 'Däniken and his flying machines' in *Encounter*, June 1977, and the correspondence columns in *Encounter*, August 1977.

MARRIAGE IS A SACRAMENT TO ANGLICANS

Not at all. The 25th of the Thirty-Nine Articles in the prayer-book of the Church of England will prove that marriage is expressly excluded as a sacrament. "Those five commonly called sacraments, that is to say, Confirmation, Penance, Orders, Matrimony, and Extreme Unction, are *not* to be counted for Sacraments of the Gospel . . . There are two Sacraments ordained of Christ our Lord in the Gospel, that is to say Baptism and the Supper of our Lord".

THERE ARE CANALS ON MARS

It is a pity that space exploration has reached the stage at which this fallacy is now virtually extinct, for when it finally passes beyond we shall no longer be able to recount the tale of Dr Barnard, Director of the Lick Observatory when it possessed the largest telescope in the world who, when asked whether he had made many observations of the canals, replied that he regretted his telescope was too powerful to show them.

For the mournful record of human gullibility, the Martian 'canals' were first observed by Schiaparelli in 1877 and subsequently by hundreds of others. Percival Lowell founded the Lowell Observatory specifically to study Mars: see his article on the 'hydraulic artifacts' in *Nature*, vol. 82 (24 February 1910, pp. 489-91). The 'canals' were reinterpreted as fracture systems in 1963, linear dunes in 1964, strips of vegetation in 1965, rift zones in 1966, and giant cliffs in 1972 even after the Mariner 9 photographs of 1971 had dispelled the optical illusion of canals by revealing a complex picture of channels, canyons, volcanoes and zones dotted with hummocks, furrows, knobs and grooves.

Sources include: Thomas A. Mutch and others, *The geology of Mars* (Princeton, 1977).

MARS HAS TWO ARTIFICIAL SPACE-STATIONS PLACED THERE BY MARTIANS

This is the view not of a crazy amateur but of Dr Iosif Shklovskii, credibly described by Patrick Moore as "one of the world's leading astrophysicists". He believes Phobos and Deimos, the two natural miniature satellites of the planet Mars, to be artificial space-stations. As they were noted before the visits to Mars from Earth, Shklovskii came to the conclusion that Martians (who do not exist) had placed them there. This conclusion was reached from the observation of alleged irregularities in the movement of Phobos. "These calculations have since been found to be wrong", states Moore, "and in any case the Mariner 9 pictures of Phobos, taken in December 1971, show a body which looks decidedly natural",

Source: Patrick Moore, *Can you speak Venusian?* (London, 1976, p. 112).

MATHEMATICAL FALLACIES

Dr E. A. Maxwell of Queens' College, Cambridge, has written a useful (if brief) introduction: *Fallacies in mathematics* (Cambridge, 1959) in which he explains that a mathematical fallacy "leads by guile to a wrong but plausible conclusion", whereas a mistake is an error of little consequence and a howler denotes an error which leads innocently to a correct result. Dr Maxwell devotes his final chapter to howlers, no space at all to mistakes, and ten chapters to fallacies. Among the geometrical fallacies are: "To prove that every triangle is isosceles"; "To prove that every angle is a right angle"; "To prove that, if ABCD is a quadrilateral in which AB=CD, then AD is necessarily parallel to BC"; and "To prove that every point inside a circle lies on its circumference".

The algebraic and trigonometrical fallacies include: "That $4=0$"; "That $+1=-1$"; "That all lengths are equal"; and "That the sum of the squares on two sides of a triangle is never less than the square on the third".

Dr Maxwell also disposes of the fallacies that $0=1$; that $2=1$; that $\pi=0$; that a cycloid has arches of zero length; and some 'limit' fallacies.

MECHANISTIC FALLACIES

This group of fallacies has been defined by R. M. MacIver, in *Social causation* (2nd ed., New York, 1964). It treats the various components of a social situation, or of any organized system, as though they were detachable, isolable, homogeneous, independently operative, and therefore susceptible of being added to or subtracted from the causal complex, increasing or decreasing the result by that amount. But even a slight acquaintance with the mechanism itself should teach us to avoid this fallacy.

Two examples of this fallacy, so prevalent in historical and philosophical writing, are provided by J. B. Bury in his *History of the later Roman Empire* (2 vols., New York, 1958, vol. 1, pp. 308-9) and by the eminent French mediaevalist Marc Bloch in *Feudal society* (Chicago, 1961, pp. 35-8).

Bury eliminated depopulation, the Christian religion, and the fiscal system as causes of the dismemberment of the Roman Empire, stating that a combination of some or all of these could not have been responsible for the Empire's dismemberment by the barbarians in the West since the same causes operated in the East, but there the Empire survived much longer intact and united. But, as Morton White explains in *The foundations of historical knowledge* (New York, 1965), the three causal elements which Bury rejects may have interacted with each other, and with other elements, in such a way as to produce results in the West very different from those in the East.

Bloch considers the cessation of Scandinavian pillaging in the Middle Ages *not* to be explicable by the fact that the Scandinavians were converted to Christianity, noting the false generalization that no Christian people would indulge in pillaging: "there was apparently no difficulty in reconciling ardent faith in the Christian mysteries with a taste for violence and plunder, nay even with the most conscious glorification of war". Yet when Bloch tries to explain the beginning of the Scandinavian invasions, he accepts the explanation that the Scandinavian countries were overpopulated at the time. However, he would deny, surely, that the people of every overpopulated country invade in the manner of the mediaeval Scandinavians.

MEDICAL MAGNETISM

The wealthy American Gaylord Wilshire (died 1927) made a cure-all called 'I-on-aco'. The healing energy was drawn directly from an electric light plug linked by a lead to a collar worn by the patient. The collar was sold by salesmen offering convincing testimony at US $58.50, and sales declined only after exposure by the American Medical Association and the Better Business Bureau. The medical doctrine underlying Wilshire's wonder cure has been eloquently summed up as "the left hind foot of a rabbit caught in a churchyard at the dark of the moon".

Source: Eric Maple, *Magic, medicine and quackery* (London, 1968, pp. 175-6).

ADVANCES IN MEDICINE ARE OFTEN MADE BY DOCTORS

A detailed refutation of this idea was made by W. Bulloch of the London Hospital in a lecture to the Hospital Officers' Association on 18 January 1918. The research, discovery and experimental work are mainly due to pathologists, bacteriologists, botanists, anatomists, and others working in laboratories, and the consequent advances were made in the overwhelming majority of cases *not* by doctors, and *not* at the patients' bedside. The diagnosis of diseases is done mainly by pathologists and none of the following are the work of practising doctors or nurses: diphtheria serum, X-rays, anti-typhoid inoculation, the use of penicillin, and insulin.

Source: A. S. E. Ackermann, *Popular fallacies* (London, 1950, p. 172).

MENSTRUATION FALLACIES

The dread of blood which is common throughout human societies seems to be responsible for most of the irrational fears connected with the perfectly natural process of menstruation. The loss of blood is often exaggerated: it is in fact no more than an average of two fluid ounces a month, according to John Camp in *Magic*,

161

myth and medicine (London, 1973, p. 181). Other errors are: that intercourse with a menstruating woman will make a man sick, and produce feeble-minded children if the union is fertile; that women should not eat cold (especially frozen) food, or bathe, during menstruation; that women are in some way 'unclean' at that time; and that they will contaminate a temple (in Hindu Bali).

Pliny reports that at the approach of a menstruating woman, seeds become sterile, plants become parched, and fruit drops from the trees. Lest we laugh at Pliny, remember that nowadays it is still widely believed that a girl cannot bear a child until she begins to menstruate; that the process is controlled by the moon; and that only human females menstruate (females of all apes and monkeys menstruate: see S. Zuckerman, *Functional affinities of man, monkeys, and apes*, London, 1933, p. 40).

MERMAIDS EXIST

The basis of this fanciful invention of love-starved seamen is the sea-cow family: the manatees found along the coast of Latin America and as far north as Florida; and the dugong found in the Indian Ocean, the Indonesian island chains, and as far as Australia. When they surface, these mammals project their rounded heads above the water in a manner not unlike that of a drowning human being, and at a distance could certainly be mistaken for a human.

Sources include: Osmond P. Breland, *Animal facts and fallacies* (London, 1950, pp. 40-1).

THE HUMAN EYE CAN MESMERISE WILD ANIMALS

By building up a relationship with certain animals, particularly the dog, human beings can affect their actions. They have no power at all over wild animals, or even over those domestic animals which choose not to obey, as cat-lovers will agree with alacrity. Francis Galton, in *Inquiries into human faculty and its development* (London, 1883), states that man "has no natural power at all over many other creatures. Who, for instance, ever succeeded in frowning away a mosquito, or in pacifying an angry wasp by a smile?"

METEORITES HAVE SPECIAL POWERS

Many meteorites are enshrined as religious objects, among them one protected and kissed by Muslims at the Holy Ka'ba in Mecca. Australian aborigines carry fragments on their persons at all times in the belief that they give protection against disease and ill luck, while the Geological Survey of India reports that a team has urgently to be sent to a newly-arrived meteor to prevent its being cut up and sold in pieces as charms. The mediaeval French chained meteorites at night to prevent them returning unseen to their point of origin!

It was not until the research of Chladni (Riga, 1794) that the true nature of meteorites was satisfactorily resolved as natural lumps of metal or stone falling from the sky and thus offering valuable information as to extra-terrestrial materials.

Source: G. J. H. McCall, *Meteorites and their origin* (Newton Abbot, 1975).

METOPOSCOPY

A fallacy, like phrenology (q.v.), based on the irrational and base-less notion that physical appearances can denote character. Metoposcopy, or the study of interpreting frontal wrinkles, seems to have been invented by Girolamo Cardano (q.v.) whose Latin *Metoposcopia* (Paris, 1658) was followed the same year by a French translation, neither reprinted in the complete edition of Cardano's works (1663).

Cardano claimed to have discovered a localization of the planets on the forehead similar to that found by astrologers in the case of the bodily members, with Saturn at the top of the brow and the moon just above the eyebrows. A wavy wrinkle is said to indicate sea-travel, for instance, and in Cardano's eight hundred figures, most of the wrinkle-permutations are explained. If we were to encounter an agreeable person whose forehead is marked with six parallel horizontal lines and a short vertical line, we may be sure, says Cardano, that she is an adulteress and will end as a beggar.

Source: Émile Grillot de Givry, *Picture museum of sorcery, magic and alchemy* (New York, 1963, pp. 249-55).

'MIDDLE-AGED SPREAD' IS INEVITABLE

There is nothing inevitable about a young man's acquiring a paunch or other indications of incipient obesity. This can be prevented by increasing the amount of exercise taken and reducing the amount of calories consumed.

THE MIDDLE CLASS IN ENGLAND ROSE DURING THE TUDOR PERIOD

Louis B. Wright's *Middle-class culture in Elizabethan England* (Chapel Hill, North Carolina, 1935) identified a close interactive causal connection between the rise of the middle classes and the rise of the Tudors, an allegedly 'bourgeois' dynasty, whatever that term might mean.

J. H. Hexter's closely-argued analysis of Wright's argument exposes the tautology: everyone who is rising is admitted to the middle class. Hexter finds that "there is little evidence, then, that the Tudor period saw any extraordinary development in the middle class of group consciousness, group pride, or will to power", and no proof of the proposition that Tudor monarchs favoured commerce in any special way, or that they manifested "middle-class characteristics in any intelligible sense".

More significant than all this is the common desire of certain modern European historiographers to discover the 'rise of the middle class' in every period from the twelfth century to the twentieth.

BIRDS MIGRATE ON THE SAME DAY EACH YEAR

Dozens of fallacies concerning bird migration can be found in standard works such as A. Landsborough Thompson's *Bird migration* (London, 1949) or J. Dorst's *Les migrations des oiseaux* (Paris, 1956), but it will be sufficient to explode one of the commonest which, despite regular scientific refutation by one ornithologist after another, recurs annually. According to Californian newspapers, the cliff swallows nesting at the San Juan Capistrano Mission there always leave the Mission on 23 October for their southward migration and return on 19 March, even taking account of leap years! The fact remains that their departure date varies from year to year.

Source: Osmond P. Breland, *Animal facts and fallacies* (London, 1950, pp. 113-14).

A MILDLY INFECTIOUS PERSON CAN TRANSMIT ONLY A MILD INFECTION

The fact that this fallacy has been so widely held shows how dangerous common fallacies can be! How 'mild' an attack becomes depends entirely upon the ability of our system to withstand the attack: the infection itself has nothing to do with the case. An infected person will consequently transmit the disease to another seriously, if the latter is weakened, or mildly, if the latter is strong.

Source: A. S. E. Ackermann, *Popular fallacies*, 4th ed. (London, 1950, p. 145).

AT THE MILLENNIUM THE MESSIAH WILL RETURN

There have been hundreds of false Messiahs since Jesus Christ (see vol. 8, pp. 581-8 of Hastings' *Encyclopaedia of religion and ethics*, New York, 1913-1922), the most spectacular being Sabbatai Zvi (1626-1676) and the most detestable Jacob Frank (1726-1791). The fall of an Empire always raised the Jewish people's hopes of a new Messiah. As Hugh Trevor-Roper wrote in *Historical essays* (London, 1963, pp. 148-9), "when Popes and Kings allied themselves with the blind prejudices of the Church and the mob, such patronage availed the Jews no more than the Moriscos of Spain or the Huguenots of France. Whither then were the persecuted remnant to turn for relief? Whither indeed but to that stock refuge of the oppressed: mysticism, the Messiah, the Millennium. As the defeated humanists of Spain sank into private ecstasies, as the *marabout* on his African dunghill promised a Mahdi to the dejected beduin, as the Anabaptists of the seventeenth century manipulated their Scriptural logarithms to hasten the Apocalypse, so also the Jews of the Dispersion deviated into mystical heresies, counted the days to the Millennium, or discovered the Messiah".

Millions believe that Christ is coming again on a specific date, and repeated disproofs of their fallacy against rebirth fail to destroy their gullibility.

The Massachusetts farmer William Miller, after studying *Daniel* and *Revelation*, came to the conclusion that Christ would return on 22 October 1844. A number of Millerites were convinced, but most lost interest after the date passed. Ellen Gould Harmon, a young woman who was to marry the sectarian minister James White, kept true to the faith and became leader of the

Seventh Day Adventists before dying at the age of 88 in 1915. The sect takes Saturday to be the Sabbath and claims to be the only group which keeps all the Ten Commandments.

Another American sect, founded by the English doctor John Thomas, is the Christadelphians or 'brothers in Christ'. Thomas emigrated to the U.S.A. in 1832 and taught that Jesus Christ would return in 1866-8. They are akin to the Seventh Day Adventists in believing there is no Hell: they claim that the wicked die, whereas the Adventists claim that the wicked sleep.

The Panacea Society claim that there have been eight prophets, and that the Coming of the Messiah is close at hand. The first prophet was Jane Lead (1666), and others include Joanna Southcott, a servant-girl from Devonshire who left behind a Box, to be opened by twenty-four bishops of the Church of England in the hour of Britain's utmost danger, which contains the writings of Joanna Southcott destined to lead the nation to salvation.

The most memorable true account of a fundamentalist belief in the Second Coming in English literature is Edmund Gosse's *Father and son* (London, 1907), which recounts Philip Henry Gosse's fanaticism. In the *Life of Philip Henry Gosse* (London, 1890), the son declares how his father was 'invulnerably cased in fully developed conviction on every side'. He refused to take a meal with a Christian of any other sect, and broke even with the Plymouth Brethren, founding his own group in Devonshire. The group was greatly annoyed when the political turmoil of 1848 did not bring about the Second Coming. P. H. Gosse's *Omphalos* (London, 1857) suggested that God deliberately created the world with fossils embedded in the rocks and other apparent signs of evolution to deceive mankind and test their faith.

The Aetherius Society (q.v.) claims that Jesus has returned already, not to Earth but to Venus.

CLARK ON MISTAKES

Although not all mistakes are fallacies, all fallacies are mistakes. In *The mistakes we make* (London, 1898), C. E. Clark included a large number of popular errors under the following headings: Things that we call by their wrong names; mistakes we make about places and their names; mistakes we make about plants and their names; mistakes we make about animals; some literary stumbling-blocks; common errors in speech and writing; words, phrases, and things that are misunderstood; misstatements by famous authors and others; common mistakes of many kinds; historical mistakes; mistakes we make in connection with religious history; and, mistakes we make in connection with ancient history.

Clark's sequel, *More mistakes we make* (London, 1901), covered: Orthographical vagaries; murdered traditions; murdered quotations; the patriotic ill-treatment of foreign words; an arabesque of confusion; on natural history; pictorial mistakes; and a miscellaneous assortment.

MOLEOSOPHY

A fallacious technique purporting to foretell or diagnose character by interpreting the moles on the human body. A mole on the right hand implies success in business; on the left hand, possession of an artistic temperament; on the right knee, a happy marriage; on the left knee, possession of a bad temper.

But anyone foolish enough to be taken in by such nonsense will presumably not have had the intellectual curiosity to read so far.

Source: P. Showers, *Fortune telling for fun and popularity* (Philadelphia, 1945).

MONARCHY

"True believers and true scientists cannot be other than monarchists".

Or, if you are an anti-monarchist, read "anti-monarchists". Each statement is equally illogical, since monarchy is an institution that has nothing to do either with belief in God or with science.

Source: Pierre Félix, *L'équivoque démocratique* (Paris, 1906).

A SNAKE CANNOT KILL A MONGOOSE

There is a theory that the mongoose is protected against snakebite by eating a certain plant, thus obtaining a preventative antidote. This is not true. A mongoose can easily be killed by a snake if it does not immediately seize the snake behind the head to render it powerless and then break its backbone by biting it or cracking it like a whip. If the mongoose makes a mistake in this process, it can easily be bitten to death, an occurrence seen frequently in India.

IF YOU LEFT A CROWD OF MONKEYS ALONE WITH TYPEWRITERS LONG ENOUGH THEY WOULD BE ABLE TO RECREATE THE WHOLE WORKS OF SHAKESPEARE

This type of fallacy is normally used to ridicule the human faculty of creativity, particularly in the case of avant-garde writing or indeed any other literature which the reader is too lazy to appreciate.

Darrell Huff, author of the important exposure of statistical fallacies *How to lie with statistics* (London, 1954), has exploded this particular error in *How to take a chance* (London, 1960).

Random tapping of typewriter keys by one monkey would produce the initial 'd' of *dear sir* at the rate of one a minute; three monkeys over ten weeks could between them produce the word 'dear' with the letters in the right order; but to make the words 'dear sir' including the space in the right place would take 10,000 monkeys a hundred and fifty years. It is therefore inconceivable that any product of the human imagination could be replicated in any comparable way by random methods (which devalues among other examples the story *La biblioteca de Babel* by Jorge Luis Borges, in *Ficciones*).

Sir Arthur Eddington pointed the same moral in a limerick (though I am aware of the fallacy that 'all limericks are *ipso facto* true'):

> *There once was a brainy baboon*
> *who always breathed down a bassoon,*
> *for he said "it appears*
> *that in billions of years*
> *I shall certainly hit on a tune".*

TRAVEL TO THE MOON IS IMPOSSIBLE

Not only that: see also **AVIATION IS IMPOSSIBLE**.

As Dr Dionysius Lardner stated, addressing the British Association for the Advancement of Science in 1838, "Men might as well project a voyage to the Moon as attempt to employ steam navigation across the stormy North Atlantic Ocean". Jules Verne, writing science fiction in *De la terre à la lune* (Paris, 1865), was more farseeing and accurate than the distinguished American astronomer Forest Ray Moulton, who asserted in 1935: "It must be stated that there is not the slightest possibility of such a journey

... There is no theory that would guide us through interplanetary space to another world even if we could control our departure from the Earth; and there is no known way of easing our ether ship down on the surface of another world, if we could get there''.

On 18 October 1948, the London *Daily Mirror* offered "our candid opinion . , . that all talk of going to the Moon, and all talk of signals from the Moon, is sheer balderdash—in fact, just moonshine". As recently as January 1956, Sir Richard Woolley (for a period Astronomer Royal) described space travel as "utter bilge", an off-the-record comment which nevertheless found its way into the London daily press.

Failure to follow and appreciate the technical achievements of Russian and American space exploration research was characteristic of the popular press in all countries until, on 4 October 1957, the Russians successfully launched the pioneer artificial satellite Sputnik 1.

Source: Patrick Moore, *The next fifty years in space* (London, 1976).

HAVING TWO FULL MOONS IN A MONTH MEANS WET WEATHER

No. We know that there is absolutely no connection between changes of the moon and changes in the weather, since various scientists have taken the trouble to check the erroneousness of such superstitions. Horsley found that the weather tables of 1774, published by the Royal Society, showed that only ten changes of weather out of a total of forty-six occurred on days of lunar influence, only two of them being at the new moon, and none at all at the full ...

Source: Richard Inwards, *Weather fallacies*, in *Nature*, 15 August 1895.

THE PROPHET MOSES IS THE AUTHOR OF THE PENTATEUCH

The books of the Bible attributed to Moses, and indeed those attributed to David, Solomon and Daniel, were written long after the times when they lived.

Source: *The Bible and criticism*, by W. H. Bennett and Walter F. Adeney. The Christian orthodoxy of the authors is not in doubt, the former having been Professor of Old Testament Exegesis at Hackney College (London) and the latter Principal of Lancashire College, Manchester.

MOTHS EAT CLOTHES

Not quite so simple. What actually happens is that clothes-moths lay eggs on cloth, and these eggs develop into larvae which then eat tiny particles of cloth. The larvae change into pupae, each forming a tiny cocoon, and after a time the fully-grown moths emerge from the cocoons. The adult moths do not eat cloth.

BLACK IS THE COLOUR OF MOURNING

White is the prevalent colour of mourning, particularly in the Far East, Ancient Rome, and Sparta. In England mourners wore white up until the Middle Ages, and Henry VIII is recorded as having worn it for Anne Boleyn (who wore *yellow* for Catherine of Aragon). Yellow is worn in Egypt and Burma. Deep blue was worn during the Republican Roman period. Greyish-brown is the traditional colour of mourning in Ethiopia and pale brown in Iran. Among the Celts and Gypsies the prevalent colour of mourning is red.

LIFE CAN BE CREATED BY THE ACTION OF SUNLIGHT AND MUD

Shakespeare attributed to Lepidus in *Antony and Cleopatra* (II, vii, 29-31) the belief that certain forms of life were created by the action of light on mud. "Your serpent of Egypt", he declared, "is bred now of your mud by the operation of your sun; so is your crocodile", and the hardy sceptic of his time, Sir Thomas Browne, asserted in the 17th century that the sun was "fruitful in the generation of Frogs, Toads and Serpents". This belief was overthrown during the 19th century (in some places). See also **FROGS CAN RAIN FROM THE SKY.**

Sources include: Thomas Browne, *Pseudodoxia epidemica* (London, 1646).

MUMPS IN MEN CAUSES STERILITY

"A team at a London hospital has published a study of nearly 200 men who had mumps in the five years before, and there was no evidence that the condition stopped them from fathering children".

Source: John Camp, *Magic, myth and medicine* (London, 1973, p. 176)

170

MURDER WILL OUT

"Truth will come to light; murder cannot be hid long; a man's son may; but at the length, truth will out", is a dramatic point made by Shakespeare in *The Merchant of Venice* (II, ii, 75) but though many believe that both truth and murder do eventually emerge, nothing is less axiomatic. Truth will only emerge if someone has the wit, courage and energy to compel it to do so, for it will not emerge of its own accord. So with murder.

William F. Kessler and Paul B. Weston, in *The detection of murder* (New York, 1961), open their book by declaring that "nowhere in the world is the investigation of unexplained or unexpected death so casual and haphazard as it is in the United States. Of the close to 300,000 deaths in the United States each year from suspicious or violent causes, only a little more than 10,000 are officially recognized as murders".

One in thirty detected as *murders*? And few of those with a conviction in the case? It looks as though neither in the U.S. nor elsewhere will 'truth' or 'murder' out.

IT IS POSSIBLE MEANINGFULLY TO COMBINE GEOMETRY WITH MYTHOLOGY

The year after publishing the fanciful *Essay on the sentiments of attraction, adaptation, and variety. To which are added a key to the mythology of the ancients* (Edinburgh, 1822), the poet and philosopher William Howison produced *A grammar of infinite forms; or, the mathematical elements of ancient philosophy and mythology*.

The fallaciousness of Howison's enterprise can be comprehended from a single example, which demonstrates an awesome ignorance of the manner in which myths arise and become disseminated. Howison deals with Perseus under the heading "the evolution of diminishing hyperbolic branches".

N

"The narrower the range of man's knowledge of physical causes, the wider is the field which he has to fill up with hypothetical causes of a metaphysical or supernatural character."—ANDREW LANG, in *Myth, ritual and religion* (London, 1899).

THE ORIGIN OF **NAPOLEON BONAPARTE**

All we know for certain is that he was a pure Semite (Eugène Gellion-Danglar, *Les sémites et le sémitisme*, 1882); of Germanic origin, to be traced back to Conrad and his wife Ermengarde (Wencker Wildberg, *Commentaires sur les Mémoires de Napoléon*); Greek, 'Bonaparte' being a translation of Calomeros (Princess Lucien Murat, *Les errants de la gloire*, 1933); the son of an Italian bandit (pamphlet of 1814 cited in Jean Tulard, *L'Anti-Napoléon*, 1965); a descendant of Totila, king of the Ostrogoths (*Mémoires curieux*, 1821); a descendant of Tedix of Cadolingi, Count of Pistoia in Italy (*Annuaire generalé héraldique universel*, 1901); a descendant of Corsican hussars (*Bonaparte démasqué*, 1814); and a Florentine named William, who took the surname of Bonaparte in 1261 (Hubert N. B. Richardson, *A dictionary of Napoleon and his times*, London, 1920).

NAPOLEON I WAS THE FIRST TO CALL ENGLAND 'A NATION OF SHOPKEEPERS'

He merely quoted Adam Smith's *Wealth of nations* (London, 1776), having it first from Barère, who publicly used it of England in the French Convention of 11 June 1794, in allusion to Howe's battle of 1 June: "Let Pitt, then, boast of his victory to his nation of shopkeepers".

Adam Smith actually wrote, "To found a great empire for the sole purpose of raising up a people of customers, may at first sight appear a project fit only for a nation of shopkeepers. It is, however, a project altogether unfit for a nation of shopkeepers;

but extremely fit for a nation that is governed by shopkeepers".

Napoleon's actual words were, "L'Angleterre est une nation de boutiquiers".

NATURALISTIC FALLACY

A term coined by G. E. Moore in *Principia ethica* (Cambridge, 1903, p. 10). Moore wrote, "It may be true that all things which are good are *also* something else, just as it is true that all things which are yellow produce a certain kind of vibration in the light ... But far too many philosophers have thought that when they named those other properties they were actually defining good; that these properties, in fact, were simply not 'other', but absolutely and entirely the same with goodness. This view I propose to call the 'naturalistic fallacy' ..."

NATURE HAS 'LAWS'

The 'laws of nature' are observed and recorded by men, and thus as clearly man-made as penal or commercial laws. They, like penal or commercial laws, must also be modified in the light of changing circumstances to conform to new facts.

Julian Huxley wrote in his *Essays of a biologist* (1923): "A law of Nature is not (and I wonder how often this fallacy has been exploded, only to reappear next day)—a law of Nature is not something revealed, not something absolute, nor something imposed on phenomena from without or from above; it is no more and no less than a summing-up in generalised form, of our own observations of phenomena; it is an epitome of fact, from which we can draw general conclusions".

I would add only this: where agreed 'laws of nature' are attacked explicitly or implicitly by those writers whose ideas are generically termed 'fallacies' throughout this book, the onus is clearly upon them to prove that the 'laws of nature' have been changed (and to show where and how). The onus is not upon those who accept the current but perennially-mutating 'laws of nature' to show why they do so.

NATUROPATHY

A medical cult not to be confused with the simplicity of diet and regular exercise which it recommends in common with orthodox medicine.

Naturopaths believe that the body will keep naturally healthy instead of having to cope with unnatural foods, customs, and medicines. They object to food grown with the aid of artificial fertilizers, yet it is farming (the systematic interference with nature to provide food) together with similar methods of adapting environment to needs which has enabled man to survive in competition with creatures that possess wings, claws, power, bulk or speed. As to avoiding medicines, the chemists have yet to produce anything as lethal as the 'natural' poisons of some medicinal plants. All chemicals (to which naturopaths illogically object) are made from naturally-occurring raw materials.

Naturopathy had no single founder, but grew up as an anti-scientific reaction to the gradual development of drugs in eighteenth- and nineteenth-century Europe. An early U.S. pioneer was the Seventh Day Adventist John H. Kellogg, and even now Adventism stresses nature therapy.

Though numerous books and magazines testify to the extremism of most naturopaths, nothing has yet equalled the great five-volume *Encyclopaedia of physical culture* (1912), by Bernarr Macfadden, with its injunctions against the internal use of drugs and medicine and against consulting orthodox doctors. Most suggested cures involve diets, exercises, and water therapy; cancer for instance should be treated by fasting, exercises, and a 'vitality building regimen'. Macfadden subsequently recanted his views on cancer (he now believes that it can be cured by a diet consisting solely of grapes).

Sources: Martin Gardner, *Fads and fallacies in the name of science* (New York, 1957); and Peter Wingate, *The Penguin medical encyclopedia* (2nd ed., Harmondsworth, 1976).

THERE IS A RACIAL DIFFERENCE BETWEEN 'NEGRO BLOOD' AND 'WHITE BLOOD"

When the American Red Cross agreed to segregate the blood of negroes from that of 'whites' in its blood banks, its officials may well have been aware of the fallacy that there is a racial difference between the two, but silently succumbed to the common error to avoid giving distress to white soldiers resisting the idea of a transfusion of 'mixed blood'. Like most such attempts to smother the truth, this one failed because it caused equal distress: to the negro soldiers.

The ancient, and still widely-held, fallacy that blood can carry hereditary characteristics comes from literary metaphor: 'he is of noble blood' meaning that his ancestors were more ambitious, greedy and successful than the ancestors of others. But blood is merely a device by which food and oxygen are transported to the body's cells and waste matter carried away. Negroes have all the blood groups that 'whites' have and every characteristic of their blood is similar to that of white blood.

Source: M. F. Ashley Montagu, 'The myth of blood', in *Psychiatry*, vol. 6, 1943, pp. 15-19.

NEGROES HAVE UNDERDEVELOPED BRAINS AND THICK SKULLS

Racial prejudice ought to be decreasing with increasing educational programmes to offset the many fallacies which are dangerous to world harmony and community peace. There certainly seems to be a correlation between lack of higher education and the holding of racial beliefs which conveniently give the holder the highest possible prestige. Thus, while it is true that the negro brain is on average forty cubic centimetres smaller than that of 'white' (that is to say, 'pink') Americans, it is equally true that the 'white' man's brain is smaller than those of American Indians, Eskimoes, Japanese, Kaffirs, and Polynesians, according to T. Wingate Todd's paper on 'Cranial capacity and linear dimensions in white and negro' in *American Journal of Physical Anthropology*, vol. 6, 1923, pp. 97-194.

As regards the thickness of the skull, we have the word of M. F. Ashley Montagu (who has seen many 'white' and negro skulls sawn through) that there is no difference in their thickness.

Source: Bergen Evans, *The natural history of nonsense* (London, 1947).

NERO FIDDLED WHILE ROME BURNED

The violin was not invented until the 16th century, so that story must surely die soon. Was the instrument a lyre or lute-type then found in Rome? It is known that he played an instrument and also that he wrote poetry (Suetonius records having seen his notebooks with his own erasures), but he was at Antium when the fire that ruined half of Rome broke out in 64 A.D. The rumour that he had had the fire started began to circulate when he took the opportunity to build on the ashes his own colossal Domus Aurea. Nero himself put the blame on Christians, who were no more likely to have started the fire than he was.

Source: *Oxford Classical Dictionary* (Oxford, 1949).

NESTS ARE USED BY BIRDS FOR SLEEPING

It has been observed that a mother bird will infrequently doze off while sitting on her eggs, but of course birds are as clean as pigs in their habits and leave their nests at dusk to sleep in tree branches. Town children often imagine birds asleep in their nests at night.

NICOTINE IS THE GREATEST DANGER TO HEALTH IN CIGARETTE SMOKING

A pamphlet issued by the Health Departments of the United Kingdom in August 1976 states that "tar is regarded as a greater danger to health than nicotine", and lists cigarettes sold, despite this warning with a tar yield (mg/cig) varying from under 4 (including Embassy Ultra Mild, Player's Mild De Luxe, and Silk Cut Extra Mild) to 34 mg/cig (Capstan Full Strength, Pall Mall King Size, and Player's No. 3). The Health Departments continue, "Our advice is: STOP SMOKING" and add the now proven facts that "Cigarettes cause lung cancer, bronchitis, heart disease".

If one needed an epitaph for human reason, it could well read 'THEY SMOKED CIGARETTES'.

"THE NIGHTINGALE, IF SHE SHOULD SING BY DAY,

When every goose is cackling, would be thought
No better a musician than the wren"

says Shakespeare in *The Merchant of Venice* (V, i), falling into the popular error of believing the singing nightingale to be the hen-bird. Only the cock nightingale can sing.

NIGHTINGALES SING ONLY AT NIGHT

No known species of nightingale sings only by night, though both *Daulias luscinia* and *Daulias vera* (common in Britain) are more usually heard at night.

Source: A. S. E. Ackermann, *Popular fallacies* (4th ed., London, 1950).

NORTH AMERICAN INDIANS USED TO MASSACRE WHITE PIONEERS

At the time when Columbus 'discovered' America, there were just short of a million Indians in the area now known as the United States; the figure at the end of the 19th century was about a quarter of a million. At least a thousand massacres by white men are recorded, but in *The Gospel of the Red Man* (1939), Ernest Thompson Seton cannot identify a single massacre of Whites by Indians.

The record begins with the Christmas Eve massacre by the Pilgrim Fathers at Cos Cob, Connecticut, resulting in the killing of 400 peaceful men, women and children. In 1631 John Winthrop used the Bible to justify Puritan seizure of Indian lands.

Forcible 'protection' on reservations limited Indian hopes even further by the 1880s. The Allotment Act of 1887 gave tiny 'farms' to individual Indians and the huge areas left over were sold to wealthy white speculators. In 1958 the annual budget of the Indian Bureau was alleged to be $250 million, but the average per capita income of American Indians was reported to be $19.20 per year. President Kennedy recognized the injustice done when in 1961 he stated: "America has much to learn about the heritage of our Indian people. Only through this study can we as a nation do what must be done if our treatment of the American Indian is not to be marked down for all time as a national disgrace".

EVERYTHING IS NUMBER

The profound teaching of Pythagoras (c. 588-500 B.C., if he ever lived at all: Greek *python*, a soothsayer), included the above saying. By 'numbers', he meant the common whole numbers and the fractions obtained by dividing one whole number by another, such as $\frac{3}{4}$, $\frac{11}{9}$, $\frac{6}{25}$ and so on. These together are the 'rational numbers'. It followed that both a side and a diagonal of any square would be measurable by (rational) numbers. But if a side of a square is measured by a (rational) number, a diagonal of the same square is *not* measurable by any (rational) number. So not everything is 'number', even in mathematics. The square root of two is an irrational number.

Plato followed Pythagoras in the irrational worship of number, and John Dee (1527-1608) wrote in his preface to the first English translation of Euclid's *Elements*: "All things (which from the very first original being of things, have been framed and made) do appear to be formed by reason of numbers. For this was the principal example or pattern in the mind of the Creator" [spelling modernized].

The fallacy was perpetuated in 1935 by Sir Arthur Eddington, and is still a commonplace.

Source: Eric Temple Bell, *The magic of numbers* (New York, 1946, p.111).

THERE ARE NUTS IN MAY

On this fallacy depends the popular children's song "Here we go gathering nuts in May". As Brewer states in *A dictionary of phrase and fable*, the phrase "is a perversion of "Here we go gathering *knots of may*", referring to the old custom of gathering knots of flowers on May Day, or, to use the ordinary phrase, "to go a-maying". Of course there are no nuts to be gathered in May".

"One of the first duties of man is not to be duped."
—CARL BECKER.

AN **OCTOPUS** CAN STRANGLE A MAN

Pure fantasy. It has been reported rarely that a swimmer has been held by one of the eight suckers of an octopus, but no harm has ever resulted, at least to the swimmer. Octopuses are also alleged to have bitten human beings with their beaklike mouths and to have injected venom, but no consequence has ever been more serious than a slight and temporary swelling.

ROGER BACON ON **OFFENDICULA**

Roger Bacon (c. 1214-1294) recognized four categories of *offendicula*, which might be translated 'impediments to thought'. These are 'excessive reliance on authority', 'slavery to custom', 'subjection to the weight of popular opinion', and the 'concealment of ignorance by pretending knowledge'.

Source: Roger Bacon, *Sumule dialectices* (written about 1245) in Bacon's *Opera hactenus inedita*, ed. by Robert Steele (fasc. 15, Oxford, 1909).

OMENS

Primitive people (in all civilizations) have always, in lieu of seeking actual experimental knowledge which requires the acquisition of books, the art of reading and writing, leisure for study, diligence, and native ability, tried to master their unmanageable lives by 'finding out what to do' themselves or by resorting to those who claim to be able to foretell the future. It is still commonplace to hear an otherwise intelligent person declare, "that's a good omen".

Fallacies involving telling the future (see also **I CHING** and **TAROT**) include aeromancy (divination from cloud-formations in the air), alectryomancy (from cockerels), alphitomancy (from grains of wheat), alveromancy (from barley), amniomancy (from the amniotic membrane occasionally enveloping the head of the newborn), axinomancy (from an axe and

hatchet), clidomancy (from keys), cromniomancy (from onions)
. . . And that it is a selection from only the first three letters of
the English alphabet!

The credulity of men can be estimated in direct contrast to their
willingness and ability to learn. See also **DIVINATION**.

THE "ALL MEN ARE DRIVEN BY ONLY **ONE THING**" FALLACY

In *Leviathan* (London, 1651), Thomas Hobbes the English philosopher declared: "In the first place, I put for a general implication
of all mankind, a perpetual and restless desire of power after
power, that ceaseth only in death". And his book is based solely
on that supposition.

Robert Ardrey, in his *Territorial imperative* (New York, 1966),
argues that man's territorial attitude is the key to much of his
activity, for good and ill.

Gordon Rattray Taylor, in his *Sex in history* (New York, 1954)
seeks to demonstrate not merely "how closely attitudes to sexual
matters interlock with other social attitudes" but also how they
"dictate them". For him, as for countless other writers past and
present, all men are driven by only one thing. They only differ
in their opinion as to what that is. Let the reader, young and old,
beware of the writer who simplifies phenomena essentially complex. Some men may be driven by the urge for power, or territory,
or sex. But not all. One might as well say that all men are driven
by the urge to collect stamps or learn Danish. Evelyn Underhill
deserved the last word for a generalization of this type which will
be prized by every collector of human fallacies: "There is a sense
in which we may think of the whole life of the Universe", she
wrote in *Worship* (New York, 1936), "seen and unseen, conscious
and unconscious, as an act of worship, glorifying its Origin,
Sustainer, and End".

OOSCOPY AND OOMANTIA

Divination by eggs.

Suetonius relates that Livia, anxious to know whether she would
be the mother of a boy or a girl, kept an egg in her bosom at a
proper temperature, until a chick with a beautiful cockscomb
came forth. Oomantia denotes a method of divining the signs or
characters appearing in eggs. According to Pliny, Umbricius—
who was the most skilful physician of his own time—stated that the

vulture laid thirteen eggs; that with one egg it purified the others and its nest, and afterwards threw it away. (The Egyptian vulture, presumably the bird Umbricius knew, lays just two yellowish white eggs during February-March according to Heinz Brüll in Grzimek's *Animal life encyclopaedia*, vol. 7 (New York, 1972) pp. 399-400).

Source: William Jones, *Credulities past and present* (London, 1880, p. 449).

WORDS CANNOT MEAN THEIR OPPOSITE

For the student of words from the careful listing of Roget to the subtle imagination of Lewis Carroll, nothing is more enchanting than words in any language which mean their own opposite, something which is regularly believed by the unwary to be impossible.

Let formerly meant to prevent, as when Hamlet, intent on following his father's ghost, shouts at those who would stop him, "Unhand me, gentlemen. By heaven, I'll make a ghost of him that lets me!" Nowadays, he would say that he would make a ghost of anyone who would *not* let him follow his father's spectre.

Scan means to scrutinize with great care; or to glance so briefly that one takes in the headlines or main points only. For instance, "The bibliographer scanned the first edition carefully to ensure that it was perfect in every detail", and "The traveller barely scanned the front page before handing the magazine to his wife".

Shame*ful* and shame*less* are virtually the same thing; so are valuable and *in*valuable. *Nice* in mediaeval usage meant 'foolish, dull, strange, or stupid'. I can *distract* (entertain) a reader without, I hope, *distracting* him (sending him out of his wits).

THE ORANG-UTAN BELONGS TO THE HUMAN SPECIES

The *orang-utan* (properly *orang hutan*, Malay='man of the forest'), is an anthropoid ape, that is a member of the ape family. The popular American writer on animals, Ivan T. Sanderson, wrote in *Animal treasure* (1937) that both the orang utan and the gorilla "I can only regard . . . as a retrograde form of human . . . life".

There is perhaps more excuse for the Scottish judge Lord. Monboddo (1714-1799), who described in *Of the origin and progress of language* (6 vols., 1773-92) and *Antient metaphysics* (6 vols., 1779-99) his pet orang utan as an example of "the infantine

181

state of our species" who could play the flute but "never learned to speak". Thomas Love Peacock (1785-1866), with de Quincey the most underrated English writer of the early 19th century, wrote a hilarious conversation-piece on the unfortunate Monboddo: *Melincourt, or Sir Oran Haut-ton* (1817). Mr Sylvan Forester, a wealthy young philosopher, has trained an orang-utan in everything but speech, and bought him a baronetcy and a seat in Parliament. The amiable, chivalrous Sir Oran plays the flute to perfection and enchants the company.

Source: C. B. Tinker, *Nature's simple plan* (Princeton, N.J., 1922).

ORGONOMY

Wilhelm Reich (1897-1957) was a psychoanalyst under Freud and held a number of important teaching and administrative posts in Viennese psychoanalytical organizations. A Marxist, he published an extraordinary book, partly inspired by the anthropologist Malinowski, called *The function of the orgasm* (1927) in which he stated his theory that the sexual frustration of the proletariat caused a thwarting of its political consciousness, and it was only though uninhibited release of the sexual urge that the working class could realize its historic mission. The Marxist authorities were unimpressed, labelling his book "un-Marxist rubbish" and he soon parted too from Freud, being formally expelled from the International Psychoanalytical Association in 1934.

In the 1930s Reich seems to have lost his mental balance, and in 1939 he became obsessed with 'orgone energy', inventing the term 'orgonomy' to describe the science of this new type of energy. He issued the *International Journal of Sex-Economy and Orgone Research*, later renamed the *Orgone Energy Bulletin: The Annals of the Orgone Institute;* and numerous books and pamphlets to try to demonstrate that he had discovered the biological basis that Freud had been seeking for his theory of the libido, or sexual energy.

Orgone energy, according to Reich, is a non-electromagnetic force permeating all nature. It is the life force of Bergson made accessible and usable by means of a therapeutic box called an Orgone Energy Accumulator. According to a former translator, Dr Theodore P. Wolfe, this box is the "most important single discovery in the history of medicine, bar none". It consists of a short phone-box type of structure made of sheet iron on the inside, and an organic material (such as celotex or wood) on the outside. Orgone energy is allegedly attracted by the organic substance on the outside, and is passed to the metal which then radiates it inward. The metal reflects orgone, so the box soon acquires a high concentration of the energy. Reich's anonymous booklet *The Orgone Energy Accumulator* (1951) advertised it as a cure for hay fever, anaemia, cancer in early stages, acute colds, chronic ulcers, and any kind of lesion or abrasion.

(Incidentally, Reich also invented a rainmaking device called C.OR.E, or Cosmic ORgone Engineering which does not spray the clouds. As Irwin Ross reported in the *New York Post* (*Sunday Magazine*) for 5 September 1954, it merely draws orgone out of them, weakening their cohesive power and causing them to break up.)

Legal action to prevent 'orgone energy accumulators' being shipped interstate and to prohibit the distribution of publicity matter mentioning orgone energy was taken by the U.S. Food and Drug Administration in 1954. They estimated that a thousand of the orgone boxes had been sold. After a series of careful tests, FDA official scientists concluded that "there is no such energy as orgone and that Orgone Energy Accumulators are worthless in the treatment of any disease or disease condition of man. Irreparable harm may result to persons who abandon or postpone rational medical treatment while pinning their faith on worthless devices such as these". After being diagnosed by a psychiatrist as a paranoid, he became intensely religious and started to pray. He identified himself with Christ in his book *The Murder of Christ* (which I suppose is one step more logical than identifying Christ with *amanita muscaria* as John Allegro has done in his book *The sacred mushroom*) but he made a number of valuable contributions, including *The sexual revolution* (1930), re-issued in 1969.

Sources: *Humanist*, February 1970 (pp. 46-7), and Martin Gardner, *Fads and fallacies in the name of science*, 2nd ed. (New York, 1957, chapter 21).

AN **ORPHAN** IS PARENTLESS

It is often stated that an orphan is one who has lost both father and mother, but the *Shorter Oxford Dictionary* defines 'orphan' as 'one deprived by death of father or mother', so that a child with one parent still living should properly be referred to as an orphan.

OSTEOPATHY

A theory invented by Andrew Taylor Still (a man with no identifiable medical training) in 1874 which states that diseases are caused by a malfunctioning of the nerves or blood supply, which is due chiefly to the dislocation of small bones in the spine. These dislocations, or "subluxations of the vertebrae", press on nerves and blood vessels and prevent the body from manufacturing its own curative agents. Still's eccentric autobiography (shown by investigation to be full of invention and fraudulent claims) records that by his system of spinal rubbing, he grew three inches of hair in a week on a head completely bald, and that by his methods of spinal manipulation he 'cured' malaria, yellow fever, diphtheria, diabetes, dandruff, obesity, piles and constipation.

There are 11,000-odd practitioners of osteopathy in the United States today. As Martin Gardner quietly points out, "the back rub feels pleasant—especially for patients with repressed sexual longings (or homosexual if the practitioner is of the same sex)".

Osteopathy should not be confused with reputable manipulative surgery. As Sir Herbert Barker wrote in *The Daily Telegraph* of 7 February 1935: "My correspondence, the lay and professional press, and my friends, all make it very apparent that practically the entire public believes that osteopathy and manipulative surgery are one and the same thing . . . Bone-setting, or manipulative surgery—a British and very much older system of therapeutics—deals only with injuries, and derangements of the joints, ligaments, muscles and tendons, and some acquired deformities".

Sources include: Martin Gardner, *Fads and fallacies in the name of science* (New York, 1957).

OSTRICH WINGS ARE USELESS, AS THE BIRD CANNOT FLY

The ostrich cannot fly, but uses its wings to turn sharply when eluding a hunter. Ostriches can both jump and swim.

OSTRICHES BURY THEIR HEADS IN THE SAND

This curious fallacy probably arose from the observation that, when sighting danger from afar, they occasionally drop to the ground with their necks parallel to the ground and watch intently. Then, if danger approaches, they do what every other animal with strong legs is likely to do: they run like hell.

President Woodrow Wilson is only one of a thousand politicians and orators who have used the picturesque figure of speech, obviously thinking it a fact and not a fallacy. In a speech on 1 February 1916 he declared: "America cannot be an ostrich with its head in the sand". To which one is tempted to add "neither can an ostrich", for it would quickly suffocate.

OSTRICHES CAN DIGEST COINS AND KEYS

Metallic and other hard substances are taken into the gizzard by ostriches, much as common fowl take small sharp pebbles, but they are not digested, despite Shakespeare:

"Ah, villain, thou wilt betray me, amd get a thousand crowns of the king by carrying my head to him; but I'll make thee eat iron like an ostrich, and swallow my sword like a great pin, ere thou and I part" (Jack Cade to Alexander Iden)—*King Henry VI*, Part 2 (IV, x).

But the fallacy that such metal objects are actually digested by ostriches was repudiated by Sir Thomas Browne in *Pseudodoxia epidemica* (London, 1646), Book III, chapter 22: "The common opinion of the Ostrich, Struthiocamelus, or Sparrow Camel, conceives that it digesteth iron, and this is confirmed by the affirmations of many: besides swarms of others, Rhodiginus in his prelections taketh it for granted, Johannes Langius in his epistles pleadeth experiment for it; the common picture also confirmeth it, which usually describeth this animal with an horseshoe in its mouth. Notwithstanding, upon inquiry we find it very questionable, and the negative seems most reasonably entertained . . ."

Ostriches eat vegetables and grass in the wild; in captivity according to the London Regent's Park Zoo they will eat almost anything, from meat to keys and coins, but of course they cannot *digest* these latter. Cuvier shall have the last word: "The powers of digestion in this bird are certainly very great, but their operation is confined to matters of an alimentary character".

THE OUIJA BOARD CONNECTS THOSE PRESENT WITH DISTANT EVENTS OR PERSONS

The '*ouija*' board (combining the French and German words for 'yes') is a flat piece of polished wood with the letters of the alphabet in a line, semi-circle or circle along one side. On this a small board, mounted on casters, slides about when participants place their hands on it and may spell out words and sentences by the pointing of an arrow. In other cases an upturned wine glass slides towards a letter which the participants allege is chosen by spirits directing them.

Michael Faraday investigated the ouija board phenomena and came to the following conclusion: "It is with me a clear point that the table moves when the parties, though they strongly wish it, do not intend, and do not believe that they move it by ordinary mechanical power. They say the table draws their hands; it moves first and they have to follow it". After testing various substances with different electrical properties, Faraday found that "No form of experiment or mode of observation that I could devise gave me the slightest indication of any peculiar natural force—nothing but mere mechanical pressure exerted inadvertently by the turner".

The ouija board is a method of autonography midway between table-turning and automatic writing (qq.v.).

Sources include: D. H. Rawcliffe, *Illusions and delusions of the supernatural and the occult* (New York, 1952) and Richard Cavendish, ed., *Encyclopedia of the unexplained* (London, 1974).

AN OVATION IS A MAJOR TRIUMPH

The popular press frequently refers to an ovation accorded to a figure deserving of every reward. But the Latin *ovatio* is, to quote Cassell's *Latin dictionary* (1948 printing) merely "a kind of lesser triumph in which the victorious general proceeded to the Capitol on horseback or on foot". An ovation is thus a secondary triumph.

OXFORD BELLS ARE MAGICAL

Louis Pauwels and Jacques Bergier, in *The dawn of magic* (London, 1963), claim to "have studied certain reports of the occult section of the German Intelligence Service—notably a lengthy report on the magical properties of the bells in the belfries of Oxford which were thought to have prevented bombs from falling on the town".

With breathtaking understatement the authors add: "It is undeniable that there is an element of aberration here; but the fact that it affected supposedly intelligent and responsible men, thereby illuminating certain aspects of both visible and invisible history, is equally undeniable".

OZONE AT THE SEASIDE IS GOOD FOR YOU

There is no ozone at the seaside, for the simple reason that the ozone layer is roughly fifty kilometres above sea level. The *University Correspondent* (1 July 1914) reported that "The existence of ozone in air has always been doubtful, the chemical evidence for its presence being quite unsatisfactory . . . The smell attributed to it at the seaside really arises from decaying seaweed".

Sir Edwin Ray Lankester, a valuable popularizer of science, explained to readers of *The Daily Telegraph* (26 February 1912) "that the presence of ozone . . . in respired air in even very minute quantities acts as an irritant to the air passages and is highly injurious. It produces no effect whatever on the respiratory processes which go on in the lungs, but it is not altogether negligible from the point of view of fresh air and ventilation".

"Concentrations of even one part in the million are too irritative, and quickly depress the metabolism and lower the temperature of rats, and are unpleasant to man . . .", reported Dr Leonard Hill and Dr Martin Flack in their paper *The influence of ozone in ventilation* to the Royal Society of Arts (7 February 1912).

P

Populus vult decipi. ("The people want to be deceived").
—ANCIENT ROMAN SAYING.

PAPAL INDULGENCES WERE ABOLISHED IN THE MIDDLE AGES

An American visitor records having bought four different *bulas* (bulls) over the counter of a Spanish bookshop as recently as 1911. The first, costing 50 *centimos*, bought permission to eat meat when Catholics elsewhere are fasting. The second and third, costing 75 *centimos* each, bought plenary indulgences for either the buyer or for someone else. The fourth was known in Spain as the 'Thieves' *bula*', since it allowed the buyer to keep illgotten property whose owner's name and address was unknown (such as a pickpocket's victim). This cost 1.15 *pesetas* for articles valued up to 15 *pesetas*, beyond which a further *bula* had to be bought. This gave rise to the Spanish phrase "Tengo una bula para todos"— I've permission to do whatever I like.

Source: Joseph McCabe, *A rationalist encyclopaedia* (London, 1948).

THE 'PANAMA' HAT COMES FROM THE CENTRAL AMERICAN STATE OF PANAMA

A Panama hat is one made from the undeveloped leaves of the stemless screw-pine (*Carloduvica palmata*) and has nothing to do with the nation of Panama.

PARAMNESIA

A common psychological phenomenon defined as 'distortion or falsification of memory or recognition', so that one is wrongly conscious that 'all of this has happened before' or 'I can guess what will happen next' or 'I was here in a former (or later) existence'. This illusion is also known as 'déjà vu' (French, 'already seen').

The significance of this fallacy is that Plato's firm belief in extrapolation from past experience induced him to use it as an argument for his belief in a previous existence.

Source: James Drever, *A dictionary of psychology*, revised by Harvey Wallerstein (Harmondsworth, 1964).

PARAPSYCHOLOGY HAS NOW BEEN ACCEPTED AS A SCIENTIFIC DISCIPLINE BY A MAJORITY OF SCIENTISTS

This is the unfortunate, and untrue, premise of Arthur Koestler's *The roots of coincidence* (London, 1972). Because Mr Koestler has become gradually more convinced of this himself, he feels able to speak on behalf of the majority of scientists, and this is certainly premature, if not completely erroneous. In his first chapter, 'The ABC of ESP', he claims that ESP has been generally accepted as a mysterious but demonstrable faculty, and that parapsychology is rapidly becoming established as an academically respectable subject.

As Chris Evans observes in the *New Humanist* (September 1972, p. 198), "During the 'thirties and 'forties it is true, thanks to [J. B.] Rhine's vastly publicized work at Duke University, parapsychology acquired a fleeting academic respectability, but the horrible failure of parapsychologists to produce a repeatable experiment led at first to increasing scepticism and, more lately, to a simple lack of interest on the part of the average scientist . . . Even the famous Parapsychology Lab at Duke University (never a university department incidentally) no longer exists—it folded in 1968 with the retirement of Rhine, and the university authorities decided not to appoint a successor . . .'

J. Beloff, reviewing another batch of books on the subject in the *Times Literary Supplement* of 17 December 1976, writes of Nona Coxhead's *Mindpower* (London, 1976): "Those who already look upon parapsychology as the preserve of cranks may well have their suspicions confirmed. For parapsychology can all too readily degenerate into pseudo-science and the author lacks the discrimination necessary to tell the one from the other. Charlatans are accorded the same uncritical reverence as reputable academics. We meet here such engaging characters as Tony Agpaoa, the Filipino psychic surgeon; the American, Cleve Backster, with his emotionally sensitive plants and eggs; and the Czech, Robert Pavlita, with his "psychotronic generators" by means of which he claims to be able to store purely psychic energy sufficient to

"magnetize almost any material" (shades of Mesmer!). All of
these she seems to accept at their own valuation. The result is a
brisk conducted tour of Wonderland by an Alice who is sadly
deficient in that ingenuous common sense that was the saving
grace of the original Alice".

PARROTS CAN LIVE TO BE A HUNDRED

Not so far as the experts have been able to obtain reliable records.
"Hundred-year-old parrots certainly belong in the realm of the
fable; nevertheless a raven in captivity reached an age of 69
years".

Source: Grzimek, *Animal life encyclopaedia*, vol. 7 (New York, 1972,
p. 73).

THE PATHETIC FALLACY

An error of "imaginatively endowing inanimate objects with
life", according to Toynbee (in *A study of history*, London, 1935,
vol. I, p. 18).

It permeated Greek religion as both anthropomorphism (human
forms) and anthropopathism (human feelings), and can be found
throughout such masterpieces as the *Iliad*, the *Odyssey*, and the
Oresteia of Aeschylus. The fallacy was attacked as early as the
sixth century B.C. by Xenophanes of Colophon, but it persists to
this day in such various guises as the 'Statue of Liberty' or the
'two faces of Communism'. Theodore Roosevelt even went to the
absurd length, in a drafted speech, of comparing nations of the
world to specific animals, including monkeys, hyenas and hippo-
potami. Max Lerner (in *America as a civilisation*, 2 vols., New
York, 1961, vol. I, p. 28) wrote of a national compensation in the
U.S.A. for "the sacrificial slaying of the European father". The
psychoanalytic approach to history is fraught with such fallacies,
and is invariably simplistic to the point of absurdity.

See also **APATHETIC** FALLACY.

ST. PATRICK WAS AN IRISHMAN

St. Patrick (385?-461?) seems to have been born near the west
coast somewhere between the Clyde and the Severn estuary, but
in any case not in Ireland. A Romano-Briton, he merely *evangel-
ized* the Irish, but of course there were Christians in Ireland long

before Patrick began to preach the Gospel there. The Irish bishop of the time was Palladius.

Source: E. MacNeill, *St Patrick, Apostle of Ireland* (1964).

PATRIOTIC FALLACY

A nationalistic extension of the fallacy of egoism, the fallacy of patriotism is to assume that one's own country or region is superior to that of other men. The fallacy is still held almost universally, though not officially, even at the United Nations and other international organizations.

Antoine de Rivarol, in *De l'universalité de la langue française* (Paris, 1784), claimed that "English literature is not worth a second glance", and much worse judgments, private and public, have led beyond fights and duels to full-scale wars completely based on prejudice. "The West", stated Gobineau in his absurd *Essai sur l'inégalité des races humaines* (1853-1855), "has always been the centre of the world". Think about it.

A PEAL OF BELLS IS THE NAME OF THE EIGHT BELLS IN THE BELFRY

An appeal (or summons) of bells was early corrupted to 'a peal' and in campanology refers to 5,040 changes, or the varying of the order in which the bells come down as they are being rung. The bells peal, but are not in themselves a peal.

A PEDAGOGUE ORIGINALLY MEANT A TEACHER

The Greek *paidagogos* was "a slave who led a boy to school, *hence* [my italics], a tutor, instructor", and not originally the boy's teacher. It was in Latin that *paedagogus* came to mean "a preceptor", and this usage passed into French and other modern languages with its changed meaning.

Source: Walter W. Skeat, *An etymological dictionary of the English language* (Oxford, 1888).

PERPETUAL MOTION CAN BE ACHIEVED BY AN 'OVERBALANCING WHEEL' MECHANISM

This idea has been 'discovered' time and again by inventors the world over. Henry Dircks, for instance, illustrates in his *Perpetuum mobile* (London, 1861; second series, 1870), machines of this type by the Marquis of Worcester and Dircks himself. The weight of each smaller ball and its attached rod slightly exceeds that of the larger ball; in consequence, it extends or contracts the lazy-tongs when the rod is vertical (in other positions the rod is prevented from sliding by stops inside the hub). In spite of the fact that the larger balls on one side of the wheel are much farther from the centre than those on the other, the wheel has no tendency to rotate.

If ingeniously made, the mechanism *wastes* very little power, but cannot generate any.

Source: Rupert T. Gould, *Oddities*, 2nd ed. (London, 1944), for the chapter *Orffyreus' wheel*, pp. 89-116.

ST. PETER WAS THE FIRST BISHOP OF ROME, OR 'POPE'

It is on Jerome's questionable assertion (4th-5th centuries) that Peter was Bishop of Rome for twenty-five years that this common fallacy depends, but while it cannot be disproved that he was ever at Rome, it is likely that the passage in *Acts* XII, 3 *sqq.* on the persecution of the Church by Herod which mentions that after release from prison, Peter "first went to the house of Mary, the mother of John Mark, and afterwards went to 'another place' " refers not to Rome or indeed to any other city, but to another place in Jerusalem. The New Testament nowhere says that St. Peter went to Rome. His name of course was not Peter, but Simon. Jesus called him 'Kepha', the Aramaic word for 'rock' (John, I, 42), of which the Greek equivalent becomes 'Peter' in English.

Source: Donald Attwater, *The Penguin dictionary of saints* (Harmondsworth, 1965).

ST. PETER'S IS THE CATHEDRAL OF ROME

A widespread fallacy, accounting for the fact that when I last visited St. John Lateran (San Giovanni in Laterano) in Rome it was almost completely deserted, though it is in fact not only the Cathedral of Rome, and the Metropolitan Church of its bishops, but "Mother and head of all churches in the city and the world" as its façade inscription pronounces ('omnium urbis et orbis ecclesiarum mater et caput').

Sir Paul Harvey's *Oxford Companion to English Literature* (entry PETER'S, St., Rome) perpetuates the error of calling the Vatican church 'the metropolitan church of the Roman see'.

A LIGHTED CIGARETTE WILL IGNITE **PETROL**

The signs on filling-stations exhorting one to extinguish cigarettes always impressed me (as a non-smoker), but when I perhaps foolishly tried to ignite petrol from a lighter with a friend's cigarette, I failed. When the glowing tobacco was dipped into the petrol it was extinguished. (This is not a recommendation for anyone to smoke at filling-stations, or indeed at all.)

A CHILD OF 11 MAY BUY A CAT OR DOG FROM A **PET SHOP**

In Britain this is not true. The Pet Animals Act of 1951 makes it illegal to sell an animal as a pet to a person under 12.

ALL COMBUSTIBLE SUBSTANCES AND ALL METALS SUSCEPTIBLE TO CALCINATION CONTAIN **PHLOGISTON**

The phlogiston then escapes when the substance is ignited. This idea was originated by Georg Ernst Stahl (1660-1734), who considered that after the escape of the 'phlogiston' only the 'calx' or ash remained. Different substances contained different 'calces' but the 'phlogiston' was common to all. The theory "was self-consistent in most respects, and proved an adequate basis for explaining the results of the very important chemical investigations carried out especially by Black, Priestley, Scheele, and Cavendish", according to D. L. Hurd and J. J. Kipling in *The origins and growth of physical science* (vol. 1. Harmondsworth, 1964, p. 85), but only because the many modern descriptions of chemical reactions could be described in terms of the phlogiston theory as a result of the virtual interchangeability of the concepts of 'uptake of oxygen' (which occurs) and 'evolution of phlogiston', which does not.

The erroneous theory of phlogiston was supported by Marggraf (1709-1782), Macquer (1718-1784), Black (1728-1799), Cavendish (1731-1810), Priestley (1733-1804), Bergman (1734-1784), Scheele (1742-1786) and many more. Dr Joseph Priestley's last scientific work was a vain attempt to argue the truth of the discredited theory.

PHRENOLOGY

A pseudo-science founded by the otherwise able Viennese anatomist Franz Josef Gall on the intrinsically unlikely notion that the outward shape of the skull, when analysed, can reveal the owner's character. The shape of the brain has no influence on the shape of the skull: phrenology has therefore no basis in fact at all, but it it is still widely held to be scientific by cranks and the ignorant, despite the fact that a majority of its own members voted to put the British Phrenological Society into voluntary liquidation in 1967, when most of its important library was divided between University College London and Cambridge University.

See also **METOPOSCOPY**.

Sources: J. A. C. Brown, *Pears medical encyclopædia* (London, 1967) and David de Giustino, *Conquest of mind* (London, 1975), the latter on the British phrenologist George Combe (1787-1852).

PHYSIOGNOMY

The doctrine of a mystical connection between the human body and the universe. The Rosicrucian Robert Fludd attempted in 1619 to demonstrate the link between the microcosm (man) and the macrocosm (universe). This is illusory, but even more so is the supposed indication of destiny by an interpretation of 'the mystery of the human head' which Fludd purported to unravel by dividing the face into three 'worlds'. The 'divine world' is the forehead, the 'physical world' comprises the nose and eyes, and the 'material world' comprises the inverted triangle based on the jaw and chin.

Lavater defined physiognomy as "the knowledge and realisation of the link between the exterior and the interior, the visible surface to the invisibility which it covers".

PI IS EQUAL TO THREE AND ONE-EIGHTH EXACTLY

Despite the fairly widely-acknowledged fact that *pi*, the ratio of the circumference to the diameter of a circle, is equal to roughly 3.14159265 . . . , James Smith (1805-1872) of the Mersey Harbour Board wrote extensively to prove that *pi* was equal to exactly $3\frac{1}{8}$.

For those curious to learn Smith's reasons for his monomania, his books include *The ratio between diameter and circumference in a circle demonstrated by angles, and Euclid's theorem, Prop. 32, Book 1, proved to be fallacious* (Liverpool, 1870) and *The quadrature and geometry of the circle demonstrated* (Liverpool, 1872).

Source: Augustus de Morgan, *A budget of paradoxes* (2nd ed., 2 vols., Chicago, 1915, vol. 2, pp. 103—). Incidentally, de Morgan's great collection of popular and scholarly errors contains many other references to *pi*.

THE 'PICTS' OF SCOTLAND HAVE A KNOWN ORIGIN

T. F. O'Rahilly, in his *Early Irish history and mythology* (Dublin, 1946) refers to the wild speculations of 'archaeologists', some of them professional, historians and linguists on the question of the race and origin of the *Picti*, 'the painted people' (unfortunately for identification, all the *Britanni* tribes were painted). Bede began the wild goose-chase with a theory that the Picti came from Scythia, an Irish tradition. Modern writers have described them as 'Goedels', as 'Brythons', as Celts who spoke a Gallo-Brythonic dialect allied to both Gaulish and Brythonic, and as a pre-Celtic people of non-Indo-European origin. They arrived in Britain in the Early Bronze Age, the Middle Bronze Age, the Late Bronze Age, and in various phases of the early Iron Age, depending on the 'expert' that you happen to read. Affinities have been found for them among the Eskimoes, the Finns, and the Illyrians. The Pictish question has been 'settled', but seldom to the satisfaction of more than the writer, by H. M. Chadwick, V. Gordon Childe, T. Rice Holmes, Henri Hubert, Joseph Loth, R. A. S. Macalister, Eoin MacNeill, Adolf Mahr, O'Rahilly himself, Julius Pokorny, Joseph Raftery, and W. J. Watson. F. T. Wainwright has said that in some of these explanations "the element of fiction, even fantasy, is so pronounced that Bede's story of Scythia appears (by comparison only) to be a model of scientific sobriety".

Insufficient evidence is available at present for the 'Picts' to be identified either by race or origin.

Source: F. T. Wainwright (*editor*), *The problem of the Picts* (London, 1955).

HOMING PIGEONS HAVE AN UNERRING INSTINCT FOR RETURNING TO THEIR POINT OF ORIGIN OVER HUNDREDS OF MILES

Common knowledge, indeed. But not to anyone who has had to train a homing pigeon, beginning from ten feet. Rewards are given to the pigeon for each success, and not for each failure. A homing pigeon cannot be taken completely out of sight of any known landmark and expected to return, so its 'instinct' is in fact

195

simply the use of a visual memory. This is assisted by careful breeding of the birds with the best proven memories. As for the ability of *carrier pigeons*, the U.S. Army Signal Corps (the largest breeder and trainer of carrier pigeons) does not expect its best birds to return over a distance exceeding twenty-five miles, and then only after repeated training flights over the same territory.

Sources: William Rowan, *The riddle of migration* (Baltimore, 1931, p. 81) and *New York Times Magazine*, 27 April 1941, pp. 14, 19.

PLANETS MOVE IN CIRCLES

'Having been created by God, the Universe must be perfect', a false idea, combined with the notion that the circle is the perfection of symmetry to form a non-sequitur 'that planets must necessarily move in circles, or if not in circles, then in curves compounded out of circles'.

This concept, originally formulated by Hipparchus in the 2nd century B.C., led to such complexity that the King of Castile, when the system was explained to him, was driven to remark that had he been present when the universe was constructed, he could have given the Deity some good advice.

Source: W. F. G. Swann, *Error in physics*, in Joseph Jastrow, *The story of human error* (New York, 1936, pp. 130-31).

IF THE WORLD'S PLANKTON ARE POISONED THE MAJOR SOURCE OF OXYGEN WILL BE DESTROYED AND ALL LIFE ON EARTH WILL PERISH

J. Piccard wrote in *Time* (8 November 1971) that "Phytoplankton generate most of the Earth's oxygen. All you need do is knock out the surface phytoplankton and the entire marine life cycle is disrupted". Other writers took up the theme, and the newspapers ran 'scare' stories prophesying the end of the world, which always makes a good story. It is always possible, but not by destroying plankton. L. C. Allen had already quietly pointed out (in *Nature*, 25 July 1970, p. 373) that only 0.0001 % of our oxygen comes from living plants. Most of the rest is the accumulation of 2,000 million years of photosynthesis. Atmospheric carbon dioxide has probably grown by some 11 % since 1890, but carbon dioxide still constitutes less than 0.033 % of our air.

THE **PLEISTOCENE ICE AGE** WAS CAUSED BY A COMET HITTING THE EARTH

This fallacy has been promulgated by a number of theorists, most notably by Ignatius Donnelly (1831-1901), an American lawyer, in his popular *Ragnarok: the age of fire and gravel* (New York, 1882) and by Velikovsky (q.v.).

According to Donnelly, the unstratified clay and gravel found on Earth are not so-called 'till' deposits produced by moving glaciers (as they are stated to be by professional geologists) but the congealed dust from the tail of a comet which also destroyed Sodom and Gomorrah.

This giant comet hit the earth with "world-appalling noises, thunders beyond all earthly thunders, roarings, howlings, and hissings, that shook the globe". After it had passed, and the fires had subsided, an 'Age of Darkness' began and with it the Ice Age.

PNEUMONIA ALWAYS ARRIVES ON AN ODD-NUMBERED DATE

"To take up another of the million fallacies which decline to die of old age or succumb to the teaching of science; just as, 200 years ago, the belief prevailed that the seventh son of a seventh son was foreordained for the medical profession, so today many persons believe that the crisis in such diseases as pneumonia always comes on an odd day—the third, or the seventh, or the ninth. One idea is as ridiculous as the other".

Source: Dr Leonard K. Hirshberg in *The North American*, 11 September 1910.

N.B. If Dr Hirshberg thought that the former belief had died out in 1710 and so convinces my readers, I refer them to p. 84 of my *Come with me to Ireland* (1972), reporting the case of the currently popular Cavan 'doctor' Finbar Nolan. "He is the seventh son of a seventh son, and in Ireland such a prodigy (unless a daughter intervenes) is a born healer".

ELECTIVE **POLARITY**

About 12,500 years ago α Lyrae was the pole-star, according to Frances Barbara Burton's *Elective polarity the universal agent* (London, 1845). She attributes the great size of the now fossil animals to a star of such 'polaric intensity as Vega pouring its magnetic streams through our planet'.

But Miss Burton is reported to have been good at Hebrew.

BRITAIN IS A SOCIETY WITH LESS **POLICE** SURVEILLANCE THAN ANY OTHER

Not according to the *Police Review*, discussing in a 1976 editorial the Police National Computer-Unit based in Hendon, whose experts predict that by 1979 this unit will have on file more than 36 million names and entries. "It is to be far more comprehensive than any other computerized intelligence service in the world". The police claim that the computer contains data only on stolen vehicles and convicted criminals, but the size and structure of the installation is such that it must contain information about innocent members of the public which could then be used against them by friendly or unfriendly governments who obtained licit or illicit access to the computer.

After U.S. Pentagon intelligence officials disclosed that dossiers had been compiled on 25 million innocent American citizens, the U.S. Government ordered most of the dossiers to be destroyed. The U.K. National Health Service computers contain secret and personal details about many millions of people. The patient has no right to see his own medical record, but those who happen to obtain access to the computer can check on it at any time for whatever purpose can be justified. The British M.P. Brian Walden, a member of the Franks Committee to examine the Official Secrets Act in 1971, concludes that "Some of the activities of the state security services are grossly intrusive and some of the consequences of their actions are very unfair to individuals".

POLITICAL FALLACIES

The standard work is still *The book of fallacies* (London, 1824) by Jeremy Bentham, in its revision by Harold A. Larrabee (Baltimore, 1952).

Bentham defines a fallacy as "any argument employed or topic suggested for the purpose, or with the probability of producing the effect of deception, or of causing some erroneous opinion to be entertained by any person to whose mind such an argument may have been presented".

He lists four causes of fallacies: self-conscious sinister interest, interest-begotten prejudice, authority-begotten prejudice, and self-defence against counter-fallacies.

There are four major types of fallacy in Bentham's view: fallacies of authority (including our ancestors); of danger (including distrust of innovation); of delay (including the procrastinator's argument); and of confusion (including sham distinctions, allegorical idols, and question-begging epithets).

BRITISH **POLITICS** IS GOVERNED BY LOGICAL CONSIDERATIONS

"I profoundly distrust logic when applied to politics, and all English history justifies me. [Ministerial cheers]. Why is it that, as contrasted with other nations, ours has been a peaceful and not a violent development? Why is it that, great as have been the changes that have taken place in this country, we have had none of those sudden revolutions and reactions for the last three hundred years that have so frequently affected more logically-minded nations than ourselves? It is because instinct and experience alike teach us that human nature is not logical, that it is unwise to treat political institutions as instruments of logic, and that it is in wisely refraining from pressing conclusions to their logical end the path of peaceful development and true reform is really found".

Source: Austen Chamberlain, speaking in the House of Commons against the Geneva Protocol on 24 March 1925, as reported in *The Times*, 25 March 1925.

PUBLIC OPINION **POLLS** ARE AN INVENTION OF THE 20TH CENTURY

Quite untrue. The *Harrisburg Pennsylvanian* of 24 July 1824 reported a random sampling of 532 electors in Wilmington (Delaware) which showed a clear lead for Andrew Jackson over John Quincy Adams and the other two candidates. The fact that none of the four candidates obtained a majority that year and the House of Representatives elected Adams as President does not prove that all polls are unreliable; it merely points to the fallacy of believing polls either reliable *or* unreliable. Polls are merely an indication of probability: the larger the sample, the greater the probability that they are correct.

POLTERGEISTS

From the German 'Polter' (noise)+'Geist' (spirit), an alleged 'ghost' capable of making its presence known by noises; often extended to the phenomena of 'throwing spirits'. There is of course no such thing as a poltergeist in Germany or anywhere else, despite works such as Nandor Fodor and Hereward Carrington's *The story of the poltergeist down the centuries* (London, 1953).

Literally thousands of cases have been reported by the gullible public to the cynical media over the centuries. In France, there was the case of St Jean Marie Baptiste Vianney (1786-1859), Curé d'Ars. In his book *The Curé d'Ars* (London, 1927), Abbé Francis Trochu says of the villagers and Vianney, "The name of M. Vianney got into their low songs; anonymous letters, full of the basest insinuations, were sent to him, broadsheets of a like nature were placarded on the door of the presbytery, and at night a wild hubbub took place under his windows ... His front door was splashed with dirt, and for a space of eighteen months a miserable creature stood, night after night, under his windows, insulting and reproaching him as if he had been guilty of leading a disorderly life".

Despite these known natural phenomena, it was apparently necessary to attribute to the Devil and to poltergeists subsequent phenomena such as blows "struck against doors" and shouts "heard in the yard in front of the presbytery". Just as Vianney was able to fall asleep, "he would start up, awakened by shouts, mournful cries, and formidable blows. It seemed as if the front door were being battered in with a sledge-hammer. Suddenly, without a latch having been moved, the Curé d'Ars perceived with horror that the Devil was close to him". But of course, it was merely the villagers' further vindictive attempts to get rid of him.

A similar case of a 'poltergeist' at Epworth Rectory in North Lincolnshire was recorded during December 1716 and January 1717, by Samuel Wesley's wife and daughters. Many studies have been devoted to the story, one at book length in Dudley Wright's *The Epworth phenomena* (London, 1917). Frank Podmore, in *Modern spiritualism* (vol. 1, London, 1902, pp. 38-39) attributes the phenomena to Wesley's daughter Hetty, a suggestion scorned by G. W. Lambert as 'ridiculous'. Lambert, in vol. 38 (June 1955) of the *Journal* of the Society for Psychical Research, blames the tidal river Trent (actually four miles from Epworth). The likeliest explanation, as offered by Trevor H. Hall in *The Rationalist Annual* (vol. 83, 1966, pp. 3-14), is the same as the most reasonable explanation of the Curé d'Ars affair, that is to say that the noises were caused by vindictive neighbours and parishioners who wanted to get rid of a clergyman they hated. This is all the more likely when one realizes, in the words of W. H. Fitchett (*Wesley and his century*, London, 1906), that "The stubborn fenmen did not take kindly to those who, like the Wesleys, were not of their stock . . . They stabbed the little rector's cows, maimed his sheep, broke the dams at night to flood his little fields. They harried him for his debts, [and] tried, not unsuccessfully, to burn his parsonage over his head. Then they accused him of having set fire to it himself".

But poltergeist traditions occur all over the world, and once a timid mind has been tamed with threats of an inimical spirit, it soon grows to fear any falling object or strange noise. 'Spontaneous' throwing or falling is invariably attributed to one person in the family, and spiritualists explain this by suggesting that that person is 'psychic' and attracts the poltergeist. In fact, the person (usually an adolescent boy or girl) is solely responsible for the phenomena, and maladjusted children, often bored, seek to draw attention to themselves by causing the phenomena—many cases are documented in the literature of psychical research. As Lyall Watson writes in the otherwise credulous best-seller *Supernature* (New York, 1973), poltergeist phenomena are "produced unconsciously by someone in the vicinity suffering from a frustration of pent-up aggression".

Tinnitus is a recognized complaint which consists of hallucinatory noises, usually singing, caused by inflammation of the middle ear. Some tactile hallucinations are due to the early stages of psychosis, while the reports of elderly people that they are being pricked or nudged by poltergeists are attributable to neurotic delusions. The delusions are real enough, but there are no poltergeists!

WAS THERE A 'POPE JOAN'?

A scandalous story, still widely believed, alleges that in 855, between the pontificates of Leo IV and Benedict III, a woman was unanimously elected Pope. The philosopher Leibniz lent his support to the following absurd tale. A young Englishwoman called Joan, born at Ingelheim near Mainz, travelled in a monk's habit from Fulda to Athens, and later in Rome so delighted churchmen by her learning that, still in male attire, she became known as 'the Roman wonder'. After being elected pope, she had an affair with her valet, which came to light when, in the course of a procession from the Colosseum to the church of S. Clemente, she gave birth to a child and died. Friedrich Gontard, who writes of Pope Joan in *Die Päpste* (Munich, 1959), suggests that "the fable probably originated in the tenth century when, over a period of sixty-seven years, each pope was more sinister, more worthless, and more dangerous than the one before him". The story continued to obtain credence until the 16th century, for the tradition says that every Pope up to Leo X (1513-21) had to undergo a sex test. At the enthronement ceremony an antique chair with an open seat (the *sella stercoraria*) was occupied by the newly-elected Pope; after due examination a deacon called out *Habet!* ('He has'), whereupon the people of Roman chorussed *Deo gratias!* ('Thanks be to God!').

A papal bust of 'John VIII, a woman from England' in Siena Cathedral was renamed 'Pope Zachary' by Pope Clement VIII (1592-1605). See also Lawrence Durrell's amusing novel on the non-existent woman, *Pope Joan*, which of course merely had the effect of reawakening the popular fallacy that such a pope had once existed.

POWDERED GLASS IS POISONOUS

Oddly enough, there is quite a literature refuting this fallacy, topped by Dr Richard Mead, physician to King George II, who offered, if someone gave him two large diamonds, to crush one to a powder and eat even that!

It is alleged, without documentary proof yet known to me, that oriental monarchs were poisoned by drinking powdered glass in coffee. If the glass were so coarsely powdered as to produce mechanical injury to the alimentary canal (which would not be *poisoning* at all), it would presumably be noticed by the drinker; if on the contrary it were finely powdered, it would cause no injury of any kind. Details of experiments proving this were made available in Pierre Jean George Cabanis' *Les curiosités de la médecine*. The same error has been dealt with by Sir Thomas Browne in Book II, chapter V, section 2 of his *Pseudodoxia epidemica* (London, 1646) and by John Phin in his *Seven follies of science* (New York, 1912, p. 211).

PREFORMATION

A group of seventeenth-century zoologists claimed to discern all the necessary parts of an adult being preformed in the individual egg. Charles Bonnet suggested about 1750 that every female contains the germs of all her descendants, enclosed one within another. He actually did see a new generation forming within and emerging from the body of the plant-louse and felt justified in formulating his idea as a general principle. He did however combat the erroneous scientific explanation of the vitalistic philosophy by pointing out that the bodily functions work on mechanistic principles and that the use of the "soul" as an explanation is merely a facile begging of the question.

Source: Howard M. Parshley, *Error in zoology*, in Joseph Jastrow, *The story of human error* (New York, 1936).

IT IS BAD GRAMMAR TO END A SENTENCE WITH A **PREPOSITION**

It would instead be accurate to state that "if it is possible to end a sentence less awkwardly than with a preposition, the preposition should be avoided". But it would sometimes be much more awkward to avoid the preposition. What about this sentence, culled from a war-time *Reader's Digest*?

"Little Tommy, ill upstairs, complained to his mother as she sat down to read to him: 'What did you bring that book I didn't want to be read to out of up for?' "

"It is a good rule to go by" is a better sentence than the clumsy "It is a good rule by which to go".

NO WOMAN OR NEGRO CAN BECOME **PRESIDENT** OF THE U.S.A.

Both these categories of U.S. citizen *can* in fact become President of the U.S.A., who must be a natural-born citizen, be at least 35 years old, and at least 14 years a resident of the U.S.A.

Source: *Our American government* (Washington, 1963).

PRIVATE MEANINGS FOR PUBLIC WORDS

One commits a grievous fallacy when discussing matters with words of commonly agreed meanings yet with a private significance. In the B.B.C. Brains Trust programmes during and just after World War II, Professor C. E. M. Joad earned a remarkable notoriety for his refusal to be bamboozled by such ambiguities: "it depends what you mean by . . . " was his method of clarifying any given points to be debated.

He would have been rightly impatient with the nineteenth-century lady who complained that she did not like a house because it was 'very romantic'. Sir Lewis Namier, in his essay 'History and political culture' in the symposium *Varieties of history*, ed. by Fritz Stern (New York, 1956), records that when her puzzled correspondent asked her why she should not have wished it to be 'very romantic', the lady replied, 'When I said *romantic* I meant *damp*'.

THE FALLACY OF **PROJECTION** IN AESTHETICS

"It has to be recognized that all our natural turns of speech are misleading, especially those we use in discussing works of art. We become so accustomed to them that even when we are aware that they are ellipses, it is easy to forget the fact. And it has been extremely difficult in many cases to discover that any ellipsis is present. We are accustomed to say that a picture is beautiful, instead of saying that it causes an experience in us which is valuable in certain ways.* The discovery that the remark, 'This is beautiful', must be turned round and expanded in this way before it is anything but a mere noise signalling the fact that we approve of the picture, was a great and difficult achievement. Even today, such is the insidious power of grammatical forms, the belief that there is such a quality or attribute, namely Beauty, which attaches to the things which we rightly call beautiful, is probably inevitable for all reflective persons at a certain stage of their mental development.

Even among those who have escaped from this delusion and are well aware that we continually talk as though things possess qualities, when what we ought to say is that they cause effects in us of one kind or another, the fallacy of 'projecting' the effect and making it a quality of its cause tends to recur. When it does so it gives a peculiar obliquity to thought and although few competent persons are nowadays so deluded as actually to hold the mystical

---

*"We can diagrammatically represent the delusion as follows. What actually occurs is that A, a work of art, causes E an effect *in us*, which has the character B; A *causes* E. We *speak* as though we perceived that A has the quality B (Beauty); we are perceiving A; and if we are not careful we think so too. No one of our recent revolutions in thought is more important than this progressive rediscovery of what we are talking about. It is being inevitably followed by wide changes in our attitudes to the world and to fellow-creatures. One current in this change is towards tolerance, another towards scepticism, a third towards far more secure founding of our motives of action. The startling philosophical changes in the general outlook sometimes predicted for Relativity (or for popular ideas about it when once they become widespread) appear likely, if they occur at all, to be engulfed by these more unobtrusive but more domestic changes".

view that there is a quality Beauty which inheres or attaches to external objects, yet throughout all the discussion of works of art the drag exercised by language towards this view can be felt. It perceptibly increases the difficulty of innumerable problems and we shall have constantly to allow for it. Such terms as 'construction', 'form', 'balance', 'composition', 'design', 'unity', 'expression', for all the arts; as 'depth', 'movement', 'texture', 'solidity', in the criticism of painting; as 'rhythm', 'stress', 'plot', 'character', in literary criticism; as 'harmony', 'atmosphere', 'development', in music, are instances. All these terms are currently used as though they stood for qualities inherent in things outside the mind, as a painting, in the sense of an assemblage of pigments, is undoubtedly outside the mind".

Source: I. A. Richards, *Principles of literary criticism* (London, 1967, pp. 13-14). The whole book is of the highest value in its alertness to aesthetic fallacies.

PROPHECY

If one out of every hundred predictions comes true, as seems more than reasonable according to statistical probability, that hundredth prediction is greeted by the gullible as a prodigy, when it is of course a mere coincidence. Nobody has ever bothered to count up all the predictions that went wrong: it is much more exciting to tot up the right ones. 'The End of the World' is, however, one of the frequent prophecies that seems to be honoured more in the breach than the observance, but thousands of others can be read in world journalism. Take for instance the 'tidal wave' that was to destroy Weymouth at 3.53 p.m. on 29 May 1928.

IT IS POSSIBLE TO **PROPHESY** NATURAL DISASTERS

There are so many earthquakes in Japan and the related zones that no skill is required to anticipate further disasters of the same type. The type of prophecy which is irrational is that based on no knowledge of natural phenomena.

A recent example that comes to mind is that of the Australian house-painter John Nash. His first prediction was that Adelaide would be destroyed by an earthquake and engulfed by a tidal wave on 19 January 1976. The only result of the prophecy was that thousands irrationally abandoned their homes. When nothing happened, Nash decided to leave Adelaide and settle in Warwick, Queensland. His second prophecy was that Warwick would be the safest place in Australia. Unluckily for Nash, within a few days Warwick—like much of eastern Australia (but not Adelaide!) was hit by the severest floods ever known in that region.

All prophecies based on fear and ignorance are fallacious, and should be ridiculed.

THE **PROPORTIONS** OF THE HUMAN BODY WERE DISCOVERED BY ITALIAN RENAISSANCE ARTISTS

A large number of fallacies concerned with 'inventions' or 'discoveries' derive from the loss of knowledge through inadequate libraries and missing links in the chain of scholarship. Rediscoveries and reinvented methods or techniques are often claimed to be new, and while fraud may sometimes be involved, plain human ignorance and failure to do basic research are the normal reasons for a false claim to originality.

The proportions of the human body were investigated four thousand years before the Italian Renaissance by Egyptian artists. A human hand measured one square of a grid, and by the same grid-measure a man's height was determined at 18 squares.

Source: British Museum Egyptian Gallery, Case J: Scribes and Artists, 1976.

PROVIDENCE

'Providence' may be defined as 'obtaining one's just reward in the future by the simultaneous or successive occurrence of pre-ordained events', and is—at least thus defined—a very prevalent fallacy.

The absorbing *Curiosities of literature* (3 vols., 1791-1823) by Isaac D'Israeli (1766-1848; it was his son Benjamin, 1st Earl of Beaconsfield, who changed his style to 'Disraeli') has a chapter "Of a history of events which have not happened" (see also **PROPHECY**). It begins with an indictment of the fallacious notion of Providence. "Some mortals have recently written history, and "Lectures on history", who presume to explain the great scene of human affairs, affecting the same familiarity with the designs of Providence as with the events which they compile from human authorities. Every party discovers in the events which at first were adverse to their own cause but finally terminate in their own favour, that Providence had used a peculiar and particular inter-ference; this is a source of human error and intolerant prejudice. The Jesuit Mariana, exulting over the destruction of the Goths in Spain, observed that "It was by a particular providence that out of their ashes might rise a new and holy Spain, to be the bulwark of the catholic religion"; and unquestionably he would have adduced as proofs of this "holy Spain" the establishment of the Inquisition, and the dark idolatrous bigotry of that hoodwinked people. But a protestant will not sympathise with the feelings of the Jesuit; yet the protestants, too, will discover particular provi-dences, and magnify human events into supernatural ones".

Livy was guilty of this fallacy when speculating idly on the consequences which might have resulted had Alexander the Great invaded Italy.

PSYCHICAL RESEARCH HAS PRODUCED POSITIVE RESULTS

Speaking on "Laws, miracles, and repeatability" at a Rationalist Press Association Conference on the theme of 'Science and the Paranormal', in 1975, Professor Antony Flew, of the University of Reading, stated that "though people have gone on working in this area [of psychical research]—perhaps more has been done in the last twenty-two years than in any comparable period before—it still seems to me that the general evidential situation is just the same".

Professor Flew's conclusion in *A new approach to psychical research* (London, 1953) had been that "there was no such thing as a reliably repeatable phenomenon in the area, and there was really almost nothing positive that you could point to with assur-ance; there were some bits of negative work you could point to with assurance, but that was all".

PSYCHOMETRY

Psychometry, also known as 'object-reading', will be treated here as a fallacy since the burden of proof for the existence of psycho-metric phenomena contradicting or supplementing currently-accepted verifiable phenomena lies on those who wish to prove the case but have so far failed to do so. It is a branch of extra-sensory perception and is subject to the same criticisms which are frequently applied to other branches: that is to say that there is no evidence yet universally acceptable to the objective investigator despite the great mass of reporting which has been done.

W. G. Roll has advocated belief in psychometry in an article on Gustav Pagenstecher (1855-1942), a German doctor working in Mexico, in the *Journal* of the American Society for Psychical Research (no. 61, 1967). Pagenstecher worked with only one person, the 'sensitive' Maria Zierold, whom he 'tested' by giving her an object which was then used as the centre of object associations. The principle is that if a piece of string is detached from an identification plate used by a German soldier during World War I and shown to Mrs Zierold, she could connect it with its original associations. An ability to do this is considered virtually proven if a likely association results in one or more tests, but cases of failure are seldom or never recorded and it is impossible to double-check original results.

The controversial Dr J. B. Rhine stated his belief in psychometry in *New worlds of the mind* (New York, 1953), defining it as clairvoyant 'free association' in connection with a token object. Psychometric archaeology has been defended by John Foster Forbes in such strange works as *The unchronicled past* (London, 1938) and object association is common in radiesthesia and other pseudo-medical practices. Belief in the healing powers of sacred relics is also a form of psychometrical belief. Dowsers and other mediums claim to detect oil-bearing or water-bearing strata and spirits of the dead respectively by object association, though there is so far no evidence that success has been other than accidental or of more than average frequency.

ARCHAEOLOGY CAN BE ASSISTED BY PSYCHOMETRY

The revival of fascination with the occult characteristic of western civilization in the 1970s might be exemplified by an attractively-produced pictorial book by Janet and Colin Bord called *Mysterious Britain* (London, 1972), which attaches equal and uncritical significance to prehistoric circles, holy wells, mazes, leys and tracks, and King Arthur. A photograph of stone walls of herringbone design in Cornwall is captioned with the suggestion that these walls "show Cretan influence, this design being common in the walls on the island of Crete".

Mr and Mrs Bord repeat as factual evidence the results of a visit to Glastonbury Tor of John Foster Forbes and the psychometrist Iris Campbell in 1945. Forbes had already written two works which propounded the value of psychometry to archaeological research, so he can hardly be considered an objective investigator. He and Miss Campbell visited Glastonbury Tor specifically to record impressions that Miss Campbell received with a view to 'throwing more light on its early history'. The Bords relate that the rites practised on the Tor "were designed to restore bird and flower life forms to a more complete condition, [having] become greatly impaired due to the succession of natural calamities that had befallen the earth. The ritual involved a dance of circular motion, moving sunwise and upwards round the spiral path. A tremendous vortex of power was produced which, on an etheric level, created a canopy of a 'glazed substance'. This could act as a receiving centre for the absorption and refraction of regenerative forces to which the bird and flower life could respond".

It is not clear what this means, if anything, but its connection with verifiable archaeological evidence is inexistent, and it would be a service if commentators were to say so. John Foster Forbes' applications of psychometry to archaeology can be read in *The unchronicled past* (London, 1938), *Ages not so dark* (1939), and *Giants of Britain* (1945).

PYRAMIDS OF EGYPT

The best-known pyramids of Egypt have occupied the imagination of cranks of many countries for several centuries, and no attempt is made here to summarize the numerous occult and pseudo-scientific interpretations of these funerary monuments. All known pyramids contain or have once contained sarcophagi, and most bear the names of the kings buried within them. The pyramid of Cheops was *not* an astronomical observatory-cum-table of measurement which can be interpreted as a chronological guide to the principal events of past and future history. The methods of planning and construction are known in outline, if not in full detail, and are adequately published in I. E. S. Edwards' *The Pyramids of Egypt* (1947), though it was W. M. Flinders Petrie, in *The Pyramids and Temples of Gizeh* (London, 1883), who first proved that all the pyramids were intended and used as tombs.

One important fallacy still prevalent was first propounded by Richard Lepsius, who suggested that their size corresponded to the length of their owner's reign: this is known as the 'accretion theory'. It is odd that it should have been suggested at all, since all one needs to refute it is a chronology of Pharaonic Egypt together with a tape measure. Thus, the pyramid of Pepi II (who reigned for 94 years) should have become several times as large as that of Mykerinos, who reigned for about 18 years. In fact, the considerations involved were probably the ruler's inclination, power, and religious beliefs.

Leonard Cottrell, an excellent popularizer of Egyptology, has an absorbing chapter in *The mountains of Pharaoh* (London, 1956) entitled 'The great Pyramidiot' devoted to a handful of those cranks whose "prophecies have often been proved wrong, their calculations inaccurate, their theories unacceptable by any unprejudiced mind". Yet Cottrell rightly complains that these theorists still have their followers, especially since one of them, Charles Piazzi Smyth, was not only Astronomer-Royal for Scotland but a brilliant mathematician and a fluent, engaging writer. His absurd, fantastic works included *Life and work at the Great Pyramid* . . . (3 vols., Edinburgh, 1867); *Our inheritance in the Great Pyramid* (London, 1864); and an undignified attack, *The Great Pyramid and the Royal Society* (London, 1874), when the Society rightly rejected a paper on his interpretation of the design of the Great Pyramid.

Smyth was of course not an Egyptologist at all, and denied that the Ancient Egyptians designed the Great Pyramid, though he admits that they may have laboured on it. It was not a tomb, but a mysterious laboratory interpretable by mathematical calculations based on the dimensions, capacities and proportions of its outer structure and inner galleries and chambers. He was insp- by another crank study: *The Great Pyramid. Why was it built? And who built it?* (London, 1859) by a publisher, John Taylor. A clue to his methods can be obtained from the fact that the Pyramid's measurements were not exactly round numbers in any known system of mensuration, so Smyth invented the 'Pyramid inch', corresponding to .999 of a British inch. He then measures the base line of the Pyramid (inaccurately, according to Flinders Petrie) and after dividing it by 366 (which is not exactly the number of days in a natural year), he finds that the resultant length (roughly 24 British inches) is "a length approaching nearly one ten-millionth of the earth's semi-axis of rotation". From this meaningless figure, Smyth feels able to deduce that the architect of the Great Pyramid had "laid out the size of the Great Pyramid's base with a measuring rod 25 inches long in his hand; and in his head, the number of days and parts of a day in a year, coupled with the intention to represent that number of days in terms of that rod on each base side of the building".

The Revd. John Davidson and Edgar Stewart are others of that legion of pyramidologists whose motive was less to understand and appreciate the civilization of Pharaonic Egypt than to demonstrate to the world their own ingenuity.

Moralizing over the Great Pyramid with not the slightest idea of its purpose, Samuel Johnson wrote in *Rasselas* (1759): "No reason has ever been given adequate to the cost and labour of the work. The narrowness of the chambers proves that it could afford no retreat from enemies, and treasures might have been reposited, at far less expense, with equal security. It seems to have been erected only in compliance with that hunger of imagination, which preys incessantly upon life, and must always be appeased by some employment. Those who have already all that they can enjoy, must enlarge their desires. He that has built for use, till use is supplied, must begin to build for vanity, and extend his plan to the utmost power of human performance, that he may not be soon reduced to form another wish. I consider this mighty structure, as a monument of the insufficiency of human enjoyments". I consider this judgment a piece of pompous drivel which sheds more light on the preoccupations of the author of *The vanity of human wishes* than on the subject of his digression.

Quell: What you say often seems negative—without a principle to follow.

Finger (pleased): That's it. So many people pretending to have the whole truth, the citizens we need are those who know they haven't the whole truth: call them 'the enquirers'. They're the men who decide on a provisional solution in a particular context.—PHILIP WARD, *The Quell-Finger Dialogues* (North Harrow, 1965).

QUICKLIME DESTROYS A CORPSE

Some writers of detective stories still labour under the odd delusion that quicklime will 'eat' a dead body, and it helped to convict the multiple murderess Mrs Belle Gunness of La Porte, Indiana, whose fourteen victims were excellently preserved in the tell-tale substance.

Source: Stewart Holbrook, *Murder out yonder* (New York, 1941, p. 141).

QUICKSANDS SUCK IN HUMAN BEINGS

So do rivers, come to that, but quicksands (a mixture of sand and water) will support the human body much more easily than water unmixed with sand. A sucking sound that panicking victims fear is made only when a large object or person is pulled *out* of a quicksand. The force creating the suction is in the puller, not in the quicksand or bog, or whatever the quagmire may be. The danger lies simply in exhausting oneself by struggling; those who do not struggle seldom sink below the armpits.

So don't panic. If you sense you are getting into a quicksand, lie down and *roll* across it. If it should be too soft to roll on, lie on your back with your mouth as high as possible. The quicksand is denser than your body, and so your body cannot sink completely into it.

Source: Lawrence Perez, in *Science News Letter*, 12 April 1941, p. 232.

THE RELIGION OF THE HOLY QUR'AN IS MUHAMMADANISM

The name is totally incorrect. The religion of the Holy *Qur'an* is called Islam (surrender [to Allah, or God]), and the inference by the *Shorter Oxford English Dictionary* (3rd ed. as revised and corrected, Oxford, 1955) and similar sources is that the religion worships Muhammad, as Christianity takes Jesus Christ to be one of the Holy Trinity. But nothing could be farther from the truth: Muslims worship only God, whose most recent prophet was Muhammad.

This fallacy, perpetuated by the title *Mohammedanism* of D. S. Margoliouth's text for the "Home university library", has been repeatedly refuted, again recently in the official Egyptian Government publication *The religion of Islam* (Cairo, n.d.), where Maulana Muhammad 'Ali states: "the name Muhammadanism was absolutely unknown to the followers of that religion to which it has been given by the Western writers, and is not to be found either in the Holy *Qur'an* or in the sayings of the Holy Prophet".

R

"Reasons are not like garments, the worse for wearing."—THE
EARL OF ESSEX to Lord Willoughby, 4 January 1599.

A RABBIT SHOULD BE PICKED UP BY THE EARS

Merely because a rabbit's ears are relatively large, it does not
follow that rabbits should be picked up by their ears, as the popular theory goes. They should be picked up by the skin behind the
shoulders, as guinea-pigs should. Cats should be lifted below the
front part of the body, with the back legs resting on your arm.
Geese or swans should be picked up by the wings just behind the
back, never by the delicate legs. Small cage-birds such as canaries
should be enclosed in the hand from the back, taking care not to
grip them too tightly.

RABIES

Fallacies connected with hydrophobia or rabies include the following:
1. That it can be cured by the use of a madstone.
2. That it can be prevented if the dog that has bitten a person is
   immediately killed.
3. That mad dogs foam at the mouth and are always greatly
   excited.
4. That it can be prevented by applying to the wound some of the
   hair of the dog that did the biting. [This nonsense was attributed by Athenaios in his *Deipnosophistai*, or 'Banquet of the
   Learned' in the 3rd century A.D. to the Greek comedian Aristo-
   phanes (448-380 B.C.)]

Source: A. A. Thomen, *Doctors don't believe it* (New York, 1935, pp.
321-8).

THERE IS AN ENTITY KNOWN AS A 'RACIAL SOUL'

Racists who feel able to discern which races are inherently superior and which others inherently inferior (for purposes of their
own) have postulated not only the existence of a 'racial soul', but

even its colours, one for each race. Thus, in H. Guenther's *Rassen-kunde des deutschen Volkes* (Munich, 1922), the soul of the Dinaric people seems to be of a dark green colour.

RACIST FALLACIES

A race can be understood to refer to a 'gene pool' or 'breeding population' in the broad sense: those who share a common genetic heritage and certain observable statistical regularities in their genetic composition.

But this admission must be immediately qualified. There is so far no clear taxonomy or classification of the 'gene pools' and students of race can be divided into the 'lumpers' such as Carleton Coon, who divide races into a few great groups (in his case the Capoid, Australoid, Congoloid, Mongoloid and Caucasoid); and the 'splitters', who divide races into many thousands of species.

Gene pools have always been unstable, and this process is accelerating according to current research in biochemistry and genetics.

Finally, races are not easily definable groups. They have a statistically definable membership and a common history, but they have no group structure and no normative patterns of conduct, at least in the broad sense.

But any other interpretation of the human races' uniqueness is likely to fall foul of M. F. Ashley Montagu's too sweeping *Man's most dangerous myth: the fallacy of race* (3rd ed., New York, 1952) at the end of the spectrum which scorns the concept of race as unacceptable, or Carleton Coon's *The living races of man* (New York, 1965) at the end of the spectrum which overstates the significance of racial difference. It is politically 'liberal' to understate racial difference and politically 'reactionary' to overstate it. The objective reader will probably wish to take as a guide writers such as Stanley Garn, whose *Human races* (Springfield, Ill., 1961) avoids the hysteria usually associated with this subject.

Source: David H. Fischer, *Historians' fallacies* (New York, 1970, pp. 232-3).

RADIESTHESIA

While there is undoubtedly a basis of sensory perception to some claims made by some dowsers (see **DOWSING**), the recent cult of radiesthesia is unacceptable because it exaggerates the potential of dowsing to an impossible level. The less reputable dowsers now claim that, among other capabilities, they can forecast the future, detect the presence of thieves or stolen goods, dowse for minerals or water over maps and plans, detect the sex of eggs or unborn children, and even diagnose and cure disease. Those who see rods or pendula sway and waggle in their hands are convinced that they can thereby detect the presence of something or someone (which is a *non sequitur*), and moreover claim that there is a connection between these wagglings and some form of extra-sensory perception. Besterman has stated that practical success does not always carry with it the ability to explain itself. "However", he adds, "no speculation is altogether wasted in a field where ignorance is practically complete".

Reviewing the in-classic *Physics of the divining rod* by J. C. Maby and T. B. Franklin (London, 1939), *Nature* (1940, p, 150) concluded that "The theoretical section, by the second author, postulates some form of cosmic radiation resulting in electro-magnetic waves of ten metres wavelength. There seems to be no direct evidence for such waves, and the author's discussion of their polarization cannot be justified on our present physical knowledge. In presenting facts and theories to the scientific world, there is a well-accepted and necessary procedure. It is to be regretted that the authors have not followed this procedure, thus making the position of the scientific reviewer impossible".

D. H. Rawcliffe observes that the electro-magnetic or 'radiesthetic' theory of dowsing is merely a modernized version of the long-since-discredited theories of Mesmer, Blondlot and Grimes. Radiesthesia as a fallacious 'cure' for hysteria and other diseases is only a more modern idea than the repudiated notions of animal magnetism, electrobiology, and the 'aesthesiogenic agents' of Charcot and Bernheim, who used magnets and metals to 'cure' their hysterical patients.

RAILWAYS WERE BUILT FOR TRAINS

A virtually ubiquitous fallacy. The steam locomotive had not been invented when the first wooden railways were laid. Their purpose was to run trucks of coal from the pithead to the harbour for transportation. Such railways were first used in 1602 at Newcastle-upon-Tyne, England. It was not until 1820 that iron was used for train-tracks, and not until 1857 that iron was replaced by steel.

GUNFIRE PRODUCES RAIN

While so-called 'primitive' tribes enact rainmaking rituals in most parts of the world as they have always done, fallacies about the subject are still prevalent among the world's intelligentsia. Many otherwise intelligent people declare that atomic or nuclear tests have upset the world's climate, though they can adduce no shred of evidence for this. Heavy gunfire as a source of rain has always been criticized. British farmers petitioned the Admiralty in 1910 to postpone the Navy's gunnery exercises, fearing that the explosions would precipitate unwanted rainfall. Coincidental rainfall at the Battle of Waterloo was immediately attributed to cannonfire. Japanese rice-growers use a cannonade to make rain, while French *vignerons* let off their rockets near harvest to stave off impending showers!

Aircraft are used to induce rain to fall from large cumulus clouds at least fifteen degrees below freezing point, but it is quite fallacious to argue that these highly localized experiments can ever have a long-term or global effect. Or that any two groups of citizens would ever agree on a common rainfall policy!

Source: David Gunston, *Scientific rainmaking encounters serious limits* in *Humanist*, January 1968, pp. 22-23.

"RAIN AT SEVEN, FINE AT ELEVEN"

A popular fallacy based upon the error that rain does not last for more than four hours at a time. It might be observed that, having no clock, the rain does not know when (or where) it is seven o'clock, any more than it can recognize eleven.

Similar nonsense includes such sayings as "Fine on Friday, fine on Sunday", which depend for their usage on the general lack of interest in checking dubious generalizations about the weather against the facts. The rain doesn't know about Fridays; neither does the Sun.

See also **WEATHER.**

RECANTATION

Various creeds encourage heretics to recant on their deathbed or claim that their most significant opponents recanted. Thus, the Church of England booklet *The impossibility of agnosticism* by Leith Samuel (1950; frequently reprinted) declares that the atheist Tom Paine cried on his deathbed "Lord Jesus! have mercy upon me". However, Cobbett investigated this story on the spot where it originated and, as G. W. Foote wrote in *Infidel deathbeds* (London, 1888) "The whole story, as far as it related to recantation . . . is a lie from beginning to end".

The fact that someone has recanted is logically no test of the truth or falsehood of the opinions he held either before or after recantation.

The Churches have numerous accounts of non-believers who were converted when helpless on their deathbeds.

The fallacy is that people who are sick and dying are pre-occupied with religious matters; whereas those who have never been attracted to particular theologies during their lifetime are unlikely to take a sudden, genuine interest when their life is slipping away.

RED-HAIRED WOMEN ARE INCLINED TO ANGER

I imagine that this is only true if you are foolish enough to tell an inoffensive lady who happens to have red hair that she is inclined to anger! An old tradition, just as worthless, says that red-headed persons are deceitful and unreliable because Judas Iscariot had red hair! It is extremely unlikely that Judas had red hair (it was more likely black) but even if he had, the colour of his hair would not consequently damn all others with red hair. "Girls with particularly red hair are good or especially evil", says the *Manuel du physionomiste des dames* (Paris, 1843).

An old English rhyme has a different fallacy: a man with black hair but a red beard is the worst man of all.

"A red beard and a black head.
Catch him with a good trick and take him dead".

REINCARNATION

A fallacy known to the Greeks as metempsychosis and part of many religions' dogmas, It was known to the Ancient Egyptians, the American Indians, and still forms an integral part of Hindu and Buddhist beliefs.

Reincarnation became big business when a Colorado businessman named Morey Bernstein published *The search for Bridey Murphy* (1956). The author hypnotized a housewife, Virginia Tighe, who began to recollect an earlier existence as an Irish girl, 'Bridey Murphy'. The United States audience, conditioned to a belief in reincarnation by the medical diagnosis of Edgar Cayce, made the book a best-seller, and millions who read Bernstein's book never learned of the sequel.

Mrs Tighe had in fact been brought up in a house very similar to that of 'Bridey Murphy', one of her neighbours had been a woman called Bridie Murphy, and Mrs Tighe had been in love with Bridie's son. The events claimed by Mrs Tighe to have happened to 'Bridey Murphy' had in fact happened to her.

We are indebted to the *Chicago American* for its brilliant exposé of this particular example of 'reincarnation'. See also **KARMA**.

Sources include: *Journal American* (New York City), June 10 to June 18, 1956, *Time*, June 18, 1956 and *Life*, June 25, 1956.

EINSTEIN'S SPECIAL THEORY OF **RELATIVITY** HAS BEEN DISPROVED BY MILLER

Einstein's special theory of relativity was evolved to explain the failure of the Michelson-Morley experiment (1887) which discovered that the velocity of light, sent out from a moving object, is *not* constant regardless of how fast the light source moves.

In 1927, many years after Einstein had produced this special theory, Dr Dayton C. Miller performed the experiment again and this time detected slight variations in the speed of light which he understood to be a refutation of Einstein. He repeated the experiment again and again to his own satisfaction, and his results were published in celebrated anti-scientific works such as Georges de Bothezat's *Back to Newton* (1936). However, the fallacy of Miller's opposition to Einstein is that of all the repetitions of the Michelson-Morley experiment in dozens of nations by dozens of scientists in different conditions, only Miller's results were positive: every other repetition proved negative.

THE EFFICACY OF SACRED **RELICS**

A Duchess of Alba made her son, who was ill in Paris, drink pulverized relics and wash in them. To the great astonishment of his mother, the child nevertheless died.

Source: Pierre Antoine de La Place, *Pièces intéressantes* (Paris, 1790).

THE 'WHITE' **RHINOCEROS** IS WHITE

Both 'black' and 'white' rhinoceroses are grey-brown in colour. The term 'white' is a corruption of the Afrikaans word *wijd*, which means 'wide', and refers to the animal's lips. The 'black' rhinoceros is distinguishable by its pointed upper lip, used for browsing on thorny bushes, while the white rhinoceros feeds on grass. The rhinoceros' horn does not have a bony core, despite the common assumption: it consists of keratin, the material of which human fingernails are composed.

Source: Zoological Society of London, *London Zoo guide* (London, 1977, p. 27).

MEN HAVE ONE **RIB** FEWER THAN WOMEN

This fallacy, deriving from the Bible (*Genesis* ii. 21-22), can be refuted by anyone who takes the trouble to count on his body (and on that of his wife) or to look at Gray's *Anatomy* or any similar book.

EARTH'S **RING**

Some traditional astronomers may still not know that the Planet Earth once had a ring like that which Saturn proudly possesses to this day. Isaac Newton Vail (1840-1912) of Barnesville, Ohio, described in *Waters above the firmament* (1886) how each planet passed through a phase in which it had a ring like Saturn's. Vail took the example of the Earth's 'ring' to be the source of the flood waters recorded in *Genesis* (see **FLOOD** and NOAH'S **ARK**).

Naturally, if planets other than Saturn had had such a ring, it would have caused related phenomena which are—however—in fact missing. Yet this simple datum of astronomy is ignored by members of the Annular World Association, which courageously promulgates the theories of Vail to a hostile or uncaring world from its headquarters in Azusa, California.

Source: Martin Gardner, *Fads and fallacies in the name of science* (New York, 1957, p. 128).

ALL **ROCKS** ARE DEPOSITIONS FORMED IN SUCCESSION FROM WATER PREVIOUSLY COVERING THE GLOBE

Abraham Gottlob Werner (1749-1817) propounded the above theory, arguing that the minerals (included in his time within the general designation 'fossils') "which constitute the beds and strata of mountains were dissolved in this universal water and were precipitated from it".

Werner and his followers were known as 'Neptunists' as opposed to the 'Plutonists' led by James Hutton (1726-1797) of Edinburgh. The plutonic theory explained granite and similar rocks as the result of a crystallization of molten material far below the earth's surface and far removed from water in its nature. Basalt is formed from lava flows and could not be a precipitation from the sea. Rudolf Raspe (author of *The adventures of Baron Münchhausen*) did much to sink the Neptunist fallacy into oblivion.

Source: A. G. Werner, *New theory of the formation of veins*, translated by Charles Anderson (Edinburgh, 1809).

INDIAN ROPE-TRICK

The 'Indian rope-trick' is claimed to be a conjuring performance in which a small boy climbs a rope in full view of an audience *in the open air* and then disappears. The feat has been replicated on stage easily enough by means of ladders, mirrors, special lighting, and/or light-absorbing material for the boy's clothes. Other variants are the use of a 'rope' consisting of jointed bamboo rods, or the substitution of a monkey dressed in turban and *dhoti* for the boy.

But no Western (or indeed Eastern) conjuror has been able to repeat the stage feat in the open air, as has so often been claimed by the gullible. Lord Northbrook, Viceroy of India, offered £10,000 in 1875 to anyone who would demonstrate the Indian rope-trick. Though the offer was widely advertised, no claimant came forward.

Source: D. H. Rawcliffe, *Illusions and delusions of the supernatural and the occult* (New York, 1959, pp. 297-301).

ROTTEN ROW IN LONDON'S HYDE PARK IS CONNECTED WITH ROTTEN FRUIT OR ROTTEN BOROUGHS

Popular etymology is usually wrong, and here we go again. London's celebrated Rotten Row is merely the English spelling and pronunciation of the French 'Route du Roi' (King's Highway).

THE ROUND TABLE IN WINCHESTER CASTLE DATES BACK TO THE TIME OF KING ARTHUR

The round table which has hung on the wall of Winchester Castle for over 600 years has been the subject of much ill-informed speculation, though Norman Wymer in *The story of Winchester* (London, 1955) has stated that "any suggestion that it may be the authentic 'Round Table' is clearly ridiculous".

'The Mystery of King Arthur and his Round Table' was a BBC 2 television programme produced by Robin Bootle and shown on 20 December 1976; the programme notes in *Radio Times* asked "Did the Knights of the Round Table sit here?", but the team of scientists answered in a resounding negative. The radio-carbon dating gave a period of 1270-1390 (the median date being 1330), the tree-ring evidence showed a date of 1336, and the carpentry typology suggested a date between 1250 and 1350. This conclusive evidence proves that the table dates to about 1336, and was therefore probably made by Edward III in connection with his abortive project for an Order of the Knights of the Round Table.

Source: Personal communication from Robin Bootle, 11 January 1977.

S

"A substantial and severe collection of the heteroclites or irregulars of Nature, well examined and described, I find not: especially not with due rejection of fables and popular errors: for as things now are, if an untruth in Nature be once on foot, what by reason of neglect of examination, and countenance of antiquity, and what by reason of the use of the opinion in similitudes, and ornaments of speech, it is never called down."—FRANCIS BACON, *The advancement of learning* (1605).

THE SAHARA REGION OF NORTHERN AFRICA IS PERENNIALLY DRY

Though the North African desert is, outside the Polar Regions, the least-populated area of the globe, with fewer than two million inhabitants, there is archaeological and even more abundant geological evidence that the 'desert' was once more fertile and even now possesses seven major water regions of underground water reservoirs totalling an estimated 15,000,000 million cubic metres of groundwater. This figure is increasing by some 4,000 million cubic metres a year by the acquisition of rainwater running underground from the desert's fringe areas towards the central rockbound aquifers.

Source: UN Food and Agriculture Organization, Rome.

SANDWICHES WERE INVENTED BY THE FOURTH EARL OF SANDWICH (1718-1792)

No! The compulsive English gambler certainly ate cooked meat between two slices of bread at the tables rather than leave them for an elaborate cooked meal, but the Romans had introduced the idea throughout their Empire seventeen centuries earlier.

IT IS A PROVEN FACT THAT THE SASQUATCH EXISTS

The North American Indians have legends about a forest giant who is called Omah by the Huppa Indians of the Klamath Moun-

223

tains of Northern California; Gilyuk or Toki-Mussi by other tribes of the Pacific Northwest; and Sasquatch (which has become the best-known name) by the Salish of S.W. British Columbia. Sightings and tracks have been recorded over an area exceeding half a million square miles and over a period of a century and more, so it is remarkable to say the least that not a single specimen either alive or dead has ever been shown in a museum or zoo. That is why one must distrust Michael Grumley's assertion in his credulous and sensational *There are Giants in the Earth* (London, 1975) that "Sasquatch, undoubtedly, lives". Tracks do exist, but it is by no means sure what made the 1,000 tracks reported during the eight years from 1955.

See also **GIANTS** and **YETI**.

Sources include: John Green, *The year of the Sasquatch* (Agassiz, B.C., 1970) and *On the track of the Sasquatch* (Agassiz, B.C., 1971) and John Napier, *Bigfoot* (London, 1972).

SCIENTOLOGY

The wittiest exposé of this modern psychological and religious phenomenon is *The mind benders* (London, 1971), by the former scientologist Cyril Vosper. Chris Evans writes in the *New Humanist* (September 1972, p. 196): "Vosper's attack is focussed principally upon the aspects of the cult that, as a one-time senior administrator within it, he knows most about—the inefficient, amateurish administration, the ludicrous self-importance of its officials, the ruthless 'ethics' orders which guide and control the social behaviour of followers and the hefty fees charged for arguably valueless training".

Vosper's central argument does not prove the tenets of scientology fallacious. This is the conclusion of the report, *Enquiry into the practice and effects of Scientology* (London, 1971), issued by a commission headed by Sir John G. Foster and published by Her Majesty's Stationery Office. Lord Windlesham, in an official letter from the Home Office, declared scientology "to be harmful and contrary to the public interest", though the movement's founder, L. Ron Hubbard, was the only scientologist precluded (on 13 August 1970) from entering the United Kingdom whatever the purpose of his visit.

The then Minister of Health, Kenneth Robinson, replied on 5 December 1966 to a question in Parliament, "I do not think that any further enquiry is necessary to establish that the activities of this organisation [the Church of Scientology] are potentially harmful. I have no doubt that Scientology is totally valueless in promoting health and in particular, that people seeking help with problems of mental health can gain nothing from the attentions of this organisation".

Source: *Hansard*, vol. 737, col. 183.

"GREAT SCOTT!" DERIVES FROM SIR WALTER SCOTT

The exclamation "Great Scott!" derived from the United States General Winfield Scott (1786-1866), a notoriously fussy candidate for the presidency in 1852. Scott failed in his bid, but he has a greater—if unwanted—significance as the origin of a popular phrase.

Source: Eric Partridge, *Name into word* (London, 1949).

SCOUTING IS OPEN TO BOYS OF ALL COUNTRIES, CLASSES, AND CREEDS

Scouting has from its foundation in 1908 by Lt.-Gen. Robert Baden-Powell been restricted only to those who swear "to do my duty to God and the Queen". To overcome the discrepancy between 'theism' and 'religion', a World Scout Conference in the 1960s agreed to accept belief in a 'spiritual reality' as a condition of membership.

In 1954, after two young members of the Communist Party had been expelled from the movement, Lord Stansgate proposed the following motion in the House of Lords: "That in the opinion of this House the imposition of political and religious tests by the Boy Scout movement is foreign to its charter and purpose and repugnant to our national tradition and liberty of conscience".

SCROFULA CAN BE CURED BY THE TOUCHING OF ROYAL HANDS

A form of tuberculosis with swelling of the neck glands, scrofula was known as the King's Evil from the fallacious belief that it could be cured by the touch of royal hands. Macaulay's *History of England* (1849-58) records that Charles II touched 92,107 persons, though it is not recorded if any cures were claimed. In 1684, many of the gullible sufferers were trampled to death in the rush to one of the last persons touched by her in 1712 being Samuel Johnson, but the same prerogative was exercised by Prince Charles Edward in 1745.

The first English king to claim that he could cure King's Evil by touching was Edward the Confessor.

In *Magic, myth and medicine* (New York, 1956), D. T. Atkinson reports the fallacious cure for scrofula of flannel which had been dipped nine times in blue dye.

SCRYING

Crystal-gazing or scrying is a worldwide practice but, concludes D. H. Rawcliffe, "despite the claims of psychical research and spiritualism, there is not the least evidence of any supernatural powers accompanying the ability to scry; nor is there any logical reason why there should be. Scrying, when genuine, is simply a convenient method, one of several, of inducing visual hallucinations in individuals who possess either a strong faculty for eidetic imagery or a natural tendency to hallucination due to any one out of a number of possible causes".

It is worth emphasizing that one does not need a crystal ball to scry; in Egypt a pool of ink or blood has been used, while in classical Greece a polished metal mirror was customary, and in Arab countries a fingernail is the point on which the gazer concentrates.

Sources include: D. H. Rawcliffe, *Illusions and delusions of the supernatural and the occult* (New York, 1959, pp. 128-133).

GREEK AND ROMAN SCULPTURE WAS MONOCHROME

Almost all excavated examples of classical sculpture reveal traces of colour, so that the white or cream figures now shown in museums all over Europe, and especially in Greece and Italy, give no idea at all of the polychrome magnificence of the originals. Judging by holes in some of the Elgin Marbles in the British Museum, to give but one instance, real bridles and reins were attached to figures of horses, while humans' sandal-straps were of real leather and stone hands grasped actual weapons.

Gisela Richter writes in *A handbook of Greek art* (London, 1959, p. 46): "All stone sculpture, whether of limestone or marble, was painted, either wholly or in part. Though much of the original colour has disappeared, enough traces remain to make its general use certain, as indeed it had been in Egypt (even for coloured stone) and as was desirable in the brilliant light of Greece. Another general Greek practice was the addition of accessories in different materials. Eyes were sometimes inlaid in coloured stone, glass or ivory; metal curls, diadems and wreaths were added, and even earrings and necklaces; likewise metal spears, swords, and the reins and bridles of horses. Only the holes for attachment now generally remain".

One is mystified. As curators of museums are trained nowadays to provide display facilities to encourage a more imaginative approach on the part of their visitors, and a keener awareness of what life and art were actually like in earlier times, why is it almost unheard of for curators to reconstruct Greek and Roman sculptures in their original colours and with their original trappings? The cost would be very slight and the clues from ancient writers and traces of colour are abundant.

SCURVY CAN BE AVOIDED BY MOVING THE BODY

D. M. Occomore, writing in *The East Anglian Magazine*, December 1976 (p. 79), on Essex step-dancing, states that "The idea was that if a man moved his body he was less likely to contract that curse of seamen's ills, scurvy. The Admiralty insisted that the men dance the hornpipe. Whether this was the origin of the step-dance adopted by landsmen can only be guessed at".

The sole cause of scurvy is a vitamin C deficiency, and the disease was common in naval campaigns when fresh food was difficult to obtain. The remedy for scurvy is a diet including fresh vegetables, most fresh fruit, or lime and lemon juice. The British Navy introduced a regulation issue of lime juice in 1795, and this measure virtually eliminated scurvy; the British Board of Trade introduced a similar measure for the mercantile navy in 1865.

The association of dancing and scurvy is wholly fallacious.

DRINKING SEA WATER CAUSES MADNESS

People can go mad from thirst (and starvation), and shipwreck survivors who drink water will aggravate their thirst, hence the connection of two ideas in reality unconnected. A man requires a minimum of 800 c.c. of water a day (W. S. S. Ladell in *Nature*, 25 March 1944, p. 385), and if there is a shortfall of 200 c.c., then that amount of sea water can be added to the fresh water with beneficial results.

ASIMOV'S SECURITY BELIEFS

During a lifetime as a professional writer of popular (but care-fully-researched) science and science fiction, Isaac Asimov has drawn up a list of fallacies which in his view sustain the majority of mankind and prevent their accepting truth, reason, and responsibility:
1. There exist supernatural forces that can be cajoled or forced into protecting mankind.
2. There is no such thing, really, as death.
3. There is some purpose to the universe.
4. Individuals have special powers that will enable them to get something for nothing.
5. You are better than the next fellow.
6. If anything goes wrong, it's not your fault.

IT IS LEGAL TO SELL YOUR WIFE,
IF DONE IN PUBLIC

The *Annual Record* for 1832 describes the sale of a farmer's wife in Carlisle. The husband placed her in a chair with a straw halter round her neck and offered her for sale. She went for twenty shillings and a Newfoundland dog. The usual causes for such a sale, recorded on many occasions particularly in England in the 18th and 19th centuries, were the inability of a husband to main-tain his wife, or her shrewish tongue or idle nature.

In 1881 a woman at a London County Court produced a stamped receipt to prove that she was not living in adultery with her second 'husband', since her first spouse had sold her for twenty-five shillings some years before. A. R. Wright's *English folklore* (1928) mentions several sales occurring between World War I and World War II, but it is of course nonsense to imagine that wife-selling was ever sanctioned under English *law* at any period.

A PHRASE OR SENTENCE MEANS ONLY
WHAT IT SAYS

Linguistic philosophers have done much in the 20th century to clear away some of the confusion attaching to such problems as single, dual and multiple meanings. However, it is still common to read or hear statements to the effect that *absolute* clarity is possible in normal usage. Ambiguity lurks in most phrases, clauses, and sentences, and we only discern their real meaning in the way that we hear our partner's conversation at a noisy party:

by shutting out the alternatives. For instance, how many meanings can you find at first sight in the phrase "pretty little girls' camp"? The obvious three are "a pretty camp for little girls", "a pretty and little camp for girls" and "a camp for girls who are both pretty and little".

But if you take the word "pretty" in its colloquial sense of "quite", "fairly", or "rather", there are two more interpretations: "a quite little camp for girls" or "a camp for rather little girls".

Source: Willard van Orman Quine, *Elementary logic* (Boston, 1941, pp. 30-31).

A SEVEN-MONTH CHILD WILL LIVE BUT AN EIGHT-MONTH CHILD WILL DIE

This has always been one of the most remarkable of fallacies, for no matter how frequently it is refuted, it refuses to lie down. And it has been refuted by logic, experience, and statistics very many times. As recently as 19 February 1944, the *British Medical Journal* reverted to this error. If we exclude all cases where the foetus is unduly large or post-mature, all evidence shows that the more complete the development of the child "the better are its prospects for survival" (p. 276). The statistics are set out by Potter and Adair in *Foetal and neonatal death* (Chicago, 1940).

SEXUAL FALLACIES

Michael H. Briggs has listed the following fantasies surrounding the problems of sex, birth, and pregnancy:
1. 'Aphrodisiacs' increase sexual desire, as stated by 'Pilaff Bey' in *Venus in the kitchen* (London, 1952), from a reputable publisher. See also WATER IS AN **APHRODISIAC**.
2. Strict dieting during pregnancy will limit the size of the child, in the erroneous view of many mothers.
3. Intercourse, sneezing, and the mother's bumping into objects will affect the development of the child, in the view of L. Ron Hubbard, founder of **SCIENTOLOGY** (q.v.). All gynaecologists know that the baby is protected by amniotic fluids from even severe blows on the mother's body.
4. Numerous births are genuine. A certain Countess Margaret of Henneberg is reputed to have given birth in Easter week 1276 to 365 children the size of mice. 182 were boys christened 'John' by the Bishop of Utrecht, and 182 girls were christened 'Elizabeth'. The odd one out was hermaphroditic. This fan-

tasy is to be found in *Pepysian garland* (London, 1922), edited by H. Rollins.

5. A child's month of birth is significant in later life, according to at least one child psychologist, who claims that Spring children are more successful than those born in Autumn and Winter. This belief was tested in 1933 (see Pintner and Forlando in *Journal of Educational Psychology*, vol. 24, p. 561) by analyzing the distribution of birth months among 25,166 eminent Americans. The differences from month to month were as negligible as would have been required to prove an absence of positive evidence, though as a matter of interest the 'top month' was marginally October!

6. The view that male children are carried on the left and females on the right has been mistakenly believed since the 5th-century B.C. Greek philosopher Parmenides of Elea.

7. The age of females at marriage is thought to vary widely around the world. But it depends what you mean by 'marriage', for the Indian ceremony (which took place generally between the ages of 13 and 14 during the 1930s in India) is more akin to the western practice of engagement, or formal betrothal, and the average age at which Indian mothers (in Bombay and Madras) had their first baby at that time was 18-19.

8. Many people still think that only females menstruate, but many members of the monkey family do also. D. L. Gunn and others exploded the fallacy connecting menstruation (whose cycle averages 28 days) with the lunar cycle (averaging $29\frac{1}{2}$ days) by surveying large groups of women and finding no detectable relationship (*Journal of Obstetrics and Gynaecology*, vol. 44, 1937).

9. Writings by Wilhelm Reich involving his fantastic 'orgone energy' are not to be taken seriously because this alleged energy has not been detected by unbiased observers. Reich compares earthquakes with a sexual embrace preceding coition.

10. Sexual elixirs have been second only to elixirs of life as a trap for the unwary and the gullible. One John R. Brinkley sold one such elixir which, on analysis, proved to be 99.9% water with a trace of hydrochloric acid for flavour and methylene blue for colouring.

Source: Michael H. Briggs, 'Popular fantasies about sex' in *The Humanist*, October 1962, pp. 306-9.

SHAKESPEARE'S PLAYS WERE WRITTEN BY BACON, RUTLAND, OXFORD, STANLEY, MARLOWE, DYER . . .

The theory that Francis Bacon, Viscount St Albans, wrote the plays previously attributed to William Shakespeare appears first to have been suggested by Herbert Lawrence in *The life and adventures of common sense* (1769) but was not to surface again until J. C. Hart's *The romance of yachting* (New York, 1848). Since then the supporters of Bacon have been the chief opposition party to the Stratfordian party which remains in power.

Edward de Vere, 17th Earl of Oxford, was first suggested as a candidate for the authorship by J. T. Looney, ably supported by Percy Allen, William Kent, and others. William Stanley has been suggested since 1890, notably by A. W. Titherley and A. J. Evans. Two of the more recent figures nominated are Sir Edward Dyer (1545-1607), proposed by Alden Brooks, and Christopher Marlowe according to Calvin Hoffman in *The man who was Shakespeare* (London, 1955). But Marlowe was killed in 1593 and Mr Hoffman is forced to suggest a theory that the inquest was a frame-up, and that Marlowe was not killed, but smuggled to the Continent by his patron, Sir Thomas Walsingham, who had arranged for another man to be killed and identified as Marlowe. The real Marlowe survived and passed off his plays as Shakespeare's. They never met (though they were both in London in 1592 and as there were only two theatres there at the time it would have been extremely difficult to avoid meeting) and never influenced each other.

It seems to be fairly probable that Shakespeare is after all the author, if only because other candidates arrived so curiously late on the scene, long after Shakespeare's quality had been identified and widely studied and performed. The insuperable problem is that if *one* of the above factions is correct, as is likely, then all the other factions are presumably completely wrong (though the ingenious J. M. Robertson went so far as to consider the plays a scissors-and paste compilation!).

The testimony of Ben Jonson seems to be conclusive for the authenticity of Shakespeare's authorship of the plays: he "loved the man, and did honour his memory (on this side Idolatry) as much as any". Again according to Jonson, Shakespeare "was not of an age, but for all time".

SHARKS FREQUENTLY ATTACK AND EAT MEN

Human cowardice must be responsible, together with the usual barrel-load of scientific ignorance and refusal to shake off old prejudices, for this fallacy, recently revitalized by the best-selling novel and film *Jaws*. Actual cases of men being attacked by sharks are so rare that the U.S. Navy's Bureau of Aeronautics thought it worth stating in the pamphlet *Shark sense* (1944) that "there is practically no danger that an unwounded man floating in a life-jacket will be attacked by a shark". A foremost expert, Captain William E. Young, wrote in *Shark! Shark!* (New York, 1933) that he had never known of a shark's attacking a living man, though he thought it might happen. Bergen Evans concludes his remarks on this fallacy in *The natural history of nonsense* (London, 1947, p. 81): "Of the several hundred varieties of sharks only half a dozen have the denture necessary for man-eating, and of these not all have the disposition. Of those that have, few get the opporunity, and of those, few make the most of it".

IF AN ATTACK OF SHINGLES SUCCEEDS IN ENCIRCLING THE BODY, THE PATIENT WILL DIE

Pliny the Elder collected this theory and believed it in the first century A.D.: "It kills if it encircles". Two thousand years or so later, J. B. Harrison found himself repudiating the same notion in *Chambers' Edinburgh Journal* (1850, p. 389): "There is a vulgar error, that if the eruption completes the circle, it is fatal . . . fortunately this is not the case, but the complaint *does* seldom get quite round".

The last word belongs to F. W. Morton Palmer, in *Notes and Queries* (20 April 1940, p. 285), who explains that the popular fallacy is based on "the synthesis of two facts. An attack of shingles is *never* fatal . . . Also shingles *never* meets round the body . . ."

MOTHER SHIPTON'S PROPHECY

An oft-reprinted "Ancient prediction", circulated widely from 1862, allegedly "Mother Shipton's Prophecy" and 'dated' 1448, ran:
    "Carriages without horses shall go,
      And accidents fill the world with woe.
      Around the earth thoughts shall fly

In the twinkling of an eye.
The world upside down shall be,
And gold be found at the root of a tree.
Through hills man shall ride,
And no horse be at his side.
Under water men shall walk,
Shall ride, shall sleep, shall talk.
In the air men shall be seen
In white, in black, in green;
Iron in the water shall float,
As easily as a wooden boat.
Gold shall be found and shown
In a land that's not now known.
Fire and water shall wonders do,
England shall at last admit a foe.
The world to an end shall come
In eighteen hundred and eighty-one".

This is reminiscent of the famous hoax among the gullible when on 30 October 1938 thousands of Americans panicked at the radio dramatization of H. G. Wells' novel *The war of the worlds*, for Orson Welles adopted urgent-sounding newscasting tones to announce an invasion by Martians armed with heat rays.

The Mother Shipton hoax was admitted, in *Notes and Queries* of 26 April 1873, as a fabrication by the well-known London bookseller and publisher Charles Hindley, who wrote the above lines as a hoax in 1862.

The first reference I have been able to trace to Mother Shipton is Richard Head, *History of the life and prophecies of Mother Shipton* (1641), in which Cardinal Wolsey is reported to have been warned that he would see York but never enter the city. Of Hindley's fabrication, D. W. Hering writes in his *Foibles and fallacies of science* (New York, 1924): "It was a double duplicity— a piece of invention foisted by its author upon a prophetess whose own existence was shadowy if not mythical".

THE DOCTRINE OF SIGNATURES

A medical fallacy resting on some such analogical argument as 'foxes are thought to possess unusual respiratory powers, therefore foxes' lungs should be prescribed for asthma' or 'Bears have hairy coats, therefore bear's grease should be rubbed on the head as a cure for baldness'.

Fallacies of this type have led telepathists to confuse their alleged powers with those of radio waves, for example. The error lies in inferring a further (unwarranted) degree of resemblance from a known or observable degree.

SILBURY TREASURE

Silbury Hill is a round barrow of great size near the Wiltshire village of Avebury which has been the subject of a great deal of amateurish speculation of little or no value. The latest book on the site is *The Silbury treasure* by Michael Dames (London, 1976). "There was a time", writes Professor R. J. C. Atkinson, "when dotty books about archaeology were privately and rather badly printed at the author's expense. Now, such is the lure of the comforts of unreason, even the dottiest appear in full dress hard-back, expensively illustrated and sometimes from a publisher with no previous stake in the dissemination of nonsense . . . The author's thesis is that the plan of Silbury with its central mound and surrounding ditch, the latter water-filled from the beginning (which is hydrologically impossible) resembles the outline of certain prehistoric female statuettes which he assumes arbitrarily to represent a pan-European mother-goddess. There follows a delirium of theological pregnancies, horns of plenty, corn dollies, harvest hills and imagined sexual connotations of local place-names, all to illustrate the "meaning" of Silbury . . . What Mr Dames and his kind cannot understand is that the material and unwritten nature of prehistoric evidence imposes unavoidable limitations on the kind of inferences that can be drawn from it. Unlike documentary evidence, archaeological evidence is dumb and cannot speak for itself, however mendaciously. It has to be questioned specifically, and the answers have to be given by the questioner, within the framework of inference that the material permits . . .

It is a tribute to the influence of Alexander Thom (though one which he would doubtless willingly forgo) that no book of this kind is now complete without a metrical or astronomical treatment of the material. Mr. Dames gives us both. His "Silbury units" are based on the pattern *today* of local springs and streams. He recognizes the difficulty (which is insuperable) in supposing that this was the same in prehistory, and he solves it simply by asserting that there has been no change. His astronomical chapter deserves a prize for astro-archaeological fantasy".

Source: R. J. C. Atkinson, *review article* entitled 'Mound of the mother goddess' in *The Times Literary Supplement*, 12 November 1976, p. 1435.

SILHOUETTES WERE INVENTED BY
ÉTIENNE DE SILHOUETTE

E. F. Carter, in his *Dictionary of inventions and discoveries* (2nd ed., London, 1974), dates the invention of the silhouette to 1759 and attributes it, and most people still do, to the Controller-General of France, Étienne de Silhouette (1709-1767), but the *Encyclopaedia Britannica* is perfectly right in rejecting this explanation. The shadow outline of an object, usually a profile, obtained by projecting the shadow on to a sheet of white paper, tracing in the outline, and afterwards filling in with a dark colour, most usually black, was familiar in the first half of the 18th century.

Silhouette was named Controller-General through the influence of the Marquise de Pompadour in 1759, but before the year was out Silhouette was removed for proposing a land-tax on the estates of nobles and the reduction of pensions. In allusion to the sacrifices which he demanded of the nobles (including the conversion of their tableware into coinage), 'silhouette' came to refer to any figure reduced to its simplest outline.

SLAVERY IS FORBIDDEN IN THE
NEW TESTAMENT

There is no condemnation of slavery at all in the New Testament, and neither was it prohibited by the Church Fathers. Early in the 11th century Benedict VIII condemned the children of priests to be slaves and Clement did likewise to the whole population of Venice in 1309. Pope Paul III decreed slavery for all Englishmen who supported Henry VIII of England. Papal licences were granted to the Kings of Portugal in the fifteenth century to conquer 'heathen' countries and reduce their inhabitants to 'everlasting slavery'.

Altogether more than 1,800 years of Christianity supported the notion of slavery and those atheists who spoke out in favour of *The Rights of Man* such as Thomas Paine, or the free-thinking publisher Richard Carlile, were reviled and imprisoned.

Source: *The Humanist*, October 1959, p. 3.

SMOKING IS UNCONNECTED WITH LUNG CANCER

According to a report from the Medical Research Council, the mortality from lung cancer is twenty times greater among heavy smokers than among non-smokers. An independent medical study made in 1954 showed that for a person smoking forty cigarettes a day this chance was seventy times greater than for a non-smoker. About 80% of all lung cancer cases occurring in males today would not have occurred were it not for tobacco smoking. About 10% of males over the age of 25 who smoke in excess of 20 cigarettes daily will develop lung cancer by the age of seventy-five.

The death-rate from lung cancer is twice to four times as great in the large towns of Britain as it is in the rural areas.

SNEEZING IS CONNECTED WITH CONTRACTS

Michael Scot, a 13th-century astrologer, claimed that it is possible to foretell the business future by an accurate interpretation of sneezes. After a contract has been drawn up, if you sneeze once the contract will be kept, but if you sneeze three times it will be broken. To make your business venture successful, sneeze twice or four times, then stand up and walk about.

Scot also pointed out, from his presumably extensive knowledge of sneezing, that a double sneeze in the night for three successive nights will foretell a death in the house.

These irrational and wholly unsubstantiated opinions which were stated as facts are due to the usual astrologer's fallacious view that the universe has a great design, and the pitifully tiny Earth is the centre of the universe.

Source: L. Thorndike, *A history of magic and experimental science* (8 vols., London, 1923-58, vol. 2, p. 330).

SNOW FREQUENTLY FALLS AT CHRISTMAS

Snow never falls in Australia at Christmas of course, for Christmas is in the summer there, but even in England snow at Christmas is a rarity. Countless stories, novels, cards and paintings have kept the fallacy alive. Writing in *Nature* (28 June 1938, p. 938), Sir Richard Gregory states that "even frost at Christmas, at any rate in the London district, is a relatively rare occurrence. Over a period of eighty-three years snow fell only twice on Christmas Eve, and only six times on Christmas Day".

SOCIAL MYTHS

A short compendium of some social myths was written by Barrows Dunham: *Man against myth* (London, 1948). These fallacious ideas include:

1. That you can't change human nature.
2. That the rich are fit and the poor unfit.
3. That there are superior and inferior races.
4. That there are two sides to every question.
5. That thinking makes it so.
6. That you cannot mix art and politics.
7. That you have to look after yourself.
8. That all problems are merely verbal.
9. That words will never hurt me.
10. That you cannot be free and safe.

SOLOMON POSSESSED FURNACES FOR ORE FROM HIS MINES

The American archaeologist and rabbi, Nelson Glueck, believed in "the almost incredibly accurate historical memory of the Bible", yet J. B. Pritchard, editor of *The Ancient Near East* (Princeton, 1958), has come to the conclusion that "rarely, if ever, have these (Biblical) discoveries substantiated the truth of Biblical saga".

Glueck has ruefully had to admit this. He excavated in 1938-40 at the port of Ezion-Geber, at the head of the Gulf of Aqabah, and claimed that apertures in mudbrick walls were the flues of a smelter for copper ore. The building was a refinery for copper from 'King Solomon's Mines'!

This fallacy prevailed for a quarter of a century, until Glueck agreed that the apertures were nothing more than holes left in brick walls from the decay of the wooden beams of a granary.

Source: James B. Pritchard, *Seeds from stony ground*, in *Radio Times*, 15-21 January 1977, p. 9.

SOLOMON'S STABLES HAVE BEEN DISCOVERED

University of Chicago archaeologists, excavating at Megiddo in the Holy Land in 1928, discovered several large buildings partitioned into what they believed to be stalls for horses. The buildings looked like modern stables in plan and, recollecting and checking stories of Solomon's horse-dealing in the *Book of Kings*, the archaeologists claimed that they were Solomon's own stables.

More recent work at Megiddo has shown that the buildings date from a century after Solomon (to the time of Ahab, in fact). Beersheba has a structure of the same plan, and that functioned as a storehouse. It is highly likely, therefore, that the 'Solomonic stables' at Megiddo were neither Solomonic nor stables.

Source: James B. Pritchard, *Seeds from stony ground*, in *Radio Times*, 15-21 January 1927, p. 9.

ONE CAN FIND A SPA OR MEDICAL WATERING-PLACE FOR MOST COMPLAINTS

Horace Walpole's sardonic "One would think the English were ducks; they are forever waddling to the waters" might apply equally to European visitors to fashionable watering-places. Spas owe their origin to two factors: Roman hygiene in the example of the public bath, and Christian miracle-seeking in the case of miraculous healing springs. Aachen's fame is due to the former; and North Marston (Bucks.) to the latter. Many English springs were suppressed at the Reformation but Spa (in the Belgian Ardennes) gave its name to a new type of watering place, such as Baden, Baden Baden, Marienbad, and Ems. In England the fashion spread to Tunbridge Wells (1606), Scarborough (1622), Epsom (1625), Sadler's Wells (1683), Islington (1685), Cheltenham (1716) and the rest.

Fanciful ideas of the curative powers attributed to these spas were held by many with a vested interest in the commercial success of these spas, and by the gullible, whose cures (if effected at all) were due mainly to a change of air, a simpler diet, and rest. John Wesley, one such misguided advocate of 'healthful' watering-places, recommended cold baths for deafness, blindness, and the falling sickness. Many of the medical fallacies connected with watering places can be found in John Camp's *Magic, myth and medicine* (London, 1973, chapter 11).

SPACEMEN AND SPACEWOMEN MATED WITH EARTHLINGS

It is one of the cardinal theses of the best-sellers by W. Raymond Drake that extraterrestrial beings ruled Earth, and mated with human beings. In such works as *Gods or spacemen?* (Amherst, Wis.), *Gods and spacemen in the Ancient West* (London, 1974), *Gods and spacemen throughout history* (London, 1975), *Gods and spacemen in Greece and Rome* (London, 1976), and *Gods and spacemen in Ancient Israel* (London, 1976), Drake confuses legend and myth with unfounded speculations based on the allegedly extra-terrestrial origin of UFOs (see **UNIDENTIFIED FLYING OBJECTS**).

Theories from Velikovsky, Däniken (q.v.), and Adamski are uncritically restated, and the Bible narrative is interpreted both literally and allegorically, to suit the author's purpose. According to Drake, the deities of Greece did in fact help Athens to defeat the invading armies of Atlantis in 10,000 B.C., and inspired both the Greeks and the Trojans to fight for Helen, who was a space queen. Sodom and Gomorrah were destroyed by nuclear attack (a commonplace of UFO fantasy), the Angel Gabriel was a space being, and Martians actually came to Earth to teach men the art of war.

While science fiction liberates the imagination, pseudo-history such as that offered by W. Raymond Drake shackles the essential faculty of critical reading, logical thought, and understanding of ancient history through excavation and documents.

THE DEFEAT OF THE SPANISH ARMADA LED TO THE DECLINE OF SPAIN

This idea is believed and taught even now in many schools and colleges, but was dispatched fairly definitively in Garrett Mattingly's *The Armada* (Boston, 1959). Some scholars suggested that the defeat of the Spanish Armada in 1588 caused the decline of Spain and the rise of the British Empire. As Mattingly observes, "it is hard to see why they think so. By 1603, Spain had not lost to the English a single overseas outpost, while the English colonization of Virginia had been postponed for the duration".

To those who argue that the defeat of the Armada transferred control of the seas from Spain to Britain, Mattingly replies that before 1588, "English sea power in the Atlantic had usually been superior to the combined strengths of Castile and Portugal, and so it continued to be, but after 1588 the margin of superiority diminished. The defeat of the Armada was not so much the end as the beginning of the Spanish navy". To those who argue, on the other hand, that defeat dislocated the Spanish economy by the disruption of communications with America, Mattingly retorts "More treasure reached Spain in the years between 1588 and 1603 than in any other fifteen years in Spanish history".

Similar claims as to the 'effects' of certain defeats or reverses in war (or even certain battles) are almost invariably overstated.

TARANTULA SPIDERS SPIN WEBS AND ARE HIGHLY VENOMOUS

While most spiders spin webs, the four-inch long tarantula cannot; it depends on its sting to kill small insects, but its venom is not a serious threat to human beings.

Source: *National Geographic School Bulletin*, January 13, 1975, p. 256.

A SPIRAL UNIVERSE

The 'spiral universe', discovered by the American George Francis Gillette (b. 1875), takes as its starting-point the absurdity of **RELATIVITY** (q.v.). And while Gillette has unbounded admiration for Sir Isaac Newton, he is convinced that he himself has gone far beyond his master in explaining our 'spiral universe'. This, he explains at some length in four books such as *Orthodox oxen* (1929), consists of indivisible changeless unimotes which make us the 'supraunimote' of our universe and the 'maximote' of the entire cosmos.

Martin Gardner's essential guide to *Fads and fallacies in the name of science* (New York, 1957) quotes the following paragraph from Gillette as a sample of his expository style on the new cosmology:

"Each ultimote is *simultaneously* an integral part of zillions of otherplane units and only thus is its *infinite* allplane velocity and energy subdivided into zillions of *finite* planar quotas of velocity and energy".

Gillette was one of those fanatics who believe that the whole of the scientific establishment forms a gigantic monolithic conspiracy to keep him silent and unrecognised, comparing himself with the persecuted Galileo and Copernicus. But nothing could be further from the truth.

Specialist scientific journals exist in virtually every field, and with a delay of two or three years every new theory can be tested by the author's peers and accepted if true. Furthermore, if editors of journals have personal or otherwise subjective (or even objective) grounds for rejecting scientific papers, the author is at liberty (at least in the Free World) to have his paper printed privately and distributed to general news magazines such as *Time* or *The New York Times*, or to general science magazines such as *Nature* or *Scientific American*. If this were not enough, it must be allowed by all scientists that never has the state of science been in such a state of excitement and ferment as it is now, especially with interdisciplinary experiments and the overlapping of fields previously considered distinct. New ideas are welcomed nowadays as never before, and it is unlikely that a revolutionary concept can go long unrecognized or misunderstood.

To call 'conventional' scientists 'orthodox oxen' as Gillette does is a reflection more on Gillette than on the scientists he denigrates.

SPIRIT PHOTOGRAPHS

The first alleged 'spirit' photograph was produced in Boston, Mass., about 1860 and thereafter a spate of them followed, all turning out to be fraudulent when submitted to scientific examination. Buguet, a Parisian whose spirit photographs caused a sensation in London in 1874, was sent to prison for fraud.

Simeon Edmunds, in '*Spirit' Photography* (Society for Psychical Research, 1965-6?), concludes that "no reliable records appear to exist of a definitely recognized spirit extra being obtained on any photograph under completely fraudproof conditions".

SPONDLOTHERAPY

Dr. Albert Abrams, with a medical degree from Heidelberg (1882), settled in California to practise medicine and in 1910 produced a new theory, Spondlotherapy, which stated that each disease gave off its own peculiar series of vibrations providing a clue to the patient's condition. His box, the dynamizer, could determine the nature of the disease if the doctor placed a spot of the patient's blood in the box and linked it by means of a wire to a healthy person who faced west. Dr Abrams then tapped the abdomen and identified the disease.

A refinement came when the Doctor discarded the blood sample and replaced it with a sample of the patient's handwriting. The box was supported by Upton Sinclair and its 'powers' were vindicated by a British High Court Judge as recently as 1960!

Source: Eric Maple, *Magic, medicine and quackery* (London, 1968, pp. 176-8).

SPOONERISMS WERE A RECURRENT FEATURE OF THE SPEECH OF REV. DR. W. A. SPOONER

Spooner, Warden of New College, Oxford, heartily denied having spade any moonerisms in his life to a reporter (see *Evening Standard*, 22 July 1924). However, it was fairly early in his career that he is alleged to have announced in chapel the first line of the hymn as "Kinquering Congs their titles take".

When he was asked whether he had made any Spoonerisms, he retorted "It is a lace Bible". And on another occasion, "Ah, come in, Mr Smith. I'm afraid I have already detected several prowlers in your hose". It is of Spooner that the legendary account is told of the departure from a station which consisted of kissing the porter and giving sixpence to his wife.

THE MORE NUTS A SQUIRREL HOARDS, THE SEVERER THE WINTER WILL BE

The more nuts a squirrel hoards, the better the nut-season has been! The old country adage is completely false, as is the idea that all squirrels hibernate completely. Some squirrels hibernate completely, taking no food the whole time; the majority doze for days at a time, and take food at intervals when they wake; and others, especially in the mildest winters, do not go into a torpid state at all, remaining active, and feeding on bark and twigs as normal. During the Autumn they devour more food than is necessary, the store of fat being gradually consumed while the animals are asleep.

Source: Richard Lydekker, *A hand-book to the British mammalia* (London, 1895), who also quotes William Macgillivray.

SQUIRRELS ARE SHY

I suppose every frightened animal is shy. But tame grey squirrels, such as those in London's Regent's Park, where my family has picnicked a few feet away from inquisitive squirrels, will come very close to pick up offerings such as breadcrumbs. They are equally tame in Central Park, New York.

THE STAG WILL PROTECT HIS ENDANGERED DOE AND FAWN

A tale perpetuated by such writers as Eric Fitch Daglish (*The life story of beasts*, New York, 1931). In fact, as the specialist W. C. Allee emphasizes (*The social life of animals*, New York, 1938), "when danger appears during the rut, the stags make off and rejoin the females when it is past". Much the same fear is felt and shown by all social male animals, according to Allee, except the fully socialized male termites. The popular belief is due to sentimentalism.

STATISTICAL ERROR

This is, according to W. J. Reichmann, "the difference between an actual observed value of a variable and its 'expected' value (i.e. as derived from some assumed basic law or theory), the deviation arising from some chance effect and not constituting a mathematical mistake".

This is not to be confused with a 'sampling error', for which see IF STATISTICAL SAMPLES ARE SUFFICIENTLY LARGE, THEY ARE INVARIABLY CORRECT. See also MATHEMATICAL FALLACIES.

Source: W. J. Reichmann, *Use and abuse of statistics* (London, 1961, p. 339).

IF STATISTICAL SAMPLES ARE SUFFICIENTLY LARGE, THEY ARE INVARIABLY CORRECT

Many people are aware that small statistical samples are liable to a high degree of error, but place greater faith in larger samples.

This fallacy was exploded in the U.S. presidential election of 1936, when more than 10 million ballot papers were mailed out by the *Literary Digest*. More than 2.3 million were returned, most of them favouring the Republican candidate Alf Landon. The *Digest* thus predicted 370 electoral votes for Landon, and only 161 for the Democratic candidate. Yet Roosevelt, the Democrat, won 523 votes, and Landon only 8.

This 'sampling error' is defined by W. J. Reichmann in his *Use and abuse of statistics* (London, 1961) as "the difference between a population parameter and an estimate thereof obtained from a random sample, the difference arising from the fact that only a sample of values has been observed".

Source: Donald R. McCoy, *Landon of Kansas* (Lincoln, Nebraska, 1966).

STILTON CHEESE ORIGINALLY CAME FROM STILTON

No: it came *to* Stilton. A man from the Vale of Belvoir, Leicestershire, took a coaching inn at Stilton (in the modern county of Cambridgeshire which encompasses the former Huntingdonshire) and there both sold and distributed the Vale of Belvoir cheeses, which have always been known as 'Stilton' from their erstwhile central point of distribution.

THE STOMACH WORKS HARDEST DURING SLEEP

A number of the informants with whom I have spoken are quite convinced of the above notion, but no doctor I know will admit a possibility that it might be true. The stomach 'works' away without taking any notice whether the person is sleeping, sitting and thinking, or just sitting.

STONEHENGE

There are numerous fallacious theories about the Neolithic people who built England's most celebrated monument (Stonehenge I) and the Beaker people who may have converted Stonehenge to a temple with celestial orientations, adjusting the probably haphazard axis of the old ring. The standard *Stonehenge* (1956) by R. J. C. Atkinson has not been superseded or significantly amended by the imaginative theories of the historically naive, represented here by the most intelligent, Gerald Hawkins (*Nature*, October 1963 and June 1964, expanded in his tendentious book *Stonehenge decoded*, 1965) and Fred Hoyle (*Antiquity*, 1966, p. 262).

Atkinson, who writes that "a high proportion [of the huge mass of literature on Stonehenge] is the product of that lunatic fringe of archaeology to which Stonehenge has always acted, and still acts, as an irresistible magnet", reviewed Hawkins' full-length book in *Antiquity* (1966, 212) and exposed with great patience the fallacies involved.

Hawkins decided to use a computer to analyse the 'positions' formed by 'stones, stone holes and mounds' belonging to successive periods at Stonehenge and the relations between those positions and other points selected by various criteria as being significant.

While agreeing that the arrangement of the alignments was not a random one, Fred Hoyle (*Nature*, 1966) parted company with Hawkins on the Aubrey hole 'computer', suggesting that those holes represent the ecliptic and were used with stones representing the sun, moon, and the nodes of the moon's orbit. He suggested that priests, observing that the old divinities were eclipsed whenever the stones representing the divine sun and moon were closely associated with the stone representing the invisible nodes of the moon, would conclude that the third unseen god was the most powerful. This might be the origin of the invisible, all-powerful God of Isaiah. It might have destroyed sun-worship and originated the doctrine of the Trinity.

The principal fallacy of the Hoyle approach is not that it is intrinsically impossible, but that it demands of the builders of Stonehenge an intellectual prowess astonishing (as Hoyle himself confesses) among primitive farmers without any other known tradition of learning. "A veritable Newton or Einstein must have been at work", says Hoyle, though the term 'must' seems extraordinarily questionable.

Atkinson attacked Hawkins for his numerous archaeological howlers, the arbitrary selection of his 'positions', his failure to differentiate between the various building periods, the inaccuracy of the plans used, the faults in his method of calculating the validity of his statistics, and his insistence on taking the 'positions' F, G and H to be man-made, whereas they are in fact natural tree holes. Other specialists contributing to *Nature* declared that the 56-year eclipse cycle 'known' to the builders of Stonehenge according to Hawkins does not even exist; D. H. Sadler suggested that eclipses could be more easily predicted from forty-seven marks.

Criticism of Hoyle was more restrained, due to his achievement in other fields, but Newham, who worked for many years on the astronomical interpretation of Stonehenge, suggested that "if Professor Hoyle had been made aware of all the facts his approach would be entirely different". Eleven of Hoyle's 23 readings have been questioned.

The most exhaustive criticism of the Hawkins-Hoyle opinions has been made by Jacquetta Hawkes in *Antiquity* (1967, pp. 174-180), who concludes that "it is enormously improbable that [the builders] had script or numbers . . . ; Stonehenge was intended primarily as a sanctuary, and the intention behind the great horseshoes and circles of stone was architectural and not mechanical, [and] what went on there was mainly ritualistic and not intellectual".

STONES GROW IN FIELDS

Zincke records in his *Materials for the history of Wherstead* (1887) that several Suffolk farmers of his acquaintance believed implicitly in the fallacy that stones grow in fields, and that consequently it is useless to attempt to clear the ground by picking them up, since more will grow in their place. An educated farmer explained that the land itself produced them, arguing for the naturalness of the phenomenon on the ground that everything must be produced by something; moreover, his experience had shown him that it was impossible to clear a stone-infested field permanently. He had had one field on his farm picked over several times, but the pebbles always returned in as great a profusion as before.

The true explanation of this puzzling problem is that even the thinnest covering of soil will conceal small stones from the pickers, and if and when this cover is blown away, washed away by rain, or turned up by ploughs, it might seem at first sight that stones had 'grown' in the same place.

Source: E. and M. A. Radford, *Encyclopedia of superstitions* (2nd ed., London, 1961, pp. 175-6).

BABIES HAVE **STORK-MARKS**

Old wives have triumphantly pointed to marks on babies just where you would have expected a stork to carry a baby, if the traditional picture were not that of a baby being carried in a swinging nappy held in the stork's beak! The tiny red marks which sometimes appear at the bridge of a baby's nose, over the eyelids, and over the nape of the neck are actually areas (like all other birthmarks in other less obvious parts of the body) where tiny blood vessels lie densely just below the surface of the skin and most such birthmarks become less evident during the first year of life. Others remain throughout life and cannot be removed by plastic surgery.

While on the subject of storks, no book on common fallacies would be complete without the fallacy of mistaking correlation for cause, and no better example can be found than that provided by W. Allen Wallis and Harry V. Roberts in *Statistics: a new approach* (New York, 1956, p. 79). They report a high correlation between the number of storks' nests and the number of human births in various parts of northern Europe. The apparent explanation is not, charming as the thought may be, that storks bring babies, but that population increase correlates with an increase in building construction and that more buildings mean more places for storks to nest.

Source: Consumers' Association, *The newborn baby* (London, 1972).

UNITED STATES UNIVERSITY **STUDENT RIOTS** IN THE 1960s MADE FOR WIDER STUDENT PARTICIPATION IN RUNNING THE UNIVERSITIES

This is still popularly believed to be the case, yet Michael Davie's

In the future now (London, 1972) reports that, despite widespread demands for more contact between students and faculty, professors spent less time with their students at the University of California at Berkeley in 1970 (9.3 hours per week with 3rd- and 4th-year students) than in 1960 (12.8 hours); students still have no say there in the appointment of teachers (and some teachers they favoured have been silently removed); and the curriculum remains much the same as it was.

The American Council of Education, in its five-yearly review published in 1970, still put Berkeley at the top of its list of American universities, as 'the best balanced, distinguished university in the nation'.

KEMMERICH ON HUMAN STUPIDITY

Max Kemmerich's *Aus der Geschichte der menschlichen Dummheit* (Munich, 1912) is a sketchy summary of some kinds of popular errors divided into eight chapters: The Bible as a measure of truth; Asceticism; Belief in witches and the Devil in mediaeval Christianity; Stupidity and wars of religion; Compulsory religious education; The Devil in recent and contemporary thought; Religious garments and trinkets; The stupidity of the masses.

Kemmerich, a historian of false prophecies in his useful *Prophezeiungen*, deals in his last chapter with common errors concerning prophets and non-sensory perception, and false beliefs about such natural phenomena as comets.

SUBSTANTIALISM

An anti-Newtonian theory propounded by a Methodist minister, Alexander Wilford Hall (1819-1902), in his oft-revised *The problem of human life* (New York, 1879), which is predominantly an attack on evolution.

All forces, including the force of gravity, are in fact 'substances' according to Revd Hall, even if they are composed of atoms much smaller than those comprising 'material' substances. Light, heat, electricity and magnetism and even sounds and odours have 'substance' in the view of Revd Hall, who pursued his theories through two magazines: *The Microcosm* (1881-92) and *The Scientific Arena* (1886-88). These journals failed to elicit detailed refutation from the scientific establishment. In order to erect a scientific hypothesis, it is however a courtesy to effect an agreed demolition of prevailing opinion, and this the Revd Hall did not feel obliged to do. He attacked not only Darwin, Huxley and Haeckel, but also Tyndall, Helmholtz and Mayer. He was a bitter opponent of the wave theory of sound. His dissent from Newtonian gravity hinged on his disbelief that the action upon a body outside of a sphere is the same as if the mass of the sphere were concentrated in a single particle at its centre, and the distance between the bodies were to be accounted as the distance from the centre of the sphere. Hall wrote all this in bad verse.

THE SUN IS COLD

Sir William Herschel, discoverer in 1781 of Uranus, was the most famous astronomer of his day and when he died in 1822 he was President of the Royal Astronomical Society. Yet he believed that, beneath its hot surface, the Sun of our solar system is sufficiently cool for people to live on (he also considered it absolutely certain that there were intelligent beings on the Moon, but let that pass).

The sun is a star with a surface temperature of 6,000°C and an interior temperature at 21,000,000°C (according to Isaac Asimov, *The universe*, Harmondsworth, 1971, pp. 139-40). These figures are of course only approximate, but they are not likely to be completely erroneous. A West German, Godfried Bueren, however, stated his belief in 1952 that the Sun had a cool inner globe covered with vegetation. John Bradbury, a chiropodist in Ashton-under-Lyne, Lancashire, believes that the Sun is not only cool, but it is small and only 400 miles away. The most exhaustive statement of the theory, *The temperate sun* (1970) has been written by Revd P. H. Francis, formerly of The Vicarage, Stoughton, Chichester, Sussex. He writes, "The popular notion that the Sun is on fire is rubbish, and merely a hoary superstition, on a par with belief in a flat earth, an earth resting on the back of a tortoise or an elephant, or a sun revolving round a stationary earth . . . It rests on no sure basis of evidence; and if it is discarded, great simplifications become possible in the science of astronomy, geology and physics, and many other branches of science can be placed on surer foundations".

Mr Francis' theory could be tested by an unmanned solar probe, and it is indeed not unlikely that such a probe will be used in the future, though with results that may not agree with those of the former Vicar of Stoughton.

Sources include: Patrick Moore, *Can you speak Venusian?* (London, 1976, pp. 42-51).

THE SUN IS HOLLOW

While the American Cyrus Reed Teed was convinced that the Earth is hollow (see THE EARTH IS HOLLOW), the West German Godfried Bueren affirmed, despite scientific evidence to the contrary, that the *Sun* is hollow. The Sun's hot outer shell surrounds a cool inner sphere which is glimpsed occasionally through sunspots (q.v.), which are merely temporary holes in the burning outer crust. What went awry with Herr Bueren's notion was that he offered 25,000 marks (then US $6,000) to anyone who could prove him wrong, thinking that no serious astronomer would take the trouble to refute his idea, and that, even if they did, he could refuse to pay.

The German Astronomical Society, however, carefully pulled his theories to shreds and, when Bueren refused to pay, took him to court. The court not only awarded the verdict to the astronomers: they also ordered Bueren to pay interest and the costs of the case.

Source: *Time*, 23 February 1953.

SUNDAY IS THE SABBATH

The Sabbath is the 'seventh' (Hebrew) day of the week. Sunday, however, is the first. Yet the common confusion of identity persists, the Jews maintaining Saturday as their Sabbath, or day of rest, and the Christians maintaining Sunday as theirs. The Muslims take their day of rest on Friday.

THERE IS A SUN-SPOT CYCLE EVERY 11.2 YEARS

There seemed until very recently to be no question about this 'observation', but it has been proved fallacious. The outer layers of the sun are not constant in rotation or in the number of spots, and a period roughly 1625-1695 has been identified as having experienced few sun-spots. There has been no agreement on the coincidence of that period with the reign in France of Louis XIV, the 'Sun-God', but the designation of the period as 'the little Ice-Age' may well have been factually inspired.

Source: Professor John Jack Eddy, High Altitude Observatory, National Center for Atmospheric Research, Boulder, Colorado.

"SWANS SING BEFORE THEY DIE—

'twere no bad thing
Should certain persons die before they sing" is Coleridge's
heartless 'Epigram on a Volunteer Singer'.

Swans sing, or rather croak, no more before they die than do
thrushes or nightingales. The classical notion was that the swan,
as the Bird of Orpheus, was endowed with unusual musical gifts
exercised at their greatest peak near death. But Pliny discredited
the idea (*Natural history*, Book X, 23) and it is refuted by Scaliger.
There is absolutely no truth in the generalization, even if one or
two instances are corroborated throughout the centuries and
Shakespeare refers to it in *The Merchant of Venice* and *The Rape
of Lucrece*.

RAIN ON ST. SWITHIN'S DAY MEANS RAIN ON THE FOLLOWING FORTY DAYS

No amount of facts will change opinions held firmly enough, and
this is one of those persistent tales it would be derogatory to
attribute to old wives because old husbands also believe it. The
French go one better. "If it rains on S. Médard's Day (June 8),
it will rain for forty days" and "If it rains on S. Gervais' Day
(June 19), it will rain for forty days".

Bishop Swithun (838-62) of Winchester was canonized in 912,
at which time his remains were translated from a grave outside the
Cathedral ("where the sweet rain of heaven might fall upon his
grave") to a shrine within, whereupon he showed his grave dis-
pleasure by making rain for forty days.

Unfortunately for all such 'miracles', the act of verification
proves the fallacy. The Greenwich Observatory carefully collated
records in 1861 for the preceding 20 years, when it appeared from
the average of those years that the greatest number of rainy days
after St. Swithin's Day occurred when July 15 (St. Swithin's Day)
was dry. On six occasions St. Swithin's Day was wet, and the
average number of rainy days (up to August 24) which followed
was $18\frac{1}{2}$. In the other fourteen years, when St. Swithin's Day was
dry, the average number of rainy days which followed was $19\frac{1}{4}$.
In not one single case did it rain for every one of the forty days:
the maximum was 31 days, and that occurred in 1848, when St.
Swithin's day was dry!

Source: *Public Opinion*, 20 July 1894.

SYMBOLIC MAGIC

The occultist A. O. Spare claimed to have invented a new system of magic. "Like all magicians he believed that any desire deeply felt in the inmost centre of human consciousness was capable of fulfilment." His method was to compress his desire into the shortest possible sentence; cross out letters, so that each letter occurs once only; combine the remaining letters to form a sign; and concentrate on the sign by staring at it intently and allowing it to sink into his subconscious.

One such experiment was to cause freshly-cut roses to fall from the air by concentrating on symbolic drawings around the room and repeating 'roses' with his face screwed up. At that moment the overhead plumbing exploded, deluging Spare and his observer with sewage.

Since there can be no conceivable relation between words or letters and physical phenomena such as roses or sewage, the fallacies inherent in symbolic magic need not surely be underlined too humourlessly!

Source: Francis King, *Ritual magic in England* (London, 1970).

NATURE IS SYMMETRICAL

J. Robert Oppenheimer described as a 'gay and wonderful discovery' the classic paper *Question of parity conservation in weak interactions* by the Chinese-Americans Tsung Dao Lee and Chen Ning Yang in the *Physical Review* of 1 October 1956.

The discovery reported in their paper was the subject of an experiment by Madame Chien-Shung Wu. They questioned the hypothesis, long taken for granted, that Nature has a perfect left-right symmetry. Before the results were known, the great theoretical physicist Wolfgang Pauli wrote his pupil at Massachusetts Institute of Technology: "I do *not* believe that the Lord is a weak left-hander, and I am ready to bet a very high sum that the experiments will give symmetric results". Dr Pauli was duly proved wrong and 'parity' was observed to be overthrown. Doctors Lee and Yang were awarded the Nobel Prize in 1957. The nuclear system is now known to be asymmetrical, though the fallacy of symmetry has not by any means been completely eradicated from the popular mind.

Source: Martin Gardner, *The ambidextrous universe* (New York, 1964).

A SYMPATHETIC POWDER CAN ASSIST RECOVERY FROM WOUNDS

The famous "sympathetic powder" described by Sir Kenelm Digby in *A late discourse . . .* (London, 1658) was applied not to a wound, but to the weapon by which the wound was inflicted. The wound was closed up and no further attention paid to it. It was found to be a quite satisfactory method of dealing with the problem until some adventurous thinker tried closing up the wound without applying the sympathetic powder to the weapon. The result was identical.

SYPHILIS WAS IMPORTED TO THE OLD WORLD FROM THE NEW

This fallacy is so prevalent that it recurs in the otherwise entirely reputable *Penguin medical encyclopedia* (2nd ed., 1976): "There are no recognizable accounts of syphilis earlier than about A.D. 1500, but after the return of Columbus from the New World the disease spread as a plague from the Mediterranean across Europe. *Nobody can prove that Columbus and his men imported syphilis* (my italics), but it seems likely". In fairness to Peter Wingate, he does immediately confess that "There is, however, a considerable weight of contrary opinion, some of it well informed".

The problem is one of nomenclature, since the name 'syphilis' was not coined until 1530 (by Fracastorius, in his poem *Syphilis, sive Morbus Gallicus*), when it was fancifully derived from an unfortunate shepherd, one Syphilus, who cursed the sun during a heatwave and was punished with the 'new' disease.

Numerous characters in history have had what one might assume to have been syphilis if only the name had been applied earlier: Herod, king of the Jews, is said to have died of a malignant disease of the genitals, and the same applies to John of Gaunt (d. 1408).

Source: Howard W. Haggard, *Devils, drugs and doctors* (London, 1929, pp. 244-5, as reprinted in 1975).

T

"To know that we know what we know, and that we do not know what we do not know—*that* is what is meant by *true* knowledge."—CONFUCIUS

TABLE-TURNING HAS A SUPERNATURAL EXPLANATION

Table-turning, also known in various parts of the English-speaking world as table-tapping or table-tilting, is a simple form of spiritualism in which 'spirits' are asked questions by the people sitting round a table. They place their hands on the table, which then moves, not of course according to the will of the non-existent 'spirits' but according to the subconscious ideomotor movements of the participants. 'Answers' are given either affirmatively or negatively by touching the table with some part of the body (often hidden, like feet, thus giving the illusion that the table is moving without human assistance) in conformity with pre-arranged signals. Sometimes the table is made to rise; sometimes it is made to tap with one leg on the floor. Fraud is universal among professionals and common among amateurs, though a number of well-intentioned and honest participants are genuinely unaware of the true phenomena involved.

See also **AUTOMATIC WRITING** and **OUIJA BOARD**.

TABOO

The fallacy of the 'taboo' action or thing is based upon a combination of fear and ignorance. H. G. Barnett, in his important *Innovation: the basis of cultural change* (New York, 1953, p. 369) writes: "Taboos that have divine sanction carry with them the threat of supernatural vengeance for their infraction; and negativistic mores, sometimes called taboos, are observed because ignoring them brings social sanctions to bear that can be as frightful as divine punishment. When individual Palauans, Hawaiians, and Tahitians decided to break their dietary taboos, they did so in defiance of an awful penalty. Contrariwise, threats to unbelievers and heretics have brought many converts into religious congregations through fear of personal harm."

TALISMANS

"The amulet [q.v.] is supposed to exercise its protective powers on behalf of the individual or thing continually, whereas the talisman is only intended to perform one specific task. Thus a talisman may be placed in the ground with money or treasure, which it is expected to protect and do nothing else", according to Sir E. A. Wallis Budge's *Amulets and talismans* (New York, 1961).

But of course belief in such 'protective powers' is no less fallacious in an alleged talisman than it is in an alleged amulet. The word *tilasmān* is Arabic, and Brewer, in his *Dictionary of phrase and fable* (p. 1057) quotes the Arab usage of writing on a piece of paper the names of the Seven Sleepers and their dog to protect a house from ghosts and demons. In order to free a place of vermin a talisman consisting of the figure of the obnoxious animal is made in wax or consecrated metal, in a planetary hour. See also **CHARMS**.

TAROT

The Tarot is a pack of playing cards used in fortune-telling (q.v.). Its origin is unknown, though some have guessed without the slightest evidence that it was invented by the ancient Egyptians. The figures shown on the cards include an Emperor and Empress, a fool with cap and bells, a hanged man, and Death reaping. Though the Tarot pack varied very greatly according to era and country, the pack now considered standard has four suits of fourteen cards each: cups (or 'hearts'), coins (or 'diamonds'), wands (or 'clubs') and swords (or 'spades'); and twenty-two others, the 'major trumps'.

"There are almost as many interpretations of the Tarot—occult, Christian, gipsy, psychological—as there are interpreters. The cards contain such richness of symbolism and suggestion that no two people are likely to react to them in quite the same way", observes Richard Cavendish in *The black arts* (London, 1967). E. Gray, in *The Tarot revealed* (New York, 1960), concludes that "in the end, the seeker is told only what he cannot find for himself".

There is of course no way that a random dealing of a pack of cards can correspond to future events except by artificial readings or pure chance.

THE AVERAGE AMERICAN HAS BETTER TASTE THAN THE AVERAGE BRITON (OR VICE VERSA)

Sadly not. "The Duke of Bedford, England's most successful country-house showman", remarked to Walter Knott, the owner and operator of Knott's Berry Farm and Ghost Town in California advertised as "truly one of America's most unusual and enjoyable dining, shopping and entertainment attractions, half-an-hour's drive from Los Angeles" after examining Mr Knott's gift shop: "We have one thing in common. The uglier the things are, the better they sell".

The 'things', in Knott's case, included wall plaques of Bizet, and plaster groups of singing nuns, one of them clasping a guitar.

Source: Michael Davie, *In the future now: a report from California* (London, 1972, p. 164).

MORE TEA IS DRUNK PER CAPITA IN BRITAIN THAN IN ANY OTHER COUNTRY

Tea consumption in the Republic of Ireland was 7.76 lbs. (1200 cups) per head in 1973, surpassing all other countries in the world producing official statistics, including Great Britain and Northern Ireland.

Source: Official statistics.

TEILHARD DE CHARDIN'S EVOLUTIONARY PHILOSOPHY

The Jesuit priest Pierre Teilhard de Chardin attempted to demonstrate that Christian doctrine and evolutionary theory are compatible. His theory of hyperphysics purportedly supersedes both physics and metaphysics, combining parts of Oparin's *Origins of life*, Darwin's *Origin of species* and Lemaître's *Origin of the universe*. Teilhard concludes that "in the last analysis, somehow or other there must be a single energy operating in the world".

This very attractive concept has been taken up by a growing movement of those unconvinced by fundamentalist religion, but is in effect merely a modern version of the old argument that a Prime Mover must exist in order to account for motion (see NO-ONE HAS EVER REFUTED THE PROOFS OF GOD'S EXISTENCE). However, this has been demolished by Galileo's principle of inertia, which proved that movement may go on eternally without an external force to act on it. The theoretical physicist E. H. Hutten has carefully explained other fallacies of

Teilhard's ideas in 'The errors of Teilhard de Chardin' in *Humanist*, April 1971, pp. 115-6.

TELEGONY

The fallacious idea that a previous sire can influence the progeny of a subsequent sire from the same mother. Darwin believed in telegony, as did Agassiz. Lord Morton provided 'confirming' evidence to the Royal Society in 1820 after breeding a chestnut mare with a quagga and obtaining a hybrid. The mare then produced three foals to a black Arabian stallion, all showing quagga-like stripes and thus 'proving conclusively' that the mare had been influenced by the quagga.

This experiment, when repeated with a zebra later in the century, definitively refuted Morton, for most of the subsequent foals sired by horses had no markings, while two pure-bred foals, out of dams that had never seen a zebra, *did* have stripes. The explanation is that stripings occur naturally also in certain breeds of horse (such as some Indian breeds), to one of which Morton's Arabian stallion was presumably related.

Source: James Cossar Ewart, *The Penycuik experiments* (London, 1899), more easily accessible in its abridged form under 'Telegony' in the *Encyclopaedia Britannica* (11th ed.).

WILLIAM TELL SHOT AN ARROW THROUGH AN APPLE ON HIS SON'S HEAD

A stone in the Washington monument in the United States, contributed by the Swiss Government, bears the inscription, "This block is from the original chapel built to William Tell, in 1338, on Lake Lucerne, Switzerland, at the spot where he escaped from Gessler".

The Historical Society of Switzerland has diffidently pointed out to both governments concerned that both Tell and Gessler are wholly fictional characters, but the common fallacy persists. As long ago as August 1890 the canton of Schwyz ordered the Tell legend to be expunged (as nonhistorical) from the cantonal school textbooks. The events are usually placed in the 14th century and are first found in writings of the 15th century. Similar legends of marksmen shooting at an object on the head of a man or child are found in many countries, notably in England (William of Cloudesley) and Norway (Egil).

Source: Sir Paul Harvey, *The Oxford Companion to English Literature* (4th ed., Oxford, 1967).

ANIMALS OBEY THE TEN COMMANDMENTS

This is not a Moody and Sankey tale or a Billy Graham joke: it was stated seriously by Ernest Thompson Seton in *The natural history of the Ten Commandments* (New York, 1907), a latterday collection of moralistic animal tales in the same vein as the Greek *Physiologus* familiar throughout mediaeval Europe in a Latin translation. There is some justification for an ignorant scribe with a religious message to impart to describe a panther as 'an amiable beast, friendly to all creatures but the dragon' (the panther symbolizing Christ in the Christianized rewriting of the *Physiologus*); but for a 20th-century writer to claim that incidents from animal life in any way 'represent' the sins of covetousness, adultery and murder is an outrageous fallacy.

As a reviewer wryly remarked in *The Brooklyn Eagle*, even Mr Seton was unable to obtain zoological support for monotheism and opposition to perjury. He also omitted the prohibitions against swearing and working on Sunday.

LONDON'S THAMES IS HARBOURING LESS AND LESS LIFE DUE TO THE SPREAD OF POLLUTION

In 1958, the Thames was virtually incapable of supporting fish life, but in 1972 there were 55 species recorded as living in it, due to anti-pollution measures which also affected other British rivers.

Source: *Financial Times* (6 January 1972, p. 6).

SETTING THE 'THAMES' ON FIRE

This common error began circulation when the name 'temse' was changed to 'sieve'. A labourer working with a sieve (or temse) would be urged to shake it so vigorously that the sparks would fly from it, and one exercising too little effort would be rebuked: "You'll never set the temse on fire". It is only comparatively recently that the nonsense 'Thames' element crept in.

THEOSOPHY

'The wisdom of/about God' is the meaning of this compound, which claims to be science, philosophy and religion. It borrows from Western and Eastern hermetic philosophies and claims to be very ancient, but revealed afresh in 1875 through the Theosophical Society, formed in New York in 1875 by Helena Petrovna

Blavatsky. Born in the Ukraine in 1831, she led an adventurous life before turning up in the U.S.A., where she met her future collaborator Colonel Olcott in 1874. One of the 'spirits' materialized during her spiritualist sessions with the mediums Nelson and Jenny Holmes, the beautiful 'Katie King', later confessed that she was a Mrs Eliza White. Mme Blavatsky then formed the Theosophical Society following claims that she was in touch with adepts known as the Brotherhood of Luxor, a branch of the Great White Brotherhood operating from the Himalaya. They inspired her to write *Isis unveiled*, considered with the later *Secret doctrine* (1888) as major writings by the Society, though they are no more than a rehash of gnostic and gnostic-like speculations. An entertaining account of the beginnings and growth of Theosophy, which still counts thousands of followers and several branches, can be found in John Symonds' *Madame Blavatsky, medium and magician* (London, 1959).

THERE IS ONLY ONE METHOD OF THINKING

So-called 'logical' thought is by no means the only type of thinking, despite what many people believe. It should be evident that composers and military strategists do not 'think' in a comparable manner; neither do lifeboatmen or Zen priests.

Edward de Bono has devised the following classification in *The 5 day course in thinking* (New York, 1967):

Insight Thinking: The steps leading up to the solution are not all apparent. The solution seems to come about by virtue of a sudden jump in thinking. It is more a matter of finding the right approach than of care in pursuing an approach.

Sequential Thinking: The solution follows a progressive sequence of steps (modification, improvement, mistakes, new ideas, etc.). The sequence need not be a logical sequence; nevertheless, the steps occur one after another.

Strategic Thinking: This is concerned with the choice of the most appropriate steps out of a multitude of possible steps. The search is not for a definite solution but for a policy of behaviour that is more effective than others.

Dr de Bono, a medical research-worker and successful inventor, has invented the terms 'vertical' and 'lateral' thinking to describe logical thought on the one hand, and spontaneous, imaginative and non-discursive thought on the other. His *Use of lateral thinking* is a deliberately playful series of exercises in technical inventiveness.

THOUGHT FORMS ARE VISIBLE

This is one of the fallacies deriving from the error that thoughts are really things, not of course hard, solid and opaque but ethereal, vaporous and coloured. Visible thoughts are said to be symbolic, not pictorial, so that for example a pink fluffy cumulus-cloud effect is 'seen' to emanate from a person who is happy and at peace with the world, whereas a brown-green snakelike effect is caused by thoughts of jealousy.

Source: Annie Besant and Charles W. Leadbeater, *Thoughtforms* (London, 1905).

TIBERIUS INHERITED HIS DRUNKENNESS FROM HIS NURSE

This absurd error in Roman history and heredity is only one of the hundreds such that litter the pages of Benjamin Walker's *Encyclopedia of esoteric man* (London, 1977), issued by a reputable publisher. Walker does not believe in group thought, and questions the powers of Uri Geller as reported in the mass media. But he seems to believe in the medicinal and aphrodisiac powers of bone and bone-powder; that ectoplasm smells of ozone; that dimples on the chin are a sure sign of a flirt; that a nude female in a room wards off disease; and that an anal fixation is manifested in obstinacy and a desire to collect stamps, antiques, and money.

He also appears to credit the 'findings' of Sister Justa Smith, a Franciscan nun and biochemist, that healing rays from the hands of Oskar Esterbany, a Hungarian-born 'healer', considerably increased the activity of enzymes.

As C. Vita-Finzi concluded his review of the book in the *Times Literary Supplement* (22 July 1977), "Esoteric is perhaps the right word after all. The initiated will welcome this book. The outsiders are likely to find their minds even narrower after reading it".

IT IS POSSIBLE TO TRAVEL THROUGH TIME BY OTHER THAN THE USUAL METHOD OF GETTING OLDER

It is one thing to enjoy H. G. Wells' splendid *Time machine* (1895) and similar science fiction, but quite another to postulate the real capacity to travel suddenly and quickly forward or backward in time, as many authors have done, among them Johannes von Buttlar in his *Journey to infinity: travels in time* (London, 1975), translated from the German original of 1973. Even if unintentionally, however, Buttlar confuses the issue by bringing in the alleged 'elixir of life' which gives those who use it a longer life than those who do not and introduces the 'Comte de Saint-Germain' who is claimed to have lived for 245 years; by bringing in dreams, unidentified flying objects, Lunan's hypothesis of interstellar contact, hypnosis, and mummies, none of which is related to the central and inescapable problem that nobody at any time and in any place is known in practice to have travelled forward in time at any pace other than that of our human clocks, or to have travelled backward in time at all, despite numerous claims such as those of C. A. E. Moberly and E. F. Jourdain in their best-selling Versailles tale, *An adventure*, first published under their pseudonyms Elizabeth Morison and Frances Lamont (London, 1911), which has at last been exposed, if a little sadly, by Joan Evans, in *Encounter* (October 1976, pp. 33-47). Dame Joan comes to the conclusion that the two ladies had inadvertently strayed into a rehearsal for a *tableau-vivant* and did in fact see everything they claimed to see (it was not a willed mirage as claimed by Jastrow) but merely misinterpreted the evidence of their senses.

J. W. Dunne stated in *An experiment with time* (London, 1927) that time is "the fourth dimension", just as Einstein had done, but the difference is that Dunne holds that human beings in their sleep move freely along this fourth dimension, and so are enabled to foresee the future . . .

Dunne's theory and H. G. Wells' hasty (and hoaxing?) endorsement of it (as the author of *The time machine*) is, in the view of Eric Temple Bell (*The search for truth*, 1935, p. 36), "as hopeless a muddle of woolly thinking by means of metaphors and far-fetched analogies as any of the more childish efforts of the perpetual motion cranks to do the impossible".

Further fallacies pepper Dunne's subsequent *Serial universe* (London, 1934) and *The new immortality* (London, 1938).

TOADS DO HARM IN A GARDEN, AND TORTOISES GOOD

Toads are good for a garden, because they are insectivorous, and especially like to eat slugs and snails. Tortoises do not, and though often bought for their ability to keep down garden pests, are in fact exclusively herbivorous. It is possible that black beetles avoid them if possible, and consequently leave the garden of their own volition when tortoises are brought in, but there appears to be little evidence on this question either way.

SWEENEY TODD WAS A BARBER IN FLEET STREET

"Sweeney Todd, the Demon Barber of Fleet Street" and his delicious meat pies never existed. H. C. Porter exploded the widespread belief in *Notes and Queries* (1902, p. 345), but a major problem about fallacies is that they are disseminated by popular magazines, radio and television, and only corrected or refuted by specialist magazines with a much more limited readership, and while newspapers guarantee space for the right of reply, there is no such guarantee of time on radio or television programmes. Might I therefore beg ten minutes a week on each radio channel and each television channel for those anxious to correct errors detected throughout the previous week? Perhaps ten minutes would not be long enough . . .

MAN IS THE ONLY ANIMAL THAT CAN ACTUALLY MAKE TOOLS

Chimpanzees have long been known to be able to *use* tools in such activities as cleaning their bodies after diarrhoea (with leaves), cleaning teeth (with a twig) or weapon-throwing (with a stick). It was consequently asserted that Man differed from the apes in his ability to *make* tools. This fallacy has been exploded by Jane van Lawick-Goodall; her *In the shadow of Man* (London, 1971) describes how chimpanzees strip leaves from a stem to make a tool suitable for 'fishing' for termites. Leaves, made more absorbent by chewing *for that purpose*, are used as a sponge to sop up rainwater that cannot be reached with the lips.

So far, however, there is no indication (despite encouragement) that chimpanzees can use tools to make other tools, the next achievement in the technological cycle.

THE METALLIC TRACTORS OF ELISHA PERKINS

Perkins, born in Norwich (Connecticut) in 1741, invented these objects and launched them on to the unsuspecting public in 1796. He noticed that muscles and nerves were sometimes subject to spasmodic contractions when touched with metal tractors and two of these four-inch long devices were held together at their points and then drawn over the affected part of the body, always downwards or outwards. The advised length of 'tractoration' was twenty minutes a day and these 'tractors' were sold at £10 a pair to the general public (half price to the medical profession). When the general enthusiasm for metallic tractors began to wane in 1799, he went to New York with an antiseptic cure for yellow fever, then an epidemic disease, but unfortunately died in New York within a month of his arrival—of yellow fever.

Source: Eric Jameson, *The natural history of quackery* (London, 1968, pp. 146-7).

MUSSOLINI MADE THE ITALIAN TRAINS RUN ON TIME

A common defence of Italian fascism was that regimentation and efficiency replaced an easy-going life and inefficiency. However, questioning of people who actually lived in Italy between the March on Rome (22 October 1922) and the execution at Como in 1945 bear witness to the fact that Italian railways were no more careful of timetables than they are today.

TRAMPS ARE BECOMING LESS NUMEROUS IN BRITAIN

There have always been 'milestone inspectors' and always will be in a society which is sufficiently free to permit sleeping out without surveillance or identity cards.

And there is no sign that they are decreasing: the total of such men in Britain in the early 1970s was at least 50,000.

David Brandon, in a Christian Action publication entitled *Homeless in London*, estimated the vagrant homeless as follows:

    25,000 in common lodging houses
    10,000 in lodging houses and night shelters
    5,000 plus in prison
    3,000 plus in general and psychiatric hospitals
    2,000 in reception centres
    1,000 plus sleeping rough.

Source: Robin Page, *Down among the dossers* (London, 1973, p. 112).

THE VOICE OF THE TURTLE IS HEARD IN OUR LAND

The above translation from *Canticles*, ii. 12 was made the text of a sermon by a Scottish minister.

"We have here," he is reported to have said—"we have here, my brethren, two very remarkable signs and portents distinctly vouchsafed to us. The first shall be, that a creature which (like Leviathan himself) was created to dwell and abide in the sea shall make its way to the land, and be seen in the markets and dwelling-places of men; and the second shall be, that a creature hitherto denied the gift of speech shall lift up its voice in the praise of its Maker".

These deductions would be true enough if the original data were correct; but it was of course the voice of the turtle-*dove* that the author of *Canticles* referred to. Mistranslations have given rise to more fallacies than one would wish, in all charity, to recall.

Source: Rupert T. Gould, *Oddities* (2nd ed., London, 1944).

TWINS ARE USUALLY IDENTICAL

The first detailed study of this subject has still apparently not been absorbed by the popular mind. *Inquiries into human faculty* (1883) by Sir Francis Galton stated that "one would have expected that twins would commonly be found to possess a certain average likeness to one another; that a few would greatly exceed that average likeness, and a few would greatly fall short of it. But this is not at all the case. Extreme similarity and extreme dissimilarity between twins of the same sex are nearly as common as moderate resemblance. When the twins are a boy and a girl, they are never closely alike; in fact, their origin is never due to the development of two germinal spots in the same ovum".

The fact that the same point has been made in numerous publications over the succeeding ninety years has made little difference to the common lore on twins.

AN OBJECT CANNOT BE IN TWO PLACES AT ONCE

"But an electron suffering diffraction can. It also seems clear that though size and position is infinitely variable, everything shares the same time; but, as Einstein showed, this is not so. We must check our intuitive ideas all the time".

Source: B. K. Ridley, *Time, space and things* (Harmondsworth, 1976, p. 40).

"TYGER, TYGER, BURNING BRIGHT!

in the forests of the night", says Blake, but the tiger is of course so coloured that it blends into its surroundings at any hour of the day or night. Its legendary acute sense of smell is another fallacy, so is its quickness and its courage against a noisy enemy of roughly equivalent size.

U

"The utmost that can be said on behalf of errors in opinion and motive, is that they are inevitable elements in human growth. But the inevitable does not coincide with the useful. Pain can be avoided by none of the sons of men, yet the horrible and uncompensated subtraction which it makes from the value and usefulness of human life, is one of the most formidable obstacles to the smoother progress of the world. And as with pain, so with error. The moral of our contention has reference to the temper in which practically we ought to regard false doctrine and ill-directed motive. It goes to show that if we have satisfied ourselves on good grounds that the doctrine is false, or the motive ill directed, then the only question that we need ask ourselves turns solely upon the possibility of breaking it up and dispersing it, by methods compatible with the doctrine of liberty."—JOHN MORLEY, *On compromise* (London, 1886, pp. 83-4).

SWIMMING IS DANGEROUS WHERE THERE IS AN UNDERTOW

There is no objective 'undertow' in water that is not immediately reversed. An active and persistent seaward underflow at the bottom demands the occurrence of a correspondingly active and persistent shoreward flow at the surface. Except under doubly specialized conditions of wind direction and shore configurations, 'undertow' does not exist and never has, outside the imagination of frightened swimmers. The intermittent seaward pull as each wave slides back from the beach is reversed every few seconds by an equally temporary shoreward movement of the next wave.

Source: William H. Davis, in *Science*, 20 February 1925, pp. 206-8.

THE UNICORN EXISTS OR ONCE EXISTED

The Greek historian Ctesias (c. 400 B.C.) relates that there were in India swift wild asses with white coats, purple heads, blue eyes, and in the middle of their foreheads a pointed horn whose base was white, whose tip was red, and whose middle was black. See also Pliny's *Historia naturalis* (VIII, 31), which perhaps did more to spread the legend of the unicorn than any other single text. Isidore of Seville's *Etymologiae* (7th century) stated that one thrust of the unicorn's horn may kill an elephant—he must have been thinking of a rhinoceros. About 1892, the orientalist Schrader suggested that the idea of the unicorn may have come to the Greeks when they saw Persian bas-reliefs depicting bulls in profile with a single horn. The drawings and photographs of the addax and scimitar-horned oryx in Ernst Hufnagl's *Libyan mammals* (New York, 1972) would lead one to a similar hypothesis: in profile the horns would certainly seem singular.

Aristotle called the oryx one-horned and, as he had almost certainly never seen one, may have been misled by a confused report of a two-horned animal in flight.

Sources: Jorge Luis Borges and Margarita Guerrero, *Manual de zoología fantástica* (Mexico City, 1957).

UNIDENTIFIED FLYING OBJECTS (UFOs)

After thousands of reported sightings by enthusiasts, mainly in the United States, a study was carried out under the auspices of the University of Colorado from 1966-68 under the leadership of Dr Edwin U. Condon. Over nearly 1,500 pages of analysis of the evidence, the Condon Report refuted the allegedly extraterrestrial origin of phenomena generally categorized as UFOs. Its general conclusion was that "nothing has come from the study of UFOs in the past 21 years that has added to scientific knowledge. Careful consideration of the record as it is available to us leads us to conclude that further extensive study of UFOs probably cannot be justified in the expectation that science will be advanced thereby".

V

"El vivir en medio de errores, y estar satisfecho de ellos, y transmitirlos de generación en generación, sin hacer modificación ni mudanza, es propio de aquellos pueblos que vegetan en la ignorancia y envilecimiento: allí el espíritu no se mueve, porque duerme" (To live in the midst of errors, and to be content with them, and transmit them from one generation to the next without change or correction, is characteristic of those peoples who stew in ignorance and degradation: there the spirit does not move, for it lies sleeping)—JAIME BALMES (1810-1848).

NATURE ABHORS A VACUUM

This idea of Aristotle was universally accepted until Torricelli (1608-1647) showed that if a tube closed at one end is filled with mercury and inverted, the mercury will stand up to the top of the tube only if the tube is less than 30 inches long; evidently Nature's abhorrence of a vacuum is limited.

Source: W. F. G. Swann, *Error in physics*, in Joseph Jastrow, *The story of human error* (New York, 1936).

VELIKOVSKY

Comets coming near the Earth, or actually hitting it, have caused endless damage, according to enthusiasts such as the Irish-American lawyer Ignatius Donnelly (1831-1901), (see THE PLEISTOCENE ICE AGE WAS CAUSED BY A COMET HITTING THE EARTH).

The Russian Jew Immanuel Velikovsky has achieved a similar success in the U.S.A., publishing a sequence of books of such scientific naïveté that they were at first ignored in derision by the scientific establishment, and of such immense popularity among the general public that scientists were at length, against their own better judgment, forced to explain the fallacies inherent in such best-sellers as *Worlds in collision* (New York, 1950). In this work Velikovsky asserts that, some time before 1500 B.C., a brilliant fiery object was expelled from the planet Jupiter and entered a long elliptical orbit around the Sun. This was Venus. It came close to Earth about 1450 B.C., and as Earth passed though the comet's tail (so Velikovsky claims), the catastrophes recorded in *Exodus* occurred, among them the plagues of Egypt. The Earth's axis itself changed direction, so that according to some observers 'the Sun stood still' or darkness persisted longer than was normal. It was through a gap in the Red Sea created by the comet's pull that the Israelites fled. The manna falling from Venus (see also MANNA MACHINE) was the classical 'ambrosia', a kind of sweet carbohydrate formed by bacterial action in the hydrocarbons of Venus' atmosphere. The petrol we use in our cars today derives from these "remnants of the intruding star which poured forth fire and sticky vapour".

Venus was also responsible for producing the effects mentioned in the Bible when Moses was given the Ten Commandments on Mount Sinai; a visitation from Venus was the cause of the collapse of Jericho's walls.

Venus next pulled Mars out of its orbit in the mid-8th century B.C., when Mars drew close to the Earth, an event which caused more catastrophes on Earth, among them the founding of the Roman Empire in 747 B.C. with Mars as its god. Numerous cataclysms occurring in no records other than those of Dr Velikovsky complicated classical history until, once, the Earth temporarily somersaulted, so that for a time the Sun rose in the west and set in the east. Dr Velikovsky seems to think planets can change into comets and *vice versa*. His time-scale is ridiculously short to account for geological eras. He is astonishingly ignorant of world mythologies, and cites writers like Hevelius and Pomponius Mela as if they enjoyed any scholarly respectability for accuracy.

Velikovsky's later books are a farrago of unrelated detail, anachronisms, and wild speculations based on a wide range of sources, many quite unreliable. *Ages in chaos* (New York, 1953), *Earth in upheaval* (New York, 1956), *Oedipus and Akhnaton* (New York, 1960), and *Peoples of the sea* (New York, 1976) propose a radical revision of ancient history, on the lines of Velikovsky's early, scarce *Theses for the reconstruction of ancient history* (1945) and the notorious *Worlds in collision*. In *Ages in chaos*, Velikovsky simply removes six centuries from ancient Egyptian history.

Martin Gardner puts the case against the early books succinctly in his *Fads and fallacies in the name of science* (New York, 1957, pp. 31-2): "Dr Velikovsky is an almost perfect textbook example of the pseudo-scientist—self-taught in the subjects about which he does most of his speculation, working in total isolation from fellow scientists, motivated by a strong compulsion to defend dogmas held for other than scientific reasons, and with an unshakable conviction in the revolutionary value of his work and the blindness of his critics".

Yet such is the persistence of men and women in *idées fixes* that, between 1972 and 1975, the Student Academic Freedom Forum of Portland, Oregon, sought 'fair play' for Velikovsky in their magazine *Pensée*, articles from which were collected in a book, *Velikovsky reconsidered* (London, 1976); while in 1974 a Society for Interdisciplinary Studies was founded in Britain with the function of "encouraging a rational approach" to the master's theories.

We are indebted to the cuneiformist Abraham Sachs, of Brown University, Rhode Island, for a minute verbal critique in 1965 of the shortcomings of Velikovsky's use of Mesopotamian sources (on cuneiform tablets from c. 3000 B.C. to 1st century A.D.); agreeing for instance that Venus is omitted by a certain text, he goes on to point out that all the other planets are missing too . . .

Velikovsky's theory of catastrophes caused by comets had been anticipated by William Whiston, who succeeded Newton as professor of mathematics at Cambridge University, in his *New theory of the Earth* (1696); and by Ignatius Donnelly of Minnesota in his *Ragnarok: the age of fire and gravel* (New York, 1882).

See also **COMETS** and **PLEISTOCENE ICE AGE**.

Sources include: John North, *Venus, by Jupiter* in *Times Literary Supplement*, 25 June 1976, pp. 770-1.

THE SATELLITE OF VENUS

During the 17th and 18th centuries this well-known satellite was observed by Cassini il Vecchio in 1672 and 1686, by James Short in 1740, by Mayer in 1759, by Montaigne in 1791, and so on. All agreed that it was about a quarter of the size of Venus, or about 200,000 miles in diameter.

Unfortunately for these astronomers, however, we are quite sure that Venus never had a satellite of this size, and we are *almost* certain that she has never had one at all. If the satellite had fallen on to the surface of Venus her aspect and orbit would have been altered, while if it had fallen into the Sun, we should be aware of the event. Some of these observations were proved by Dr Paul Stroobant, of the Brussels Observatory, to have been 'ghosts' caused by reflections within the telescopes, which would be particularly noticeable for an object as bright as Venus. Other observers had described the satellite as starlike, and Stroobant, by calculating the positions of Venus at the dates in question, could identify in seven cases which star the observer had mistaken for a satellite. It is possible, though not certain, that the 'satellite' seen by Roedkiaer at Copenhagen on 5 March 1761 was the planet Uranus, twenty years before its recognition by Herschel. There remained little else of the observations except some statements so vague as to inspire no confidence. So final was Stroobant's critique that the earlier belief in 'Neith', the satellite of Venus, has been virtually forgotten.

Source: J.A., *Sky and telescope*, vol. 13, August 1954.

VERONICA'S VEIL

The legend, for which there is no shred of evidence, tells how a woman of Jerusalem was filled with compassion on seeing Jesus bearing the Cross to Calvary and wiped his face with a cloth; the cloth received an image of his features and a cloth allegedly the original veil is shown to visitors in S. Peter's, Vatican City, having been there possibly from the early eighth century. Yet the Roman Martyrology contains no 'St. Veronica', probably because the word 'veronica' ('true image', or 'vernicle') only in later centuries became a girl's name.

'VIKING' RHYMES WITH 'LIKING'

It rhymes on the contrary with 'licking', as *vik* (Icelandic) means 'creek, inlet, or bay', and *ingr* (in Icelandic; in Anglo-Saxon *ing*) means 'people of', or 'belonging to'. The Anglo-Saxon word *wicing* is therefore a borrowing from Scandinavia.

If it is argued that long incorrect usage makes the incorrect into the correct, it should be remembered that a language as far removed from Scandinavian as Italian has always employed the correct pronunciation in *vichingo*. The correct pronunciation appears in the Scottish coastal town of Wick, and all such compounds as Ler*wick*.

Source: Walter W. Skeat, *An etymological dictionary of the English language* (Oxford, 1888).

MODERN MAN'S **VIOLENCE** IS A RESULT OF HIS DESCENT FROM THE FEROCIOUS AUSTRALOPITHECINE 'APE-MAN'

The above view is stated by the popularizer Robert Ardrey in his best-selling *African genesis* (London, 1961) and is very widely believed.

However, relics found near Lake Rudolf in Kenya have shown that the ancestor of Man and Australopithecus were two distinct species, and while modern man can be said to be violent in some senses of the word, it is fallacious to state the cause in Ardrey's terms.

BROWNE ON **VULGAR ERRORS**

Sir Thomas Browne, the great English stylist of *Religio medici* (authorized ed., 1643) and *Hydrotaphia* (1658), is to be credited with the first attempt at a comprehensive survey of vulgar errors (as opposed to a classification of them) in *Pseudodoxia epidemica: or, enquiries into very many received tenents, and commonly presumed truths* (London, 1646), a book usually referred to as *Vulgar errors*.

Pseudodoxia epidemica is divided into seven books, the most interesting being the first, which is introductory. This deals with the fallibility of human nature as a source of fallacies, including credulity, false deduction, supinity, adherence to antiquity, tradition and authority. Browne considered himself absolutely free from heretical opinions as a Christian (the *Religio medici* appeared in Paris, where he was thought a Roman Catholic), but the Vatican placed the work on the *Index Expurgatorius* to be on the safe side. Browne gives a list of those authors to be treated with caution. Among them is Pliny, whose *Historia naturalis* is condemned in words that really demand to be reproduced: "there is scarce a popular errour passant in our dayes, which is not either directly expressed, or diductively contained in this worke, which being in the hands of most men, hath proved a powerfull occasion of their propogation . . .". It is worth mentioning, for those readers sceptical of Browne's wholesale disapproval, that Howard M. Parshley echoes Browne's view in *The story of human error* (New York, 1936) edited by Joseph Jastrow: "Pliny's *Historia naturalis* was so stuffed with errors of the time that it undoubtedly takes the palm as the greatest single repository of misinformation known to man".

Book two of Browne's work is devoted to errors concerning minerals and vegetables; book three is on animals; book four on man; book five is on "many things questionable as they are described in pictures" and on various superstitions; book six on geographical and historical fallacies; and book seven on religious errors, and a pot-pourri of such picturesque errors as those "that the Army of Xerxes drank whole rivers dry" and "of the wandring Iew".

Like all writers on fallacies, Browne knew that he was fallible, and added a caveat in his preface that "we are not Magisteriall in opinions, nor have wee Dictator-like obtruded our conceptions, but in the humility of Enquiries or disquisitions, have only proposed them unto more ocular discerners". Again like all writers on fallacies including myself and beyond, he was credulous about some beliefs which later ages exposed as fallacious and, to his discredit, gave testimony at Norwich in 1664 which led to the death of two 'witches', the wretched Amy Duny and Rose Cullender.

'Thomas Browne Redivivus' is the pseudonym of Caroline Frances Cornwallis, whose *Exposition of vulgar and common errors* was published in 1845.

FOVARGUE ON VULGAR ERRORS

Stephen Fovargue's *A new catalogue of vulgar errors* (Cambridge, 1767) is a collection of thirty-six essays, some of them discursive and a few even digressive, which indicate some of the commonest fallacies of the mid-eighteenth century in England. I append a complete list of Fovargue's fallacies.

1. That the more ammunition is put into a fowling piece, the farther it will do execution.
2. That the heron makes a hole in the bottom of her nest, through which her feet hang, when she sits upon her eggs.
3. That the bittern puts his bill or beak into a reed, and that the reed gives, by the breath and motion of the beak of the bird, that deep and low note which we so frequently hear him make as he lies in a Fenn.
4. That the tone of a violin is to be brought out, by laying on like a blacksmith.
5. That the farther you go south, the hotter is the climate.
6. That exactly under the Aequator is always the hottest climate on the globe.
7. That the more hay is dried in the sun, the better it will be.

8. That the violin is a wanton instrument, and not proper for psalms; and that the organ is not proper for country-dances, and brisk airs.
9. That the Organ and Harpsichord are the two principal instruments, and that other instruments are inferior to them in a concert.
10. That every key in music ought to have a different effect or sound.
11. That a piece of music which has flats set before it, is in a flat key on that account, and vice versa with sharps.
12. That apparitions or spectres do exist, or that the ghosts of men do appear at, before, or after their deaths.
13. That bleeding is proper for a patient, who is apt to be sick in a morning. [On scurvy.]
14. That no thing which moves upon the surface of the earth, is so swift as the wind. ["Even pigeons and swallows can go faster".]
15. That there is now, or ever was, such a science as astrology. [Fovargue would be astonished to find this error still widespread two centuries later.]
16. Most Londoners are mistaken when they think that they have wit enough to impose on countrymen. [Wrongly phrased; Fovargue does *not* think this a fallacy; he himself was a Fenman.]
17. That a pointer, if he lifts up his foot, when he comes upon game, does it in order to shew his master the spot where the birds lie. [It is coincidental.]
18. That the way to make boys learn their books, is to keep them in school all day, and whip them.
19. That clogging their parts with long grammar rules, will make them bright scholars.
20. That teaching boys Bawdy Books will make them religious men and good clergymen. [The 'Bawdy Books' are by that 'Master of Intrigue' Ovid and that 'Libertine' Horace.]
21. That the present age is a duller Age, and less ingenious, than those which are past.
22. That the musical composition of this present age is inferior to that of the last.
23. That the hearing of musical performances, is apt to soften men too much, and by that means to give them an effeminate manner.
24. That the Italian operas consist of effeminate musick.

25. That nothing is poetry but what is wrote in rhyme.
26. That kicking up the heel behind, and twisting round upon one leg, is fine scating.
27. That using hard words and long sentences, in discourse or in writing, is an indication of scholarship.
28. That the way to get a sailing boat off the shore, when she is fast by any accident, is to let go both or all the sails, and stand at her head, and push with a sprit.
29. That planting aquatics upon banks of the Fenns will preserve and strengthen them, so as to render them more able to resist the force of a flood.
30. That those who lived 2000 years ago, were larger than the present race of mankind.
31. That bleeding in May will preserve the constitution against illness during the ensuing summer.
32. That negroes are not a part of the human species. [Refutes with the aid of Locke's *Essay concerning human understanding*].
33. That negroes are the descendants of Cain, and that the colour of their skins is that mark which was set upon Cain, after killing Abel.
34. That Love is nothing but concupiscence to a high degree, or that love and lust are the same thing.
35. That the Hedge-Hog is a mischievous animal; and particularly that he sucks cows, when they are asleep in the night, and causes their teats to be sore.
36. That a person is the better or the worse for being of any particular calling or profession.

W

"The whole history of civilization is strewn with creeds and institutions which were invaluable at first and deadly afterwards"—WALTER BAGEHOT.

WAGNER IS MAD

"Wagner est évidemment fou", wrote Berlioz in a letter dated 5 March 1861. D.-F.-E. Auber, cited in *Le Ménestrel* (27 September 1863) declared: "Wagner, c'est Berlioz moins la mélodie".

Max Kalbeck described Wagner in the *Wiener Allgemeine Zeitung* (28 April 1880) as the artistic incarnation of the Anti-Christ.

These three judgments commit the fallacy of forming a judgment before a phenomenon (such as the new musical style of Wagner) can be fully assimilated, understood, and appreciated. It would have been possible to compile a book twice as long as the present dictionary with erroneous value-judgments by journalists and hack reviewers on major writers whose contribution was undervalued principally because it exceeded the horizons of the day in terms of imagination, style, or 'daring' content.

In art, major errors have been committed in attacking (usually for the wrong reasons) Picasso, the French Impressionists, abstract art, Whistler, Neizhvestny and indeed all Russian artists failing to conform to the doctrine of socialist realism, Jackson Pollock and other action painters, the surrealists, Courbet and Corot . . . The list is endless because it is *normal* for artistic taste in the public to lag at least a generation behind the achievement of the artists. In music, Debussy, Stravinsky, Webern and Berg have been bitterly attacked, while Puccini was condemned almost universally during his early years for operas which now grace every opera house in the world. In literature, Byron, Dylan Thomas, Dostoevsky, Balzac and James Joyce have all been insulted. *Blackwood's Magazine* called Keats' *Endymion* "drivelling idiocy". Even now it is impossible to buy more than one or two of the novels of Benito Pérez Galdós in paperback in Spain, though the wealthy (hence presumably the non-revolutionary) can buy expensive hardback editions. The fallacy here is that the criticism of human nature is potentially or actually deleterious to the society thus criticized; in fact, the stifling of criticism (as in Czarist Russia) is usually more dangerous to a state's stability.

WAR IS CONDUCIVE TO PEACE

Long before George Orwell's *1984* and *Animal farm*, Friedrich von Bernhardi is alleged to have stated: "It is a matter of humanity to wage ruthless, pitiless war, in order that war should be concluded more rapidly". This is one of the most fearsome of fallacies.

Source: Pierre Loti, *L'horreur allemande* (Paris, 1914). There is an English translation of Bernhardi's original work by K. von Donat (*On war of today*, 2 vols., London, 1912-1913).

WASHINGTON CUT DOWN A CHERRY TREE BELONGING TO HIS FATHER

Mason L. Weems' biography of George Washington relates the now-celebrated story that the boy cut down a cherry tree belonging to his father and, when asked if he had done it, admitted the deed, adding "I cannot tell a lie". Despite the fact that Weems' fabrication of this entirely apocryphal incident was exposed shortly after its publication, Newnes' *Pictorial Knowledge* (vol. 2, London, 1947, p. 159) repeats that "George Washington is known as 'The boy who could not tell a lie' . . .", and countless children repeat the fairytale as fact. Another error is to think of the boy Washington as a pacifist. On the contrary, he was praised as 'first in war and first in peace' after a successful military and political career.

WASPS AND HORNETS SHOULD BE KILLED

This pernicious belief should be killed instead. Both wasps and hornets destroy many garden pests, and only a few of the many varieties of wasp or hornet sting.

They should not be destroyed unless they build nests in your attic rafters, porch corners, or where children habitually play.

Source: Alma Chesnut Moore, *How to clean everything* (New York, 1972).

A WATCHED POT NEVER BOILS

The only way to stop it would be to cool it down rapidly, but the proverb's point seems nonetheless acceptable to many of those who realize that is in fact completely *untrue*. Proverbial lore is often fallaciously considered to be the treasury of wisdom built up by previous generations, yet for its naïveté, shallowness and frequent contradiction there is very little to recommend it above the prattling of infants. The sententious fool can justify any course of action by quoting "He who hesitates is lost", "Look before you leap" or "More haste, less speed". Cervantes poked fun at the Spanish propensity for these saws by writing a complete interlude in proverbs, but all other peoples are equally subject to the same gullibility for proverbial 'wisdom'.

WATT INVENTED THE STEAM ENGINE

James Watt (1736-1819) is the familiar hero of the tale you heard at your mother's knee: holding an egg-cup in steam from the spout of a kettle, he saw the steam condense on it, scalded his fingers, dropped the egg-cup which caused it to break and his granny to scold him for his idle daydreaming.

The steam engine was apparently first designed by Edward Somerset, Marquis and Earl of Worcester in 1655 and patented by Robert Hooke in 1678. The pumping steam engine was invented by Sir Samuel Morland in 1682. A model pumping steam engine was first exhibited by Denis Papin in 1685. Still before Watt's birth, Thomas Newcomen erected the first practical working steam engine at Tipton, Staffordshire, in 1712. Watt's achievement was a great improvement in efficiency by condensing the steam in a separate closed vessel instead of in the cylinder itself; he also closed the top of the cylinder and used low-pressure steam instead of cold air to drive the piston down.

There goes another childhood fantasy!

Sources include: L. T. C. Rolt's article 'Steam engine' in *Eureka!* (ed. by Edward de Bono, London, 1947, p. 71).

SEA WAVES CAN BE AS TALL AS A MOUNTAIN

Despite Virgil (*Aeneid*, I, 81-123), who was in no position to measure, and would not have heeded the measurement if he had been, the maximum height from crest to trough of an Atlantic wave which has been accurately recorded is 42 feet. Not even a small hill.

Source: John Timbs, *Things not generally known* (1st ser., 1860).

THE WEATHER CAN BE FORECAST WITH ACCURACY

Partly as a result of widespread publication of forecasts, it is almost universally believed that meteorologists can predict what the weather will be with a great degree of accuracy. This is completely irresponsible. Meteorologists study the 'motions and phenomena of the weather' (*Shorter Oxford English Dictionary*) and the connection of this scientific study with forecasting the weather is no closer than the study of philology with forecasting the languages or linguistic developments of the future. As Richard Inwards, President of the Royal Meteorological Society, wrote in *Nature*, 15 August 1895, "all the great authorities agree that in the present state of our knowledge no human being can correctly predict the weather, even for a week to come". Techniques of more accurate forecasting since Inwards' time, including radio-sonde balloons, aeroplanes, rockets and man-made satellites, have made his statement less comprehensively accurate, since it is possible to forecast, depending on present conditions, certain weather changes (based upon current awareness of similar conditions) over a very limited period. However, fraudulent 'long-range weather forecasts', often issued with the best intentions to assist farmers or seamen, should be ignored as guesswork.

CHANGES IN THE WEATHER CAN BE PREDICTED BY OBSERVING THE BEHAVIOUR OF PLANTS AND ANIMALS

No changes in the weather can be predicted with complete accuracy since, outside the realms of (some) pure science and experimental physics and chemistry, nothing whatever can be predicted with complete accuracy, for the unforeseeable can intervene.

E. J. Lowe, F.R.S., the meteorologist, tested signs generally 'accepted' to indicate change and carefully noted what happened after each sign. He did not state that *all* indications from animals and plants are useless, since he did not test them all, but those he did test seemed to fail the test.

He took the well-known signs of bats flying about in the evening, many toads appearing at sunset, many snails about, busy bees, fish rising more than usual in lakes, locusts appearing, cattle becoming restless, flies and gnats becoming troublesome, crows congregating, and ducks making more noise than usual. In 361 observations of the above signs, they were followed 213 times by fine weather, and only 148 times by wet weather; even after prognostications for rain, there was a greater preponderance of fine weather.

Even when swallows fly low, they are not an indication because, as Mr Lowe regretfully points out, they almost invariably skim the surface of the ground in late summer and autumn. There is a possibility that animals can sense the onset of a heavy rainstorm or any other sudden and highly contrasted change in the weather, but then so can man. The pimpernel and marigold do in fact close their petals before rain, because the air is getting damper, so this is not a fallacy; but it is an error, though almost universal in the countryside, that a large crop of hips, haws and holly-berries indicates a severe winter to come, 'Nature' thus providing food for the birds. As if the sight of birds dying of starvation were not sufficient to disprove this!

Source: A. S. E. Ackermann, *Popular fallacies* (4th ed., London, 1950, pp. 733-5).

WELLINGTON SAID, "UP, GUARDS, AND AT THEM!"

The famous 'saying' at Waterloo was denied by the Duke himself. According to Sir Herbert Maxwell's *Life of Wellington* (2 vols., London, 1900), "They reached the crest as a single column, containing the First and Second Battalions of the 3rd Chasseurs. There was nothing in their front, apparently, and they had neared the cross-road, when Wellington's voice was heard clear above the storm, "Stand up, Guards!" Then from the shelter of the wayside bank rose the line of Maitland's brigade". The Guards were lying down, of course, as it was the Duke's orders all troops should do under fire, when not actually engaged. Just as this book is a kind of mini-encyclopaedia in reverse: that is, it includes what *isn't* knowledge or information, so there is a need for a parallel dictionary of quotations that were never actually said, and this example would take pride of place in it. I have incidentally also pleaded, in my introduction to William Beckford's *Biographical memoirs of extraordinary painters*, 1780 (Cambridge, 1977), for a parallel National Gallery with works by artists who have never existed, such as Beckford's 'Soorcrout' and 'Insignificanti'.

WELSH RAREBIT IS A CORRUPTION OF WELSH RABBIT

Welsh rabbit is toasted cheese. Skeat dealt with the above fallacy in his *Etymological dictionary* by pointing out that those who were too dense to see the joke of calling toasted cheese 'Welsh rabbit' pretended that the name is a corruption of 'Welsh rarebit', "which is as pointless and stupid as it is incapable of proof".

It may have arisen because the original jokers thought that there were no rabbits in Wales, because in Australia there was a dish called 'colonial goose' (mutton cooked with stuffing) from the times before geese were introduced there. Similar nonsense names used in cooking include 'Irish apricots' or 'Munster plums' for potatoes; 'Gravesend sweetmeats' for shrimps; 'Essex lion' for veal; 'Glasgow magistrates' for herrings; and 'Fieldlane duck' for baked sheep's head.

WEREWOLVES

Technically 'lycanthropes', or those affected with lycanthropy, a kind of insanity in which the patient imagines himself to be a wolf, or, loosely, a beast of any kind (*Shorter Oxford English Dictionary*). The fallacy occurs when a gullible observer takes the experience to have an occult or supernatural significance. All primitive and peasant societies have such beliefs, and it is only in the last century or so that a belief in werewolves as beings different from humans has begun to die out, though in Sicily and parts of Greece the belief is still found. Secret societies in Africa use such beliefs to their own advantage by dressing in skins of the wild animal they represent (whether it be leopard, crocodile, or another), leaving appropriate tracks in the soft ground, and tearing the flesh of victims to imitate the teeth- and claw-marks of the alleged perpetrator.

The aberrations of lycanthropes are often accompanied by degeneracies such as necrophilia (sexual assaults on corpses), sadism, cannibalism, or zoerasty (sexual relations with animals). The tiger-men of Assam and northern Burma come to associate themselves with a particular tiger in the vicinity and they believe that when that tiger is caught and killed their own death will shortly follow, a belief known as *thanatomania*.

Source: D. H. Rawcliffe, *Illusions and delusions of the supernatural and the occult* (New York, 1959).

WESTMINSTER HAS AN 'ABBEY'

Not since the dissolution of the monastery, or abbey, by King Henry VIII. The official title of Westminster 'Abbey' since 1560 has been 'The Collegiate Church of St. Peter, in Westminster'. Queen Elizabeth I replaced the Abbot by a Dean.

Source: Violet Brooke-Hunt, *The story of Westminster Abbey* (London, 1902).

WHALES SPOUT WATER THROUGH THEIR BLOW-HOLES

Whales breathe through their lungs and, being unable to separate air from water as fishes do, must rise to the surface to breathe. The 'spouting' of the whale, which is commonly mistaken at a (safe) distance for water, is in fact the ordinary act of breathing out that any mammal has to perform, but in the case of the whale the intervals between breathing out are longer and the action therefore seems to be more dramatic. If the breathing out takes place under water of course it is water that is ejected, but this is relatively rarely seen, and the observer usually sees the ejection of air (highly charged with watery vapour) mixed with mucous matter.

Source: Frank Thomas Bullen, *The cruise of the "Cachalot"* (London, 1898, pp. 188-9).

A BREED OF WHITE ELEPHANTS EXISTS

No true white elephant has ever yet been reported, but Dusit Zoo in Bangkok usually exhibits a salmon-pink (albino) elephant, which is sold to the Royal Family when born since 'white' elephants are a rarity even in Asia.

The veneration of the Thais for white elephants is shown by a marvellous description written by a Siamese ambassador at the Court of Queen Victoria who wished to evoke the respect due to her in the following gallant terms; "One cannot but be struck by the deportment of the revered Queen of England. She clearly comes of a divine line of warrior kings and conquerors of the world. Her eyes, her complexion, and above all her fascination are those of a splendid and majestic White Elephant".

Source: Philip Ward, *Bangkok* (New York, 1974).

DICK WHITTINGTON HAD A CAT, WAS THRICE LORD MAYOR OF LONDON, AND WAS KNIGHTED

There is no record of Richard Whittington, a prosperous mercer born in 1358, ever having had a cat. He did marry Alice, daughter of Sir Ivo Fitzwaryn, a Dorset knight of considerable property, but was never a scullion to Fitzwaryn and in fact is recorded as having lent considerable sums of money to Richard II, Henry IV, and Henry V. Whittington was Mayor of London not thrice, but four times: in 1397, 1398, 1406 and 1419. The 'Lord Mayor' was not created as such until the middle of the 15th century, and Whittington died in 1423. As A. B. Beaven wrote in his *Aldermen of London*, "He is not styled Knight by John Carpenter, his executor who compiled the *Liber Albus*, nor by Gregory (*London Chronicle*, published by the Camden Society). He is first accorded this title in a black-letter ballad of 1641, two hundred years after his death. The first reference to the story now beloved in pantomime occurs with the licensing in 1605 of a play (now apparently lost) entitled *The History of Richard Whittington, of his lowe byrth, his great fortune*.

Source: Besant and Rice, *Life of Whittington* (London, 1894).

NATIONS HAVE A "WILL" OF THEIR OWN

Karl Deutsch, in his *Nationalism and social communication* (New York, 1953) defined "national wills" as "the set of constraints acquired from the memories and past experiences of the system, and applied to the selection and treatment of items in its later intake, recall and decisions".

The fallacy, shown by David H. Fischer in *Historians' fallacies* (New York, 1970), is that "nations do not make decisions—only people do. Sometimes people may tend to make similar decisions within a national group, but that kind of normative decision making is very different from Deutsch's collective national will".

AN ORGANIZED SOCIETY OF WITCHES EXISTED IN MEDIEVAL AND EARLY MODERN EUROPE

In *Europe's inner demons* (1975), Norman Cohn has sought to discover and to expose the origins of this curiously persistent fallacy. Earlier writers traced the origin to the Inquisition's campaigns against the Cathars in southern France and northern Italy during the 13th century, but their conclusions were based on forgeries and hoaxes now exposed by Cohn. In a review of two other books in *The Times Literary Supplement* (23 July 1976, p. 903), Cohn declares that "we still do not know why the great witch-hunt happened when and where it did. However ... I myself once ... advanced a tentative hypothesis: I pointed out that at the end of the Middle Ages and in the early modern period witch-craft acquired a new meaning, as the supreme expression of apostasy, and I suggested that the witch might thereby have acquired a new psycho-social function, as a scapegoat for an unacknowledged hostility to Christianity. I did not at that time know that French scholars, inspired by the researches of Jean Delumeau of the Collège de France, were already beginning to examine how in certain parts of Europe a new, more individual, more demanding type of Christianity was imposed on the laity between the fifteenth and the seventeenth centuries; how this produced, especially among the relatively privileged, an intenser, more personal sense of guilt; how the devil grew in stature, as a symbol of everything that might oppose or rebel against these developments; and what bearing that might have on notions of witchcraft and on the treatment of suspected witches".

WITTGENSTEIN

The *Tractatus logico-philosophicus* (1921) of Ludwig Wittgenstein begins "Die Welt ist alles, was der Fall ist" ("The world is everything that is the case").

But the Indeterminacy Principle demonstrated by Heisenberg states that for an object in motion no theoretically complete account of what was the case (no statement with equal exactitude of both its position and its velocity) could ever be given.

Since all objects are, have been, or will be in motion, the basis of the Wittgenstein definition is untenable. Furthermore the degree of extension of "die Welt" to the outermost reaches of the universe in Wittgenstein is by no means clear; it seems that he customarily deals with the Earth (Erde) since his observations are drawn from data furnished by terrestrial physics.

WOLVES HUNT IN PACKS

Not outside the realms of the popular movie or children's adventure story. As Stefansson remarks in *The standardisation of error* (London, 1928), *zoological* wolves go in pairs or families, never above a dozen.

Stefansson tracked down all reports of wolf-packs over a period of twenty years, and not one had been authenticated. Neither is there a single authenticated account of a wolf's having attacked and eaten a human being. This fallacy persisted so strongly that the Biological Survey in Washington carefully checked up on every published account of the killing of human beings by wolves in both the U.S.A. and Canada, and "without a single exception they proved to be purely imaginary". This might not seem so surprising, were it not for the fact that between January and March 1929, the *New York Times Index* showed reports of wolves devouring 16 Austrians, 5 Poles, an aged Bulgarian priest and many Czechoslovaks. They also 'menaced Constantinople', whatever that might mean.

MUSLIMS BELIEVE THAT WOMEN HAVE NO SOULS

The Holy *Qur'an* specifically states (in the translation by Sale):

"Verily the Moslems of either sex, and the true believers of either sex, and the devout men, and the devout women, and the men of veracity, and the women of veracity, and the patient men, and the patient women, and the humble men, and the humble women, and the alms givers of either sex, and the men who fast, and the women who fast, and the chaste men, and the chaste women, and those of either sex who remember God frequently; for them hath God prepared forgiveness and a great reward"— *Qur'an*, ch. XXXIII.

WOMEN'S BRAINS ARE SMALLER THAN MEN'S

As a generalization there is some truth in the common belief, but the various qualifications attaching to the statement render it worthless. First, not all women's brains are smaller than all men's. Second, the average woman's body is also smaller than that of the average man. Third, taking into account the proportionate size of the body, the weight of the brain is roughly equal in both sexes. Brain size varies in proportion to body weight, race, stature, and age.

Finally, the size of the brain is related neither to the gender nor to the intelligence of its owner.

IF A WORD FOR A THING EXISTS, THEN THAT THING ALSO EXISTS

E. R. Emmet deals with this hoary error in *The use of reason* (London, 1960). He first quotes John Stuart Mill: "The tendency has always been strong to believe that whatever receives a name must be an entity or being, having an independent existence of its own: and if no real entity answering to the name could be found, men did not for that reason suppose that none existed, but imagined that it was something peculiarly abstruse and mysterious, too high to be an object of sense".

Emmet adds: "To take a simple case, it is not necessarily true that because the words 'unicorn', 'centaur' exist there are in nature animals for which the words stand. This seems obvious to us now, but it was not always so.

Or again, to take a more complex example, though it may be convenient and intelligible to talk of a man having a strong Will or a good Memory, or a powerful Reason, it is generally agreed by psychologists today that this division of the personality into departments such as 'Will', 'Memory', 'Reason' is erroneous and misleading and that these words cannot rightly be thought of as standing for real entities".

WORLD-ICE THEORY

The *Welteislehre* (lit. 'World-ice doctrine') of Hans Hörbiger (1860-1931), which still has a million followers (estimate by Louis Pauwels and Jacques Bergier in *The dawn of magic*, London, 1963) teaches that the universe began when a huge block of cosmic ice encountered a sun. The ensuing explosion continues to this day, 'empty space' in the expanding universe being filled with fine ice crystals and rarefied hydrogen. The Earth's moon is covered with a thick layer of ice to a depth of many miles [the fallaciousness of this was of course proved on the first moon landing]. The Earth had three previous moons, which were all comets covered with ice which came too near the Earth, were successively drawn into the Earth's atmosphere, fell, and caused the ice ages and other phenomena of the earth's evolution.

Hörbiger's monumentally cranky *Glazial-Kosmogonie* (1913) provoked serious attacks from astronomers, but in the anti-intellectual atmosphere of the nascent Nazi party the theory came to be taken to heart as the central platform of a new party: the movement issued posters, leaflets and popular accounts of *WEL* as well as a monthly magazine, *The Key to World Events*. Hörbiger's disciples included Hans Schindler Bellamy, author of *Moons, myths and man* (London, 1936) and Denis Saurat, author of *Atlantis and the giants* (London, 1957).

Hörbiger believed that our present moon is spiralling towards Earth, heralding another Ice Age. Coats of ice also cover Mercury, Venus and Mars [the last named definitively disproved by landings]. He also believed that the Milky Way is a ring of enormous ice blocks, and when reminded that photographs have proved that the Milky Way consists of billions of stars, he stated that the prints were faked.

Other common fallacies connected with Ice Ages are discussed in Robert Ardrey's *African genesis* (London, 1961) in the chapter "Time was". They include the totally untenable theory of comets, the apparently more plausible but nonetheless erroneous theories of solar radiation and the tilting poles, and Ardrey's own bizarre hypothesis that the solar system revolves through a gas cloud every two hundred million years.

Source: Willy Ley, 'Pseudo-science in Naziland' in *Astounding Science Fiction*, May 1947.

THE DAWWADA PEOPLE OF THE LIBYAN SAHARA ARE WORM-EATERS

The fallacy will persist until their name is understood, for 'Dawwada' means 'eaters of *dud*', and their *dud* are not worms but minute shrimps which they eat in a kind of porridge. However, they also keep goats, chickens and sheep, and cultivate dates, apples, figs, pomegranates, peaches, almonds, apricots, tomatoes and onions.

Source: Philip Ward, *Touring Libya: the Southern Provinces* (London, 1968, p. 67).

XYZ

"Zeale without knowledge is sister of Folly:
But though it be witlesse, men hold it most holly"
—JOHN DAVIES, *The scourge of folly* (1611)

FACULTY X

The fallacy that man has a mysterious faculty 'X', responsible for his involvement with the paranormal, is the main thesis and conclusion of Colin Wilson's *The occult* (London, 1971). Faculty 'X' is defined as "that latent power that human beings possess to reach beyond the present . . . it is the power to grasp reality, and it unites the two halves of man's mind, conscious and subconscious". [It is not proven that man's mind is divided into two halves, however.]

According to Wilson, faculty 'X' is found in the spiritualistic seance, in the casting of runes, the fall of the Tarot pack, the predictions of Nostradamus, and the ramblings of characters like Ouspensky and Gurdjieff. One fallacy is in assuming that whatever one cannot understand is ultimately intelligible, and another that all otherwise unintelligible phenomena have the same explanation. In mathematics, 'x' can usefully be taken to mean anything, but in the history of ideas the notion of 'X' is of no help at all.

IT IS A PROVEN FACT THAT THE YETI EXISTS

Tibetan legend tells of a race of *metoh-kangmi* (unhappily translated into English as 'abominable snowmen') and Tibetans, as well as peoples of surrounding Himalayan regions such as Nepal, are terrified of them. Tracks have undoubtedly been found in the snow, but do they belong to a known animal or to a hitherto unknown animal or even hominoid?

Dozens of theories have been propounded, but none has found any degree of popularity. Colonel Howard-Bury attributed the tracks to the grey wolf, and Ronald Kaulback to a snow leopard. Dr T. C. S. Morrison-Scott, judging by Eric Shipton's photographs of tracks, asserted that the animal was a Himalayan langur (*Presbytis* (or *Semnopithecus*) *entellus achilles*). Reginald I. Pocock, judging by Frank Smythe's photograph of tracks, stated that the animal could only be the red bear (*Ursus arctos isabellinus*), and this view was supported by George Cansdale of the London Zoo.

Yet Sir John Graham Kerr was of the opinion that the footprints belonged to no animals known to zoologists. The conclusion must be that there is no direct knowledge (as in the case of all other giants such as the 'mono grande') and no example has been provided for scientific knowledge either alive or dead to show that a distinct animal which one might call a 'yeti' actually exists.

See also **GIANTS** and **SASQUATCH**.

Sources include: Ralph Izzard, *The Abominable Snowman adventure* (London, 1955); W. C. O. Hill's important article 'Abominable Snowman: the present position' in *Oryx*, August 1961; I. T. Sanderson, *The Abominable Snowman* (Philadelphia, 1961); Odette Tchernine, *The Snowman and Company* (London, 1961) and *The Yeti* (London, 1970); and J. Napier, *Bigfoot* (London, 1972).

ZOOLOGICAL FALLACIES

That inbreeding causes degeneration (it causes the intensification of known characteristics); that ants and bees are intelligent; that certain fly larvae, living as guests in ants' nests, are molluscs; that selection can gradually change the nature of an hereditary factor, or gene; that toads at the breeding season find ponds through an ability to sense water from a distance; and that fishes can sense a current as such and swim against it when unable to see or feel the bank or bottom of the stream . . .

THE LAST FALLACY

Or perhaps better to say 'the first fallacy'. To assume that, in every single case where I in my ignorance have selected what I have thought the best available advice, there is consequently no room for error. A glance behind my shoulder to similarly assured lists of popular delusions over the centuries is enough to persuade me that more than one of my foregoing assertions is incorrect, and that the reader should consult this book no less than any other with a sceptical air, as if to say "this too may be wrong: let me never trust what is offered as fact, truth, or wisdom without testing it in the light of experience and observation".

SELECT BIBLIOGRAPHY

This bibliography omits standard works such as encyclopaedias and dictionaries which mention fallacies only in passing, as well as works written to support the fallacies which are listed and analyzed in the entries concerned.

Abelard, Pierre. Dialectica. Ed. by L. M. de Rijk. 2 vols. Assen, 1956.
Abelard, Pierre. Logica ingredientibus. *In* Peter Abaelards Philosophische Schriften. Ed. by B. Geyer in *Beiträge zur Geschichte der Philosophie und Theologie des Mittelalters*, vol. XXI, 1-3 (1919-27). [Both works by Abelard reproduce and discuss the sixfold classification of fallacies of Boethius, q.v.]
Ackermann, A. S. E. Popular fallacies. 4th ed. London, 1950.
Adams, *Sir* John. Errors in school. London, 1927.
Aristotle. On fallacies, or the Sophistici Elenchi. With a translation and commentary by Edward Poste. London, 1866.
Atkinson, D. T. Magic, myth and medicine. New York, 1956.
Averroes. See Ibn Rushd, Muhammad bin Ahmad.
Ayer, A. J. The problem of knowledge. Harmondsworth, 1956.

Bacon, Francis. Novum organon. Edited by T. Fowler. Oxford, 1878. [For the *idola* see i. 38-9]
Beaty, John Y. Nature is stranger than fiction. London, 1943.
Bechtel, Guy *and* Carrière, Jean-Claude. Dictionnaire de la bêtise et des erreurs de jugement. Paris, 1965.
Bell, Eric Temple. The magic of numbers. New York, 1946.
Bell, Eric Temple. The search for truth. New York, 1935.
Belnap, Nuel Dinsmore, *jr*. An analysis of questions. Santa Monica, Calif., 1963.
Bentham, Jeremy. The book of fallacies. London, 1824. (Rev. ed. by Harold A. Larrabee, Baltimore, 1952). [Political fallacies]
Bessy, Maurice. Histoire en 1000 images de la magie. Paris, 1961. (Trans. by M. Crosland and A. Daventry as "A pictorial history of magic and the supernatural", London, 1963).
Boethius, Anicius Manlius Torquatus Severinus. De syllogismo categorico. Introductio ad syllogismos categoricos. *In* Migne, J.-P., Patrologiae cursus completus, ser. latina, vol. 64, cols. 761-832. Paris, 1860.
Breland, Osmond P. Animal facts and fallacies. London, 1950.
Browne, *Sir* Thomas. Pseudodoxia epidemica. London, 1646. (*In*

Works, Edinburgh, 1927). [This is the work usually known as "Vulgar errors"]

Budge, Earnest Alfred Wallis. Amulets and talismans. New York, 1961.

Camp, John. Magic, myth and medicine. London, 1973.

Cavendish, Richard, *ed.* Encyclopedia of the unexplained: magic, occultism and para-psychology. London, 1974. [Strong bias in favour of most phenomena discussed]

Clark, C. E. The mistakes we make. London, 1898.

Clark, C. E. More mistakes we make. London, 1901.

Corliss, William R. The unexplained: a sourcebook of strange phenomena. New York, 1976.

Cornwallis, Caroline Frances. Exposition of vulgar and common errors, by 'Thomas Browne Redivivus'. London, 1845.

Crawshay-Williams, Rupert. The comforts of unreason: a study of the motives behind irrational thought. London, 1947.

De Morgan, Augustus. A budget of paradoxes. London, 1872. (2nd ed., 2 vols., Chicago, 1915).

Draper, J. W. History of the conflict between religion and science. London, 1922.

Dunham, Barrows. Man against myth. London, 1948.

Eisler, R. The royal art of astrology. London, 1946. [One of the few useful titles in this immense field]

Emmet, E. R. The use of reason. London, 1960.

Evans, Bergen. The natural history of nonsense. London, 1947.

Fearnside, William Ward, *and* Holther, William Benjamin. Fallacy, the counterfeit of argument. Englewood Cliffs, N.J., 1959.

Fischer, David Hackett. Historians' fallacies. New York, 1970. [A valuable typology of historiographical fallacies]

Fishbein, Morris. Fads and quackery in healing. New York, 1933.

Fishbein, Morris. Shattering health superstitions. New York, 1930.

Flacelière, Robert. Devins et oracles grecs. Paris, 1961.

Flaubert, Gustave. Le dictionnaire des idées reçues, ed. E.-L. Ferrère. Paris, 1913. (The 1951 ed. also includes the *Catalogue des idées chic*). The translations into English include "A dictionary of platitudes", by Edward J. Fluck, and "A dictionary of accepted ideas", by Jacques Barzun (both London, 1954).

Foote, G. W. Infidel deathbeds. London, 1888. [False accounts of deathbed 'conversions' listed]

Fort, Charles. The book of the damned. New York, 1919. [Fort's overriding aim was to ridicule both orthodox and unorthodox scientists and his books, of which this was the first and most readable, are content to record the absurd, with virtually no serious analysis]

Fovargue, Stephen. A new catalogue of vulgar errors. Cambridge, 1767.

Gardner, Martin. Fads and fallacies in the name of science. New York, 1957.
Gautama. Nyāyasūtras. Ed. and trans. from the Sanskrit by Gangānātha Jhā (2 vols., Poona, 1939). [Fallacies in ancient Indian logic]
Gombrich, Ernst Hans. Art and illusion. London, 1960 (2nd ed., London, 1962).
Gould, George M. and Pyle, Walter L. Anomalies and curiosities of medicine. Philadelphia, 1897.
Gould, Rupert T. Enigmas: another book of unexplained facts. London, 1929.
Gould, Rupert T. Oddities: a book of unexplained facts. London, 1928 (2nd ed., London, 1944).
Grillot de Givry, Émile. Picture museum of sorcery, magic and alchemy. New York, 1963.

Haggard, Howard W. Devils, drugs and doctors. London, 1929 (Reprinted Wakefield, 1975).
Hall, Trevor H. New light on old ghosts. London, 1965.
Hall, Trevor H. The spiritualists. London, 1962.
Hamblin, C. L. Fallacies. London, 1970. [On logic]
Hering, Daniel Webster. Foibles and fallacies of science. London, 1924.
Heuvelmans, Bernard. Sur la piste des bêtes ignorées. Paris, 1955. (English trans., "On the track of unknown animals", London, 1958). [Discusses animals which are thought to exist but may well not]
Holbrook, Stewart Hall. The golden age of quackery. New York, 1959.
Holder, C. F. and Jordan, D. S. Fish stories alleged and experienced. London, 1909.
Huff, Darrell. How to lie with statistics. London, 1954.
Huff, Darrell. How to take a chance. London, 1960.

Ibn Rushd, Muhammad bin Ahmad. Tahafut at-Tahafut (The incoherence of the incoherence). Trans. from the Arabic by S. van den Bergh. 2 vols. London, 1954.

Jameson, Eric. The natural history of quackery. London, 1961.
Jastrow, Joseph. ed. The story of human error. New York, 1936.
Jastrow, Joseph. Wish and wisdom. New York, 1935.
Jones, Abel J. In search of truth. London, 1945.
Jones, John. Medical and vulgar errors refuted. London, 1797.
Jones, William, F.S.A. Credulities past and present. London, 1880.
Jordan, David Starr. The stability of truth. London, 1911.

Keith, Sir Arthur Berriedale. The place of prejudice in modern civilization. New York, 1931.
Kemmerich, Max. Aus der Geschichte der menschlichen Dummheit. Munich, 1912. [Anecdotes of human foolishness]

Kemmerich, Max. Kultur-Kuriosa. 3 vols. Munich, 1910-1936. [Absurdities of human behaviour]
King, Francis. Ritual magic in England. London, 1970.

Larrabee, Harold A. Reliable knowledge. Boston, 1954.

MacDougall, Curtis D. Hoaxes. New York, 1940 (2nd ed., New York, 1958).
Mackay, Charles. Extraordinary popular delusions and the madness of crowds. London, 1852. (2nd augmented ed. of "Memoirs of extraordinary popular delusions", London, 1841).
Maple, Eric. Magic, medicine and quackery. London, 1968.
Maxwell, E. A. Fallacies in mathematics. Cambridge, 1959.
Mill, John Stuart. A system of logic, ratiocinative and inductive: being a connected view of the principles of evidence, and the methods of scientific investigation. 2 vols. 2nd ed. London, 1946. [Fallacies are dealt with in book V]
Montagu, M. F. Ashley and Darling, Edward. The ignorance of certainty. New York, 1970.
Montagu, M. F. Ashley. Man's most dangerous myth: the fallacy of race. 4th ed. Cleveland, 1964. [Somewhat overstates a generally tenable position]
Montagu, M. F. Ashley and Darling, Edward. The prevalence of nonsense. New York, 1967.
Moore, J. Howard. Savage survivals. London, 1933. [How man's rise towards reasoning behaviour is impeded by factors in his ancestry; deals also with domesticated animals, but this section is outdated]
Moore, Patrick. Can you speak Venusian? Newton Abbot, 1972. [Sixteen groups of fallacies prominent in the early 1970s]
Morley, John. On compromise. London, 1886. [Ch. II treats "Of the possible utility of error"]

Palmer, A. Smythe. The folk and their word-lore: an essay on popular etymologies. London, 1904.
Parish, E. Hallucinations and illusions. London, 1897.
Partridge, Eric. Origins: a short etymological dictionary of modern English. London, 1958 (4th ed., London, 1966).
Petrus Hispanus, later Pope John XX or XXI. Treatise on the major fallacies. MS. Clm. 14458, fol. 1ʳ-28ʳ in the Bavarian State Library, Munich.
Phin, John. Seven follies of science. New York, 1912.
Plato. Republic. Translated by H. D. P. Lee. Harmondsworth, 1955. [For the idola see vii, 516A]
Plato. Theaitetos. Translated by John Warrington in Plato's Parmenides . . . London, 1961. [A Socratic dialogue on the definition of knowledge]

Radford, Edwin *and* Radford, M.A. Encyclopedia of superstitions. London, 1948. (Revised ed. by Christina Hole, London, 1961). ["Time, and the disappearance of the religion or philosophy that gave them birth, have made [superstitions] meaningless, and therefore irrational, but have not always deprived them of the power to influence men's lives"—C. Hole]

Rawcliffe, D. H. Illusions and delusions of the supernatural and the occult. New York, 1959.

Rescher, Nicholas. The development of Arabic logic. Pittsburgh, 1964.

Rijk, Lambertus Marie de. Logica modernorum: a contribution to the history of early terminist logic. 2 vols. in 3. Assen, 1962-7. [Vol. 1 contains "Glosses on the Sophistical Refutations", "Parvipontanus fallacies", "Summa of Sophistical Refutations" and "Viennese fallacies"; Vol. 2 contains "London fallacies", "Dialectica Monacensis" and "Tractatus Anagnini"]

Russell, Bertrand. Human knowledge: its scope and limits. London, 1948.

Schopenhauer, Artur. Essays from the Parerga and Paralipomena. Trans. by T. Bailey Saunders. London, 1951. [For "The art of controversy"]

Sextus Empiricus. Works, with a translation by R. G. Bury. 4 vols. London, 1933-49. [See vol. 2 for "Against the logicians"]

Sidgwick, Alfred. The application of logic. London, 1910.

Sidgwick, Alfred. Distinction and the criticism of beliefs. London, 1892.

Sidgwick, Alfred. Fallacies: a view of logic from the practical side. London, 1883.

Sidgwick, Alfred. The process of argument: a contribution to logic. London, 1893.

Sidgwick, Alfred. The use of words in reasoning. London, 1901.

Simoons, Frederick J. Eat not this flesh. Madison, Wis., 1961.

Stefansson, Vilhjalmur. The standardisation of error. London, 1928.

Sully, James. Illusions. London, 1881 (4th ed., 1895).

Taylor, F. Sherwood. The alchemists. London, 1952.

Thomas Aquinas, *Saint*. De fallaciis ad quosdam nobiles artistas. *In* "Opuscula philosophica" (Turin), no. 43, 1954.

Thomen, August Astor. Doctors don't believe it: why should you? New York, 1935.

Trench, Richard Chenevix. A select glossary of English words used formerly in senses different from their present. London, 1906.

Voltaire, François Marie Arouet de. Dictionnaire philosophique. Paris, 1764.

Webb, James. The flight from reason. London, 1971 (US edition entitled "The occult revival", New York, 1973).

Westaway, Frederic William. Obsessions and convictions of the human intellect. London, 1938. (2nd ed., entitled "Man's search after truth", London, 1942).

Wheatley, Harry B. Literary blunders. London, 1893.

White, Andrew Dickson. A history of the warfare of science with theology in Christendom. New York, 1896. (2 vols. in 1, London, 1955).

Zabaleta, Juan de. Errores celebrados. Madrid, 1972. [17th-century moral lessons drawn from anecdotes of classical antiquity]

Zaehner, R. C. Drugs, mysticism and makebelieve. London, 1972.

Zöckler, Otto. Geschichte der Beziehungen zwischen Theologie und Naturwissenschaft, mit besondrer Rücksicht auf Schöpfungsgeschichte. 2 vols. Gütersloh, 1877-79.

INDEX

299

301